What a Long Strange Trip It's Been

A Hippy's History of the Sixties & Beyond

by

Lewis Sanders

Still Steaming Press

What a Long Strange Trip It's Been
© 1989 Lewis Sanders
© 1994 Lewis Sanders - 2nd Edition
ISBN 0-9643083-0-4
Library of Congress
TX2.735.932

Cover illustrations — Bruce Campbell
Photo of author — Jonathon Waite

WHAT A LONG STRANGE TRIP IT'S BEEN

Brilliantly written, with sharpness & clarity. This is a treasure house of information & insight on the sixties and the continuing struggle for justice and love.
          David Dellinger -of the Chicago 8

I have searched for years for a book about the 60's which would both characterize the counterculture and provoke my comfortable upper-middle class students to creative thought. I found such in Sanders' wry, impertinent, wickedly outrageous ... chronicle of the era.
          Tim Dillon - Assoc. Professor of History
          Milligan College, TN

This is a fine survey of the American Mythos, which captures well the spread and sweep of our recent history.
          Factsheet Five

Have you ever wished that history came with a user's manual? Fear not ... have I got a book for you. Often detailed but never dry & assuming little background knowledge on the part of the reader, these are the Cliff Notes to the last generation you have been waiting for. This is a good Baedekers of the period.
          Mark Koltko
          Dupree's Diamond News

... a very important book. It's readers are sure to find a wealth of information not available in any history textbooks, & it is guaranteed to enlighten them.
          Paul Fad
          Unbroken Chain

... mingles personal experience with historical research & the result is a book that not only tells the reader what went on, but also gives a sense of what it was like ot be there, the missing element in so many history books.
          Mary Anderson
          Star Route Journal

*It's strange what long trips people take
in their lifetimes.*
—Jack Kerouac
Desolation Angels

For those who survived both Dead and alive.

Disclaimer

Don't sue me, I'm just the satirist.

Table of Contents

Foreword
Chapter 1 - Yellow Bricks & Poppy Trips; Camelot & Secret Plots; the Deathbird's shadow comes to rest over the land.
Chapter 2 - The One; God; the Earth as Terrapin Station; our purpose as evolution back to God.
Chapter 3 - Historical misfits & Misforgotten martyrs; Celestial Rebels; the Beats.
Chapter 4 - Jazz; Jericho; Fresh winds; the Revolution starts to move.
Chapter 5 - On the Road; Howl; San Francisco; the New Age.
Chapter 6 - Acid; magic spectacles; government harrassment of activists.
Chapter 7 - Preamble on Rose; Myth America; ToHellivision; Don't criticize, organize; The big balloon- decompress or bust.
Chapter 8 - Freed Spirit Entourage; Ken White Rabbit Kesey; the Prairie Gangsters; the look without the look within; the Kool-aid Parade; on the intrepid starship with no one to wake but the flood; the word goes out, assassins dispatched, & stars are felled in the nite; The Shadow lengthens.
Chapter 9 - John Fitzgerald Kennedy; the Cuban Missile Crisis; Richard Vomit Nixon.
Chapter 10 - The day they blew JFK away; the Bay of Pigs; losing hand at Dealey Plaza; the Warren Ommission.
Chapter 11 - LBJ, Vietnam, the Smothers Brothers; My Lai, the Tet Offensive; Presidential stenches; Lyndon's Humpty Dumpty; Eugene McCarthy; the Peace Movement grows.
Chapter 12 - Good & Evil; the Karma of killing; the obscene Corporate appetite.
Chapter 13 - Vietnam; America rapes a nation & blows its children's brains out in the jungle sun; the Tonkin Bay deception; Vietnamization- antipersonnel pinball.
Chapter 14 - The history of Vietnam; the 5, 9, & 10 of Wands- strife, great strength, & oppression.
Chapter 15 - The Summer of Love; New Visions; music, politics, & drugs.
Chapter 16 - Folk music as an instrument of protest. A new child is born on a new morning; amoebic cultural replication; Woodstock Nation; Bob

Dylan & the Guitar Army; the Lysergic Pipers of Pepperland; Acid Rock.

Chapter 17 - Poetry & posters; losing your mind; ship of fools & Karmic seas; the overgrown glint of the Golden Road.

Chapter 18 - Timothy Leary drops acid & out; the Underground Press; Underground Comix; Tim & Dick, the Harvard Review; Aldous Huxley; Ram Dass; dismissed but not misdosed; IF-IF; Millbrook, the Castalian marble bag; the Brotherhood of Eternal Love; sellouts; New Age charlatans on the late nite channel to hell; OM circles; the Jefferson Airplane.

Chapter 19 - Open season: Martin Luther King; Robert Kennedy; the New Left.

Chapter 20 - The Civil Rights Movement; Freedom Riders; Montgomery Bus Boycott, Rosa Parks parks it; the Civil Rights Voting Act; Teach-ins; sit-ins.

Chapter 21 - Organized student resistance against the war; the S.D.S.; Port Huron statement; Weathereports- things that go boom in the nite; Underground; speaking out; revolution roulette; anarchy's malarkey; nonviolence only; out of the rabbithole.

Chapter 22 - The Men in Black- government hit men; missing persons & the hit parade; the F.B.I. harrassment of Reverend King; Gay Edgar Hoover; JFK gets high; Marilyn dies; John Lennon murdered.

Chapter 23 - F.B.I., COINTELPRO, agent provocateurs, the Angels of Death of the New Left.

Chapter 24 - The Yippies; Levitation of the Pentagon; naked masquerades; flying pies; the White House Acid Test; still crazy after all what years; Abbie's last trip underground.

Chapter 25 - The Black Panthers.

Chapter 26 - The Native American Indian Movement takes aim right between Whitey's eyes- a Custer in every Apple's pie; white man's contributions: pollution, the seige of Wounded Knee; Leonard Peltier.

Chapter 27 - A time of risk; Fire on the Prairie, Fire on the Mountain: Norm Morrison.

Chapter 28 - Battlegrounds- Berkeley, the Free Speech Movement, People's Park, Columbia; Mark Rudd, Harvard's poison ivy.

Chapter 29 - The Chicago Democratic Convention; Mad Mayor Daley; Yips; blood in the streets; the Chicago Conspiracy Trial.

Chapter 30 - 1970- the child grows; communes; environmental consciousness; Earth Day; Greenpeace; worldwide deepening pollution; Bhopal; Chernobyl; a radiation sick world; the whales; the destruction of the rainforests; dancing toward Oblivion; N.O.W.; the E.R.A.; Speed kills; crack ups; booze & downers take you down & out; heroin kills; road kills: Hendrix, Joplin, Pigpen, Morrison; Hate on the Haight; split Scarabs;

Altamont; Charlie Manson; TV murder violence; increasing awareness among the programmed people.

Chapter 31 - Kent State; murder & cover-up; Nixon-Agnew cues; a nonmonumental event?; Jackson State; what price freedom?; Wide open season.

Chapter 32 - The Nixon violence; Spiro Asshole; the Silent Majority; TV Evangelshits; the Enemies List; the Huston Plan; the White House Plumbers; Pentagon Papers; the Ellsberg break-in; dirty tricks; Ed Muskie takes a trip & falls; tacky plans.

Chapter 33 - Watergate. The cover-up; Howard Hughes; the Watergate shakes; Dorothy Hunt takes a dive; Helms at the helm, bodies swaying from the yard arm?

Chapter 34 - McGovern- The eagle shits on George; America's Dicked again; Richard Nixon: Santa Claus from Hell's viscious Christmas gift to Hanoi.

Chapter 35 - Watergate trial; half spelt sentences; the cover-up's up; parting staff, passing gas.

Chapter 36 - The Walls are falling; the Tapes - is it Milhous or is it Memorex?; Spiro's woes, 1600 Pennsylvania Avenue - lawyers' row.

Chapter 37 - Tidbits thrown; false transcripts; Articles of Impeachment; Nixon resigns to the fact; the Mayflower sails again.

Chapter 38 - Gerry Ice-cream-cone-kid Ford sworn in; Rocky Raccoon; Attica State; the real people in power; the Trilateral Commission; the Federal Reserve System- power, greed, moral bankruptcy.

Chapter 39 - The Peanut Man; the Carter "White" House; Patty-cake Hearst; the October Surprise.

Chapter 40 - Ronald Reagan- Mr. 666; Ed Meese, Miranda won'tcha go, Miranda won'tcha go...; fascism made fashionable, there's no state like a police state; a gift for Grenada's mental hospitals, a lullaby for Libya; Ronnie & Ollie's lust for Nicaraguan blood.

Chapter 41 - Irangate. Guns, drugs, & the C.I.A.; subverting third world governments; American-sponsored dictatorships; the Secret Team; America's corporate-sponsored gang of thugs; torture the C.I.A. way; Henry Dr. Strangelove Kissinger; Elliot Scumbag Abrams; the Vatican; the murder of Pope John Paul I; inhumane government experiments on American citizens.

Chapter 42 - Iran. Won't you come home, Bill Buckley, won't you come home; Ollie Traitor North, concentration camps for all; gutterball 'round the Boland Ammendment; traitorous arms sales revelations; American scandal; illegal Contra money; cover-up once again; bad memories; silence is golden; Bud Valium McFarland; late for supper Bill Casey;

Casey's capers; Ollie on the grill; Contra atrocities. Cold War paranoia warmed over; Ronnie's lies; F.B. eyes C.I.S.P.E.S.; Ronnie's crippling deficit; the homeless; domestic spying rules loosened; air traffic chaos; South African freedom; Israeli Nazism; Drugs- TV violence, booze, nicotine, caffeine, cocaine, sugar, smack, crack, valium; poised for flite- Nancy Reagan; shattered like a Glass Goblin; the Peace Movement grows to new proportions in the 80s; nuclear arms treaties; the Great Peace March; Public Enema #1- Iraqnaphobia, No More Vietnams? Bush Diplomacy- Blind Vomit & Pink Chunks meet Tokyo Rose; Halcyon Daze; Duck Soup- Quayle tales and Bush's goose. Oh, No! Mr. Bill didn't inhale; Clinton wins by a nose; the Waco Debacle; Bosnia, slow on the draw; same white powder, same old story; The New World Odor.

Chapter 43 - The Future. A win in Paradise or loss at the toss of dice, it's up to you; Lost Angels in the arms of time; and a glance back at What A Long Strange Trip It's Been.

Epilogue
Who's Who of the 60's - Heroes Martyrs Villains Sellouts
OM Circles
Footnotes
Bibliography
Appendix
Index
Author

Foreword

I hesitated writing this book for years, for I thought that it'd all been said before, and I most likely wouldn't have written it at all had it not been for Harlan Ellison. I first came upon Harlan as a writer of science fiction, but being hopelessly addicted to Phillip K. Dick at the time, paid him little heed.

Then I read *The Glass Teat*. Without a doubt, the best fucking book I'd ever read in my life!

Here Ellison put it on the line and at the same time put himself right there on the line with it.

So this is for you too, Harlan, for you taught me that no matter how many times it's been said before, we've got to keep right on saying it-until the Truth is seen, and enough people awake from The Dream to set straight this whole lost hallucination.

With heart,
>with spirit,
>>with our lives on the line.

So on with the Chronicles of the Revolution, whose conclusion
>has only just begun.

I

Chapter 1

What A Long Strange Trip It's Been

Where to begin?

"It's always best to start at the beginning and all you do is follow the Yellow Brick Road."

And that's what kind of trip it's been. Full of witches, & Marvels, & untold turbulence, taking us unheard of places.
(...And, ah, full of Poppy dreams too.)
That the road would lead us to the bolted door of a false and aging wizard, we too would recognize this when the time did come. For the word had passed round that the Emperor wore no clothes. And it was clear for us to see, the stark & naked truth. For our spectacles had been forged by the artists & articulate of our time and finely fitted by the lensmen of Lysergia.
So it was no wonder we became so leary of our elder's lives & went searching for truths of our own. For nothing short of this in a time as dark as that would have preserved our deepest sanity nor satisfied our Souls.
For it was a time of Kings & Kennedys- of castles & of Camelots, ...assassins & of secret plots.
It was a time when the children were hunted & imprisoned for merely smoking an herb...when it was that which their elders smoked and drank, which were the real killers.
And as the winds blew chillier absurdity reigned. For the greatest danger came from those who had mesmerized the masses into accepting weapons of unheard of Evil, weapons which could destroy the entire world.
But the children fought against this madness, against it all. For there was nothing else they could do.
For evil had come to rest in their land, and so few did understand.
But we are getting ahead of our story. And what may you ask is the story? The story is about the path from here to There;
intelligent awareness,
                Spiritual evolution,
                                          mind expansion.

A Hippy's History of the Sixties

About the ongoing corporate takeover of the world and the behind-the-scenes power struggle between Good & Evil which this whole world serves to play.

About the collective individual quests for a further existence beyond this to which we all will go once we have passed the test.

      The Earthly Test.
      The Acid Test.

However many lifetimes it takes. But the beginning...

Chapter 2

In the beginning there was the One. That which is:
Intelligence, Bliss, Vibrating Consciousness.
God.
All powerful, all knowing, all being.
One who wanted other conscious beings to share in the blissful existence of eternal God-life also. To do this our Creator designed the most intricate cosmic mirage imaginable- this world.

And put into the bodies of each & every human being a tiny piece of God-stuff- the Soul.

That which is the source of the eternal yearning for fulfillment & unity with the Whole.
(The yearning to return.)

Heaven's the goal. Earth is the schooling ground...
A train station & dock by the bay.
Day by day, a constant test to see which side you're on
and which in the end, will depend if you go or stay.
So indeed we see, life is but a movie, but one nonetheless
with eternal consequences and a role we must play
till the final curtain closes.

THE CURTAIN RISES

Chapter 3

In every culture there have been those persons whose lives have lain outside the socially acceptable standards of existence.

Philosophers, Poets, Artists, Yogins, Hermits, Hippies, Gypsies, Magicians, Shamans: those who chose to go furthur.

They have surged ahead, & if clever in their wisdom, removed themselves from the presence of the normal world, so that their evolution might hasten undisturbed. Those who did not remove themselves were often crucified- while many crucified themselves. (Tho' most were hung by others.)

Lenny Bruce, Bruno, Galileo, Wilhelm Reich, Jesus.[1]

Beat but never beaten, beaten but never beat.

The Pure Spirit will always inject itself into this world thru some truth-telling Soul who's merely on their way Home.

So these celestial rebels were forever but a few in the midst of a quagmire of enforced mediocracy. "Waste Deep in the Big Muddy," so to speak.

The Shelleys, Rossettis, the William Morrises,[2] the Edward Burne Jones'; Clark Ashton Smith & the 1920 San Francisco fantasy weavers.

Illustrious one and all.

But the few have become the many.

The Spirit has infused itself thru a whole generation & the New Age is on, tho' its pangs of birth are far from over.

But the first prenatal screams of the New Age were heard from the Beats.

Chapter 4

    Music has always been the pulse-rythm of the Bohemian drive, the fire in the blood, the loftiest intoxication.
    And then there was jazz.
                     Jazz drove the vagabonds wild!
    The endless explosion of flowing notes like the roving novas in the nitetime sky, was just too much for some men's minds to handle.
           Charlie Parker, Dizzie Gillespie, Thelonious Monk.
    These cats blew, & blew, & blew, & blew and knew what they were doing. They had done it once before in Jericho, and were here to try again. The Hymn to the last falling wall of the Castle. For it was music which infused the Revolution with movement.
    The evolution away from mindless misdirection into an alternative future of Peace and abundance for all, via the doorway of artistic expression. (Anything could be, it was legal to be free.)
    It was in the haze of the reefer-filled jazz clubs of the 20's, 30's, & 40's that the first true Blows Against the Empire were heard,
and from there,
                wound down forgotten alleyways
                                    and out onto the road.

Chapter 5

On the Road.
Jack Kerouac's high-speed narrative of the cross-country odyssey of poets, beats, & benzadrine.

Speed was the key,
rushing nowhere in particular,
just straight into the eye of Eternity.

The Howl of Ginsberg in the stark raving nite, & the orgasmic screams of jazz could be heard clear across America and called all who heard to follow.

From there they wove their way straight thru the straight lace of the 50's & emerged on the verge of infinity- San Francisco, the 60's. The mystical mistress of the mist & holy misfits. And those who saw her from the far-off foggy reefs would say- "...nay, this was not just another city in the Kingdom- this was the City of Rebellion."

For as legend holds, She paid no heed to the evil dictates of the King. And it was here, that the young came seeking refuge in a land so plainly mad.

(And for awhile it seemed as if Paradise
was this Lady's name in the evening...)

For it was a city in which all the necessary elements for what was about to happen were present.
And what was about to happen was the New Age.

Chapter 6

Acid.

For all that jazz did to break people out of their molds of controlled conformity, it was but a candle to the star-filled darkness in comparison to the illumination brought about by L.S.D.

That such a tiny piece of matter could deprogram the countless years of bullshit which had been fed to us by so many normals was astounding.

A new vision came to view. Begat by the struggle for Civil Rights which peaked in the early 60's and fueled & forged by an unjust war, the stage was set for the biggest change in consciousness in humankind's history.

A fusion of the elements of compassion, politics, spirituality, self awareness, revolution & the understanding of the interaction between ourselves & the planet we live on.

A new vision indeed.

So L.S.D. served as the magic spectacles, revealing things for what they really were- ourselves, society, the Universe.

Without it the Pentagon would have forever had us fighting its corporate wars of genocide.

But the children awoke, & looking about them saw that things were not as they should be, & should not be as they were; so they set out to change them.

And for their efforts they were harrassed, spied upon, jailed, beaten and murdered.

And still are.

So you who have no idea what the 60's were about, who have never been tear-gassed & arrested, been drafted & had to resist, or have never seen the Jefferson Airplane or Grateful Dead in concert, it all goes something like this...

II

Chapter 7

"Governments are instituted among men,* deriving their just powers from the consent of the governed; that whenever any form of government becomes destructive of these ends, it is the right of the people to alter or abolish it, and to institute new government, laying its foundation on such principles, and organizing its powers in such form, as to them shall seem most likely to affect their safety and happiness."

That's a bit of American history- the Declaration of Independence of the United States- like little bits of American history. Like how we exterminated the most beautiful culture which ever existed on this planet- the Native American Indians.

And tried again in Indochina.

What terror they've unleashed upon the world in our name & in the name of freedom is ungodly.

(And tried again in Nicaragua.)

And they aren't very well taking care of our safety or happiness either.**

But how did they get away with it? Through violent assassination and by programming the masses to be dull, stupid, & impassive to what's being done in the real world around them.

Television is the big mind burn.

Murder, murder, murder,
    violence, violence, violence,
        guns, guns, guns,
            buy, buy, buy,
                stupid, stupid, stupid,
                      program, program, program.

TV has brought the S.W.A.T. team into your neighborhood without even a second thought.

That people can sit & be mesmerized by such low-level drivel is amazing.

But not really.

TV's the hypnotic eye- 60 cycles per second. It makes it very easy to control the masses; to make everyone want to be like everyone else, like

---

* ?
** Do nuclear bombs make you feel safe?

A Hippy's History of the Sixties

the image on the screen, like good Germans; or good Jews.

And if the people do get out of line the S.W.A.T. team's always there. Let's never forget that in 1985 the Philadelphia police burned down 61 homes killing 11 people (five of them children) in an effort to extinguish some radical ideas & to try to move that which will never be moved.

1984 has come and stayed.

And how about the viscious 1992 beating of Rodney King by the Los Angeles Police Department. Brutality at its worst, videotaped at length and the racist jury still let the cops off. Now that's American justice for you. And America burned in return. And so did the kids in Waco...

If you want your freedom you're going to have to fight for it from now on in. Organize. Use the polls, the process our forefathers gave us to take over. The majority of American voters are between the ages of 18 & 40.

Cause God knows these other horses' asses in power are just going to sit around & twiddle their thumbs up their butts until this whole damned world explodes.

Don't kid yourself there. We're sitting on this ever-expanding balloon that's just about ready to bust, & we can either let the air out real slowly, or pop it all at once.

Let's be a force in that decision. Let's be <u>the</u> force in that decision.

But back to history past.

Chapter 8

As the curtain rose we found the New Age winging its way thru San Francisco, picking up those chosen Souls whose Karma ordained them to become enlisted in the cause of Worldwide Spiritual Evolution. In a collision course with destiny, this Freed Spirit Entourage would integrate the elements of time, space, music, magic, acid, & enlightenment, and lay it on a whole bunch of people who were just hanging out waiting for that exact same thing to happen.

And that's when the trip really began. When the C.I.A. (they should have known better) started testing some primo California heads (a.k.a Robert Hunter, Ken Kesey) with an unheard of substance called L.S.D. to see how it could be used in their kill & be killed world. But little did they know, acid is God's magic answer to violence & war- awareness.

So Kesey in his infinite wisdom decided that others should know about this also. So he became the White Rabbit, leading others down the rabbithole to the new-found underground, taking the magic drugs home & feeding them to his friends.

They in turn became the original acidheads. Calling themselves the Merry Pranksters they got on the bus and gave the call for all to come to Wonderland & peer outside the mirror. They became the ceremonial masters of the infamous Acid Tests: renting all-night halls complete with music, inter-psychic exploratory expeditions, oratory from outer space & more; the scene complete with 55 gallon drums of acid-laced Kool-aid, opening people's minds for the very first time.

So with the hero of Paradise Neal Cassady capably at the wheel of the Bohemian drive, and fueled by the galactic alchemy of Owsley & the music of the Grateful Dead, they sped ahead, with the grand intent & much success in their endeavor to turn on the world.

And in their wake stood history's pages, still shaking their heads with wonder. And if the pages were shaking, the Lords of the vassals in the castles were trembling with fear. For many years they had ruled the land, ruled the fortunes of their fellowmen & kingdoms faraway.

But those days were growing fewer. The Black Panther phantoms in the nite & the sinister shadows of the midnight rambler sneaking thru the palace halls; the savage screams of messianic madmen that the ballroom days were over, & the airborne cries that "all your private property is target for your enemies & your enemy is we..." were all too much for the

A Hippy's History of the Sixties

forces which ruled this land.* More than once they would draw the line & more than once the line meant murder.
JFK, MLK, RFK,
Chicago '68, People's Park, Kent State;
again and again murder and violence were used to maintain a corrupt government & its policies.

Police——Policies.
For Evil had come to rest in their land, and so few did understand

---

* Jefferson Airplane, "We Can Be Together," Volunteers album.

III

Chapter 9

When I was a kid we had no TV.
When I was a kid there was John Kennedy.
If you weren't alive then you'll never know the amount of hope & peace that this man brought to us all.

Never has there been a President of the United States who so captured the imagination of its people & the people of the world and inspired them to such heights.

He was our hero. With this man in power you knew that it was going to be alright...

Yes, I was only seven years old when Kennedy blockaded Cuba from the Russian ships which were delivering missiles to Castro. I remember everyone gathered around the globe in grade school & the tension in the air. This was the tensest day in American history. War, nuclear war, was perhaps only minutes away; you could feel it hanging in the air. Yet JFK kept his cool & as stalemate moved to placate, the Russians backed down, and the world let go a sigh.

The next time I felt the imminent presence of nuclear war was in the middle of a nitetime riot at Kent State University, when after Nixon had just ordered the mining of the Vietnamese harbors of Hanoi & Haiphong in total violation of International Law, it was rumored that Russian warships were rushing in to bust up the show. Believe me, that nite with Nixon at the helm I was ready to kiss my ass goodbye.

That was the difference between
    Nixon & Kennedy, Kennedy & Nixon.
      Nite & Day, Good & Evil.

And how did such a son-of-a-bitch as Richard Nixon ever get to be the President of the United States in the first place? That's what American history's really about- those secret years. Those years of murder, secrecy, deceit, corruption & cover-up.

You see, JFK was alright. JFK smoked pot in the White House.
       JFK took L.S.D.[1]
    (Both facts of American history.)

Presidential notes show that JFK intended to withdraw the American presence in Vietnam after his re-election in 1964. But John got his head blown away and his brains stolen from the National Archives. It's all the strangest tale this country's ever seen, and the complicity & cover-up in it all is unparalleled.

>Do you remember the 23rd of November...*
>And what of it all- the day they blew JFK away.
>The C.I.A., the mafia, the glutton oil barons.²
>And this is how & why it all went down.

---

* The first day evil reigned in America 11-23-63, JFK being shot the day before.

Chapter 10

Most of it deals with Cuba & the Mafia, & a few grudge-nuts in the C.I.A. You see, the Mob had a good thing going in Cuba in the early days. By 1937 Meyer Lansky, the head of the National Crime Syndicate, had made friends with Cuban dictator Juan Batista and opened up the largest casino in the Western Hemisphere in Cuba. But it was not until 1952 when Batista regained power thru a military coup after losing power eight years earlier in general elections, that the Mob was able to change the laws of Cuba to permit the construction of hotel casino complexes comparable to those in Las Vegas. Soon the Mob was making millions on its Cuban operation & laundering the profits thru banks in Miami, New Jersey, & Switzerland. Far from the scrutiny or taxation of the U.S. government, Cuba was paradise for the Mob. Their own little country.

This all came to an end, however, when Fidel Castro led the Cuban Revolution & seized power on New Year's Eve 1958. Castro really pissed everybody off, especially the American government. They thought they had bought their man already by giving him some aid and would have him & the whole country out in the fields cutting cane for U.S. business interests after the revolution. Not so!

Both Batista & Meyer Lansky fled Cuba, & Lansky put a million dollar price tag on Fidel's head. Soon elements of the Mob & the C.I.A. began working on plans to invade Cuba, assassinate Castro, and to return control of the government to Batista, the casinos to the Mafioso, & the farmland to United Fruit Co.

The plan later materialized as the Bay of Pigs invasion. Its chief proponent in the Eisenhower administration was then Vice-President Richard M. Nixon, a longtime friend of the Mob,[1] who became the White House Project Action officer for the operation.

And one E. Howard Hunt (later caught for breaking into the Democratic Headquarters in the Watergate Hotel) so happened to be the liaison between the C.I.A. officials in D.C. and the exiled Cuban politicians who were to regain power thru the invasion. This was when the C.I.A.'s elite Operation 40 assassination unit or shooter team, led for years by Howard Hunt, was formed at the behest of Richard Nixon. It was this team made up of C.I.A. and mafia personnel which was originally created to assassinate Fidel Castro, his brother, and Che Gueverra, but after this failed turned its sights towards the head of a head of state a little closer to home. As it turned out, before the invasion plan could be implemented Eisenhower's term of office was over, Richard Nixon lost his bid for the Presidency to John F. Kennedy, and the plan itself was carried over into the Kennedy administration by the C.I.A.

As history will tell, on April 17, 1961 the Bay of Pigs invasion was launched by operatives of the C.I.A., U.S. Armed Forces & members of the Cuban exiles movement.

Once JFK finally realized what the C.I.A. was up to & the complete ramifications of it all, he withdrew most of the U.S. air support which was supposed to provide cover for the invading force as they hit the shore. Without the covert aid of the U.S. air forces & largely due to the atrocious planning & execution of the invasion itself, the whole affair turned into a bloody fiasco. Of the 1200 C.I.A.-led Cubans, 114 were killed & the rest spent 20 months in Cuban prisons until the U.S. ransomed them for 53 million dollars & they were returned to Florida where they have been trouble ever since: doing dirty work for the C.I.A.; beating up on Peace marchers; breaking into the Watergate Hotel; blowing things up; killing people; running coke; etc.

Among those left hanging was Howard Hunt, the Operation 40 assassination team which had been left on the beach, and also one Frank Sturgis, longtime soldier-of-fortune type who had fought with Castro & after the revolution had been put in charge of the entire Cuban casino scene. Sturgis was later to flee Cuba in a stolen plane & end up in the ranks commanding the Cuban exile group which was doomed to slaughter at the Bay of Pigs.

Seeing some of his best friends killed & what seemed to be the cause of freedom shamelessly abandoned, Frank Soldier-of-Fortune Sturgis vowed to get even and would, 2 years later with the squeeze of his finger & his eye on the crosshairs, watching as the top half of JFK's skull was blown to smithereens.

Sturgis would later follow his Karma with the like Karmic defecations of Howard Hunt & G. Gordon Liddy and be caught breaking into the Watergate Hotel.[2]

So the whole JFK thing was a set up. First he was suckered to Dallas by LBJ, then caught in a crossfire between Oswald in the Book Depository building & Sturgis & Hunt* & others who reportedly were dressed as

---

* According to several sources, including David Marchetti, author of *C.I.A. and the Cult of Intelligence*, & the *Independent Research Association*, a memo in Howard Hunt's C.I.A. file places him at the site of the JFK killing that day. The memo states, "Someday we're going to have to explain to one Congressional Committee or another what Howard Hunt was doing in Dealey Plaza November 22, 1963."

bums & positioned behind the infamous grassy knoll area from which dozens of witnesses claimed to have heard shots arise.

Score: 1 dead President.
(Set up like a bowling pin.)

And to tighten things up a bit, one dead Lee Harvey Oswald. And to tighten things up a bit further, one dead Jack Ruby, killer of Lee Harvey Oswald. And to tighten things up a bit further still, bunches of dead witnesses who had told their story to the Warren Commission investigating the President's death.

So the President's dead, one of the assassin's dead, the assassin's assassin's dead, witnesses snuffed; now the only thing left to do was to convince the American public that the Kennedy killing was the work of a lone crazo- case closed.

Enter the Warren Commision and puppet Gerald Ford. He & other members (Allen Dulles) of the Warren Commission did everything in their power to remold the obvious facts of the JFK assassination (notably that it was an inside hit, a conspiracy involving several planners & triggermen) into the appearance of another reality altogether. This took some doing. Like Life magazine stopping its presses on October 2, 1964 & replacing frames of the Zapruder film of JFK getting shot (which it owned) which showed an obvious strike from the front with a frame taken later in which the direction of the shot cannot be ascertained. Also by leaking information to the F.B.I. & C.I.A., some of which directly concerned the agencies themselves, Ford was instrumental in maintaining & selling their version of the President's murder to the American people.* He even wrote a book espousing the lone assassin theory. Ford would later be maneuvered into position to take over power from Richard Nixon when he was exposed for the slug that he was, & to pardon him so that he kept his mouth shut about all the things he knew about (the JFK bump off, perhaps).

So JFK got X'd by members of the C.I.A. & Cuban exiles group, with assistance from the Mob & U.S. intelligence & law enforcement agencies, backed by the Texas oil cartel upset at Kennedy's plan to repeal the 27.5% oil depletion allowance. Certainly his promise after the Bay of Pigs to scatter the C.I.A. to the wind in a thousand pieces did nothing to ensure his longevity. His firing of C.I.A. director Allan Dulles (later on the Warren Commission) and his counterintelligence chief, General Cabell

---

* An internal F.B.I. memo from December 17, 1963 discussed the various items Ford passed to Cartha DeLoach, then assistant to the F.B.I. director. Ford repeatedly did not reveal his illegal & improper actions to the other members of the Warren Commission as he continued to subvert its purpose.[3]

(whose brother was the mayor of Dallas when JFK was shot) would not be left unanswered.

For not only were members of the Bay of Pigs invading force (2506 Brigade, Alpha 66, & Operation 40) pissed at Kennedy, so was the Mob who stood to make millions, eventually billions, of dollars by regaining control of their Cuban casino interests. The fact that Kennedy was sleeping with Chicago mobster Sam Giancana's girlfiend (Judith Campbell Exner who was introduced to both men by Frank Sinatra) may also have helped put the mark on him. Thru her he passed notes back & forth to the Mafia & met Sam 10 times, brokering power with the mob. This was a mistake John Kennedy was not going to live to regret. Like the cheap hustlers on the street: don't deal with them, don't look them in the eye, don't let them into your world even a bit or they'll take you for everything you got- even your life if they can. And most important of all, don't ask the mob for their help in winning an election (voter fraud in Texas & Illinois) if you're going to prosecute them later.

Giancana would later be murdered June 19, 1975 one day before he was to go before a Congressional hearing on C.I.A.-Mafia assassination conspiracies looking into the Kennedy assassination. Coincidentally, mobster John Roselli, the original syndicate member enlisted to kill Castro, was also killed at the time because of the House Assassinations Committee and the fact that he had been talking to newspaper columnist Jack Anderson. Hmph!

Which brings us back to the original question- how did such a son-of-a-bitch as Richard Nixon ever get to be President once let alone two times?

Chapter 11

After JFK was iced by the Men in Black, darkness descended swiftly across the land. Lyndon Johnson (affectionately known to millions of TV viewers as Lyndon Elephant-Ears Johnson) was sworn in as our 36th President, & off the 7th Cavalry charged into the quicksand of Vietnam.

In 1964 LBJ enlisted renowned baby doctor & Peace activist Benjamin Spock's last minute campaign help urging parents to vote for Johnson, who promised to deescalate the Indochina conflict.

Just weeks after he won the election, however, Johnson began what was to be an immense escalation of the war. The following year, 1965, our troop involvement there rose from 25,000 to 200,000 from just spring to fall.

Spock immediately chastised him for it, & in return Johnson had Spock & 12 others arrested for assisting draft resisters. In effect the first Underground Railway since the Civil War was in operation, funnelling war resisters to safety in Canada & Sweden. Spock got off, LBJ got deeper into the bog & the Smothers Brothers got their show thrown right off the air* for doing an antiwar musical stint with Pete Seeger.

In the times to come even Dan Blocker, Hoss Cartwright of Bonanza low-riding fame, would renounce his U.S. citizenship & move to Sweden in protest of our growing involvement in Vietnam.

And even the Heavyweight Boxing Champion of the World, Muhammed Ali (formerly Cassius Clay) would be stripped of his title, lose the best three years of his boxing career & be jailed for resisting the draft. Saying in effect, I've got nothing against my yellow brothers & I'm not going to kill them for no white man's jive; here he won his greatest fight.

Signs of defiance were everywhere. At the 1968 Olympics two Black American Olympic medal winners, Tommie Smith & John Carlos, were stripped of their honors for giving the upraised fist or Black Power salute during the playing of the Star Spangled Banner.

And defiance was not limited to only those outside the military. In Vietnam resistance came in the form of desertion, refusal to fight, sabotage & fraggings. Fraggings were the killing of military commanders whose orders & actions were certain to get the men they were in charge

---

* CBS was the culprit.

of killed; but these commanders met death not from the hands of enemy fire but from their own men, & their deaths were written off as enemy fire. By 1971 there were about 500 fraggings a year taking place in Vietnam.[1]

But to those at home, it was events in Vietnam themselves which brought many to an awareness that our role there was neither just nor moral and in clear certainty was in vain.

On March 8, 1968 an American army company landed in the Vietnamese village of My Lai and proceeded to massacre the 300-400 men, women, & children who lived there.

This was standard operating procedure with the Army- it has been since they slaughtered the American Indians; that is, eradicating the native base of support of the insurgency. This practice went on day after day in Vietnam but was kept from the American TV-programmed consciousness. When the facts came out a year later Americans got a good look at what we were really doing over there- killing, raping, burning, pillaging, all for Democracy, all so the very people we were killing could be free.

But they were not lying down and playing dead before their time. On January 31, 1968 the Viet Cong launched a huge military offensive across South Vietnam, striking scores of towns, villages, provincial capitals, a dozen U.S. military bases, and even overrunning the American Embassy in Saigon. The Tet Offensive (executed on & named after the Lunar New Year) was clear proof that the Viet Cong (although suffering substantial casualties & driven back out of the cities) were still a major military force who had extensive support amongst the people of the South. This proved a significant victory for the Viet Cong as the American public had been told all along that the war was under control no problem. But Tet showed otherwise. This in turn gave further ammunition for the antiwar forces in the United States who by that time were just plain disgusted at the conduct of their country & the vulgarity of the politics of killing.

But vulgarities and the politics of killing were two subjects to which Lyndon Johnson was no stranger. In the 80's it would come out that while Vice-President, Johnson ordered the murder of a government accounting employee, Henry H. Marshall, who knew of kickbacks Johnson had arranged thru a federal subsidy program to his friends while still in Congress. Although the victim was bound & gagged & shot five times in the abdomen with a bolt-action .22 rifle and died of a head wound & asphyxiation by carbon monoxide, the case still went on record as a suicide. It was federal testimony and a book by Billy Sol Estes, one of the principal participants, which revealed his & Lyndon's role in the killing.

What a Long Strange Trip It's Been

So certainly the death of a few hundred thousand Vietnamese thru the awesome military power at his disposal was not an item which worried or would have been considered particularly vulgar by a man like that.[2]

This can best be seen in his own sense of security & personal intimacy. LBJ was immensely fond of holding private Presidential conferences in the bathroom while he sat on the executive shitter grunting heavily to relieve himself, while his conferees squirmed uncomfortably in the small, repugnant confines of this lost Cowboy's dreams.[3]

And that's when the first major victory of the New Left was won. When on March 31, 1968 Lyndon Baines Johnson appeared on the magic tube & knowing himself to be a king without subjects, withdrew from the Presidential race.

The reason for Johnson's withdrawal was the growing antiwar sentiment among voters which was apparent at the New Hampshire primary. Although winning the actual vote (by a sheer 410 votes) Johnson lost to Eugene McCarthy on purely moral grounds and could see the handwriting on the wall. This victory would have far more significance when the voting age was lowered from 21 to 18 in July of 1971 which further empowered those young people who were against the war who previously could not register their official objection to government policy thru any other way than political street action or resisting if drafted.

With McCarthy the only openly declared Peace candidate in the running, Bobby Kennedy then jumped into the race to ensure the forces of Peace had a candidate who was both capable of winning the election and stopping the war.

Chapter 12

And that's where it was at in '68- stopping the war.

Good & Evil lay clearly before each other, with ourselves like chessmen spread out amidst the forest, & foggy realms between. But the children of the land were not about to stand idly by & be pawns in the Wars of the Dark Lords...for they knew that violence and killing were wrong- for whatever the reason. And the reason it was wrong was because God had said so.

And if you want to spend another lifetime or two chained to this illusion, then murder's your door. Just like Moses & the Promised Land.

"Babe, I can hear you knockin' but you can't come in."

So for every Soul who's duped by their government to kill for freedom, they lose their own, & the laughter of Lucifer can be heard clear to Eternity's ceiling; just knowing that with the return of more Souls to Earth this whole Illusion will last just a bit longer, & with it, evil itself. And hate.

Let's talk a bit about hate. That's the real enemy. It was Peace & Love vs. War & Hate in the 60's, and if your love turned to hate then you just became one of them. There was a lot of hate directed toward longhaired activists as well as the hate felt by Vietnam Vets when they returned from doing their bidding in the jungles of Vietnam. The Vets were many times psychologically devastated because at least the protestors were on the side which was morally correct. They, meanwhile, had been brainwashed & forced by their government to kill at the drop of a hat; and afterwards these killings deeply affected their feelings toward themselves, pushing twice as many Vets over the edge into suicide as the war itself had killed. These scars are deep and hard to get over even today. But those who later realized their role in this killing was wrong will at least receive just Karmic redemption for their repentance, if never Peace in this world. And it was thru conditioning people to hate that they so easily killed. Instead people should be conditioned to love, and thru nonviolence, to bring real Peace to the world.

And how about those Vietnam Vets who still go around playing army & reliving the war. Obviously they didn't learn the lesson the first time, and sad but true, alot of people got off on the whole scene. The fact that they're still into hatred & killing proves that they're just caught in their own private hell.

What a Long Strange Trip It's Been

For the purpose of this plane is to provide a stage where our Souls may evolve away from violence & selfish desire; where they may burn away their negative Karma, while all the time fending off the Legions of Evil who form an endless line of servants holding trays heaped full of more enslaving Karma, waiting just outside your door.

"Dinner is served."
(The Last Supper.)
"No, thanks, I'm fasting."
Fasting, Praying, Waiting.

So war being the greatest manifestation of Evil indeed, in deed, those in the service of war have bound their Souls over to Satan; whether they know this or will admit this or not. And Satan is but the polar opposite of God- existing only in this world... an anti-form from which you must drift if you're ever to get to Heaven's shore.

Which is the reason for all of this anyhow. Getting to Heaven.

And bringing the Peace of Heaven to Earth. To stop suffering instead of creating it. If we were truly concerned about the welfare of all the world's people and worked as a world to provide food & shelter for all, then there would be neither the need nor the greed which is the cause of most wars.

But at the time we had a full-gear war on our hands. The corporate powers were just waiting to take over Southeast Asia & exploit the vast amount of resources there, while the C.I.A., neck deep in heroin, hoped to take over the infamous Golden Triangle poppy-growing region for their own personal profit and to finance their mercenary wars around the world.

("I expect that American oil companies will invest over 37 billion dollars in Southeast Asia during the 70's."- David Rockefeller[7])

So once again in an effort to protect their foreign interests, the corporate powers which rule this land pulled the strings in the White House and the United States military might invaded yet another country in order to make it free from the tyranny of Communism,

&

just another whore for Capitalism.

IV

Chapter 13

Vietnam.
Never have such atrocities on such a massive scale been committed against such an undeserving people in the entire history of this planet. Take heed believers of Karmic return. Better go groove with the kangaroos, 'cause someday this whole land's gonna rock & roll.

Bigtime Babylon breakdown boogaloo.

By August of 1968 2 million tons of bombs & rockets had been dropped on North Vietnam alone. That's twice as many bombs as were dropped on Europe in all of World War II! And that was before Nixon. He'd see to it we'd drop another 4 1/2 million tons before it was over. And that was just from the air. Counting naval artillery & other explosives, altogether we dropped more than 14 million tons of bombs on Vietnam.

In Laos where we waged a secret & totally illegal air war from 1964 to 1973, the heaviest concentration of bombs in history was dropped- an estimated two tons of bombs for every person in one province alone. People & children are still dying today because of the tens of thousands of unexploded antipersonnel bombs which are endlessly strewn across the countryside- in fields, the jungles, everywhere- as many as 1,000 per person in some areas.

And in Cambodia, another "secret" & totally illegal bombing war was carried out from 1969-73, disposing of 500,000 tons of bombs upon the countryside & God knows how many peasants. All courtesy of our tax dollars & our totally fucking insane leaders.

The old macho face saver "if we were allowed to fight the war the way we wanted & if we'd thrown everything we had at them we'd have won" is true only to the extreme. We stripped their forests with Agent Orange, bombed endless craters into their land making it some God-foresaken lunar nitemare, & we burned the flesh off their bodies courtesy of Dow Chemical. (Napalm burns at up to 2,000 degrees & is a creeping fire jelly, thus, in effect, bringing the ovens to the people- a much easier procedure. Dow was making 50,000 pounds of napalm a month for use in Vietnam at the time.) And you call that not trying?

Nothing short of nuclear bombs would have defeated the spirit, determination, & ultimate victory of the Vietnamese people. And the same can be said of the people in El Salvador, Tibet, China, & America today.

A Hippy's History of the Sixties

By 1969-70 we had half a million troops in Vietnam. From 1965-68 a daily bombing offensive was carried out against North Vietnam. With the exception of Hanoi & Haiphong (which themselves experienced extensive bombing, civilian targets included) there was not a stone, brick, or concrete structure left standing south of the 21st parallel when the bombing stopped.[1]

Our official reason for entering the Vietnam War was a fraud- a supposed unprovoked attack on a U.S. Navy boat when no such attack occurred. LBJ then railroaded thru Congress the Gulf of Tonkin Resolution giving him the power to begin the massive destruction of Vietnam.

And once we were beaten the fraud continued. Because of hurt pride and because they're such cold-hearted bastards, Richard Nixon & Henry Kissinger made sure that the agreements upon which the Paris Peace Accords were signed- providing American money for the reconstruction of Vietnam- were never implemented, thus following the long line of treaty breakers who have inhabited the White House.*

And in the 1980's Ronald Reagan still bombed civilians in Libya & massacred thousands of Nicaraguan citizens (12,000 by 1986) with a band of C.I.A.-Somoza thugs called Contras and our tax dollars.

To have allowed this to continue in our names, Americans showed signs of being the most politically stupid, uncaring, & spineless people on the planet.

Again, the result & response of a dulled & programmed mass. Or so it would appear. To other American's credit, they matched almost dollar for dollar the amount of money given to the Contras for military purposes with private donations given to the Nicaraguan people for humanitarian purposes and to repair some of the damage done by Reagan's hired guns.

So it was a bad thing going down here- it's still going down the tubes if we don't catch it soon.

But it was the Vietnamese people who were catching it then...bombs raining down on their heads like raindrops from Hell.

When the American people really started protesting the war, the government began a new phase of the war called Vietnamization. Namely, this was a way of reducing American casualties by putting South Vietnamese troops on the front line and turning the war into a high-tech automated air-warfare type of scene. Everything that moved was bombed. Electronic sensors were dropped in the field and would

---

* Namely, section 21 of the treaty. Nixon had promised them 4 3/4 billion dollars in a letter dated February 1, 1973. Nothing new. To date the U.S. government has broken 371 treaties with the American Indians. About every one, if not every one.

What a Long Strange Trip It's Been

transmit signals which alerted the base of some movement in the area (be it enemy, water buffalo or children) and B52s would be dispatched to make a few craters at those co-ordinates & stop enemy movements.

But even the modernest technology couldn't defeat these people.

And what about the Vietnamese people? What was their sin to deserve such terror?

Their sin was that they wanted to be free.

                              Here's their story-

Chapter 14

From 1884 until 1940 the French government ruled Vietnam from a decidedly colonial point of view.

(Lest the true nature of their barbarism go unnoticed today, although they've no empire left, the French content themselves with blowing up the ships and killing the crew members of environmental protection groups and rabidly building nuclear power plants, purposely having a meltdown, & blowing off nuclear test bombs to pollute the world.)[1]

With the collapse of the French Government to the Nazis in 1940, the Japanese moved into Indochina & took control of the French possessions there, yet permitted the French to continue to administer Vietnam, as they were doing such a "Vichy" job of it. During World War II the Vietnamese liberation army (the Viet Minh) continued to resist the Japanese presence. Led by longtime revolutionary & Vietnamese nationalist Ho Chi Minh and with the help of arms provided by the United States, they succeeded in liberating a large part of the Vietnamese countryside from Japanese control.

When the Japanese surrendered in the fall of 1945 the Viet Minh proceeded to seize power in Hanoi and, with the diplomatic abdication of Emperor Bao Dai & their near takeover of Saigon, formed a national government based in Hanoi. On September 2, 1945 Ho Chi Minh announced the independence & unification of Vietnam, asking for recognition from the respective world governments.

The Declaration of Independence of Vietnam begins: "All men are created equal. They are endowed by their Creator with certain inalienable rights. Among these are life, liberty, and the pursuit of happiness."[2]

Sound familiar? It should. Ho was patterning his government after the founding fathers of America. A free democratic country of Vietnamese people who, after countless years of French & Japanese domination, wanted to choose & govern their own destiny. For Ho Chi Minh was the George Washington of Vietnam* and had worked all his life to bring freedom to his country.

The French, however, had different ideas. Just three weeks after the Vietnamese had declared independence the French, with help from the British, wrestled control of Saigon from the Democratic Republic of

---

* Except that Ho didn't own any slaves.

What a Long Strange Trip It's Been

Vietnam and soon extended their control to all of the cities in the South.

Then the real struggle began. For the next 9 years the Vietnamese people and their democratically elected leader Ho Chi Minh (elected 1-6-46) diplomatically & militarily resisted the French forces until May of 1954, when the French, having been encircled by Vietnamese troops at Dienbienphu, held out for two months but finally surrendered.

(At the time of the French defeat it was the United States that was footing 75% of the bill, nearly 3 billion dollars by 1954 for the attempted recolonization of Vietnam.)

Two months later the French & Vietnamese met in Geneva and signed a cease fire which allowed for the temporary separation of Vietnam into North & South until the formation of a single government thru free and general elections which were guaranteed to be held by July 1956, thus finally establishing and recognizing the independence, unity, sovereignty & territorial integrity of the nation of Vietnam.

The following year, however, Emperor Bao Dai, who was back running things in the South, was unseated by Ngo Dinh Diem who then declared the southern zone of Vietnam a separate state and made himself president. He also cancelled at the behest of the American government the elections called for in the Geneva accords which were due to be held the next year. For the next four years the North tried diplomatically to persuade the South to participate in general elections, but to no avail.

In the South, meanwhile, armed insurgency began anew with the formation of the National Liberation Front (N.L.F.) of South Vietnam. The N.L.F. or Viet Cong were made up mainly of displaced Southerners, rejoining former Viet Minh compadres & gaining control of their former homelands.[3]

In the following years both the presence of the Viet Cong insurgents and American counter-insurgency advisors grew steadily in the South. Under the Kennedy Administration our committment continued to increase until Kennedy himself began seeing our involvement there as growing too deep and began steps to extricate us.

On November 1, 1963, just as 1,000 U.S. troops had been ordered withdrawn from South Vietnam, a military coup occurred apparently backed by the U.S. in which President Diem of South Vietnam and his brother were killed.[4]

Just three weeks later, however, a similar fate awaited John F. Kennedy, and he was no longer at the helm of American foreign policy in Southeast Asia.

With the assassination of JFK, Vice-President Lyndon Johnson arose to the throne & was now in command. Instead of troops being withdrawn, Johnson began an almost immediate escalation of the American involvement in Vietnam. This continued steadily, pausing briefly for him to get elected in 1964 over Republican right-winger Barry Goldwater, whose Vice-Presidential candidate General Curtis LeMay promised to bomb Indochina back to the Stone Age.

But LBJ would take care of that himself. On February 7, 1965 the United States began the daily systematic bombing of North Vietnam, which lasted 3 years and did as much to devastate Lyndon Johnson's political career as it did the countryside of Vietnam.

    It was a vulgar act from an equally vulgar man.

Chapter 15

By the time Lyndon Johnson decided not to run for re-election in 1968 we were so far into the dragon's throat that we couldn't see the fire for the smoke. But that things were getting hotter was an undeniable fact, spoken loudly by Lyndon's own political retire.

The American people were getting sick of this immoral & atrocious war, of the nitely body counts on TV, and LBJ knew that if this went on much longer, he'd have a full blown revolution on his hands. The youth were on the move & injustice was on the run. For years the Cosmos had been setting the stage for this limited engagement, and the puzzlepieces randomly floating down on the breezes of the Summer of Love suddenly found themselves joining together to bring about a hitherto unseen picture to view.

Out with the old & in with the new. Again all possibilities were possible- especially Peace. Why not?

Now Lyndon's demise was the result of the close weaving of cultural threads which formed themselves more like a noose of truth than a coat of many colours. These threads, of course, were the single cells of the still evolving culture itself; rapidly forming itself into a coat of so many colours that it virtually covered the Earth in its inborn intent of stopping the Apocalyptic course of those four well-known horsemen of lore.

These cultural threads then were woven from the looms of music, politics, & drugs; and it was from these that people's minds of the time were spun.

And are still spinning...

Chapter 16

In the early 60's it was folk music which marched shoulder to shoulder with the Civil Rights Movement which did the most to awaken people's eyes to the injustice around them and the inherent necessity for change. Music became political communique & focal point. Folk music was its roots, spreading its branches from Greenwich Village in New York City all the way to the west coast.

Troubadours & Cellar Doors.

Bob Dylan had the visionary genius to not only perceive the prophetic role which the times required, but he had the creative talent to fill that role with his own shade of aloofness & mystique; speaking for those both underground and under thumb. He gave individuals the understanding that they themselves were important forces of change, and that they were the reason the times were a' changin.

This identity with the winds of change and the rapid replication of these amoebic cells thru the unification & message of music, was what fused the few into a culture. The Human Be-In January 14, 1967 at Golden Gate Park in San Francisco was the first time this new-born babe looked in the mirror & saw itself a full 20,000 strong. Later looks would include Woodstock (half a million strong), Altamont (not strong enough), the death of John Lennon, and that which looms somewhere thru the door before us.

Other musicians of the time whose names are engraved with change were Woody Guthrie, Joan Baez, Pete Seeger, Phil Ochs, Peter, Paul & Mary, The Mommas & the Pappas, Tom Paxton, Judy Collins, & Buffy St. Marie.

On the electric side of things it was the Doors, Jefferson Airplane, Jimi Hendrix, Country Joe & the Fish, Crosby, Stills, Nash & Young, the M.C.5, the Fugs, the Stones, & the Who who might be charged with insighting the riot. Jimi Hendrix was a true voodoo child, and Jim Morrison could have been the lone panther calling in the darkness & the stars would have still come far-to-near in soaring swiftness to travel by his side.

He was a wildman.

    It was a time of extraordinary people in extraordinary roles,
        taking extraordinary chances,
            living extraordinary lives.

What a Long Strange Trip It's Been

And just as music was both serving & defining the political consciousness of the emerging culture, so too it was symbiotically responsible with marijuana & L.S.D. for the awakening of intelligence and spiritual consciousness among its members.

Marijuana had the unsurpassed quality of making one think,* & L.S.D. spoke for itself if not for God.

It was the Beatles, Donovan, & the Moody Blues who most spoke for the mystical side of the psychedelic genre; while Pink Floyd, Cream, Led Zeppelin, the Iron Butterfly, Quicksilver Messenger Service, and Ten Years After were meant strictly to melt in your mind.

But most of all it was the Beatles (masquerading as Sgt. Pepper's Lonely Hearts Club Band masquerading as the Beatles...) who molded our collective vision- our quest for outer & inner peace. Turned on themselves first to pot by Bob Dylan and then to L.S.D. by their dentist (Dr. Robert), they explored & painted the possibilities before us, in the exquisite mind-styles of Peter Max, Maxfield Parrish, & M.C. Escher.

With Revolver, Rubber Soul, Sgt. Pepper's, Magical Mystery Tour, the White Album, Abbey Road, & the movie Yellow Submarine, they defined our furthest nursery rhymes, and for a while our rhymes were real. For it was from them which our dreams were woven, drawing tight our cultural threads.

---

* Its critics have called it demotivating, but some people have to be de-motor-vated in order to sit down & think. And what follows thought is action, which is precisely why the government sees pot as a danger. They don't want people to think, let alone act!

And speaking of cultural threads, what can be said of The Dead. The Grateful Dead is the house band of the New Age. There is, was, and never will be anything like the Grateful Dead. This perhaps explains them as well as anything:

> *Just as Jesus was the mystical happening of his time so were the Grateful Dead, who transformed the hearts & minds of countless ardent seekers into the folds of a new revolution. Make no mistake about it. Those who spent half their lives on the road catching shows, bumming rides, sharing joints, & dancing in the pouring rain, were seeking religious experience; Divine Communion with their fellow humans, & with a band whose music represented nothing less than a sacred invocation to the Gods. It was thru the magic of L.S.D. & the ethereal beauty of the Dead, that these most gentle beings, dancing between the stars in the far sky and the Apocalyptic visions in the far & distant nite, offered their Souls to God. And if any tattered shreds survive the coming times, let history be read as such:*
>
> *That amidst the sullen darkness there shone a solitary lite... For it is known 'neath the sands of the Pharaohs- that deep in the land of Nite, the Ship of the Sun, is drawn by*
>
> The Grateful Dead.

What a Long Strange Trip It's Been

And what of the music itself? It was mostly the Airplane & the Dead who musically defined the term Acid Rock, which described the pure synthesis between the energy level of L.S.D. and their (the San Francisco) particular form of sound. It was Its own sound, and was something so characteristically mimical and an entity entirely divorced from the necessity of coming from one particular band that in listening back there are many times when the Sound can be found coming thru the Dead, the Airplane, the Fish, Quicksilver, Big Brother, & others, without a true clue as to which band the Sound is using as its instrument. That was the San Francisco sound, and the uniqueness of the Spirit loose at the time...
          in the town,
                    in the people,
                              in the music.

Chapter 17

But all spokespersons of the psychedelic genre were not musicians. Poetry and posters became important mediums upon which the daydreams of the New Age were displayed & expressed.

Poetry had been a moving force in the beatnik era- it freed people's Souls for a flite of freshness, giving them wings 'mong the hapless cripples. Poetry served many as life companion; charting growth and reflecting one's images of an overwhelmingly complex course of events unfolding in linear motion right before their very eyes... rolling inexplicably toward them in the material guise of the present meeting the future.

Poetry kept more than one within the bounds of sanity and recorded the slipping grips of so many others. This is just to say that sometimes it was hard to hang on to your sanity under the conditions which presented themselves in the era and in the acid-etched outer reaches thru which we found ourselves speeding at the speed of lite.

New Speedway Boogie indeed.

And sometimes it was best to let go of your mind altogether. Which is one of the ultimate lessons of this world anyway. Letting go of everything at the moment of Death and accepting what is transpiring at the time.

As the Starship says in Blows Against the Empire-

"You gotta let go you know or else you stay."

Likewise without letting go of Karmic desire and the attachment to compulsive material addictions in this life, you will never advance enough to advance.

And the fact that many never came back from those times might appear dim consolation for those who have survived and still find themselves a ways from shore; but the fact is that It's a Karmic Sea, and that's been the one truth and reassurance we've learned from all of this...the fact that most did drown by clinging to the weight of their Earthly desires. Nothing should deter the seeker; for there is a goal and tho' the path lay overgrown with age,

    the glint of its yellow bricks,

can still be seen in the fading shades of daylite.

Chapter 18

So just as poetry served as a tool of inner commune and getting things together on an individual level & expressing it outward, the poster became the main tool for assembling these individuals and getting things together on a much larger level.
          Social.   Political.   Spiritual.
The poster was both artform & town crier, and never other than in concert light shows was the psychedelic genre so well defined in visual form.

Psychedelia begins with the eye & ends in the mind. The artists Stanley Mouse, Alton Kelley, Victor Moscoso, Rick Griffin & Peter Max were the undisputed masters of this crafted renaissance.

But the loudest spokesman for the psychedelic epistle was the man from glad himself- Timothy Leary. The man with the Golden Smile. His message was clear & simple:
          Turn on.   Tune in.   Drop out.
          Create a new world on the ruins of the old.

While Ken Kesey & the Prankster crew were responsible for introducing large groups of people to L.S.D. for the first time thru personal experience at their early California Acid Tests (1965-66), Timothy Leary was the one most responsible for causing the spread of information, articles, and interest about L.S.D. in the establishment press.

In the emerging counterculture the Underground Press would develop; the finest being the San Francisco Oracle, an exquisite rag embellished with the same artistic tapestry that adorned the posters in the streets, and giving vital information to the swaddling culture at the time.

So too the Underground Comix would appear- The Furry Freak Brothers, Wonder Warthog, Odd Bodkins, Mr. Natural- written by such patriotically subversive types as Gilbert Shelton, Dan O'Neil, & the sometimes pathetically sexist R. Crumb. They too spoke to the counterculture from somewhere under the counter, addressing the politics & psychedelia of the time.

But most became acquainted with the nature & politics of L.S.D. by reading of the Robin Hood adventures of Dr. Tim in the straight press. This led to countless people wanting to try L.S.D. and experience its beneficial & enlightening effects themselves.

A professor of psychology at Harvard, Leary first took psychedelic

A Hippy's History of the Sixties

mushrooms procured from a local shaman woman in Mexico in 1960. Realizing their immense potential value to the world, he returned to Harvard and established a psylocibin research project and began psychedelic sessions among select members of the faculty and student community. Leary took psylocibin with & then made advisor to the project Aldous Huxley, author of *Doors of Perception* and prime intellesia of the early psychedelic explorers.*

Timothy Leary then met up with Michael Hollingshead, another primo head who had several mayonnaise jars full of L.S.D. which came from Sandoz Laboratories (there's no dose like Sandoz) and turned Tim on to his first acid.

Leary proceeded to do experiments with L.S.D. and positively modified the behavior of alcoholics & criminals and also to investigate its spiritual aspects as well.

His partner in the research project was Richard Alpert, a fairly yupped out assistant professor at Harvard who was to go thru some changes himself. After having his mind opened about as wide as the Milky Way, he & Leary were eventually fired for allegedly experimenting with undergraduates, who by the original guidelines were barred from the program.

Then feeling the heat coming down, he wisely went to India, met a Holy Man and came back to America as Ram Dass, guru & purveyor of the Be Here Now philosophy. Alpert's trod a pretty fair path thru the years, notwithstanding being conned by some sexual gargantuan & spiritual hydra named Joya who pretended to spontaneously bleed from the mouth when she didn't get her way with Baby Ram D. while sexually manipulating him on a power-control trip, as the rest of the ashram followed the prescribed rules of celibacy.

And you thought you had troubles!

So in May 1963 the axe came down on Leary's trip at Harvard but only to cast the entire subject of L.S.D. research and usage out in the public eye. This further reflected the tug of war as to who should have access to these chemical keys to mind expansion- the government (in this case the C.I.A. & the Army for brainwashing experiments) or the people them-selves, who in the proper setting could explore and evolve their consciousness and bring themselves closer to God. For this Leary set up the International Federation for Internal Freedom (IF-IF) and in the summer of 1963, started

---

* Huxley died the same day as JFK, and as he began to head towards the Door had his wife inject him with liquid L.S.D. in order to fully experience the transition. Huxley was a heavyweight. His books *Island*, *Brave New World*, & *Moshka* are well worth reading.

What a Long Strange Trip It's Been

a L.S.D. exploration center in Zihautanejo, Mexico. Here an L.S.D. colony was formed in which screened applicants could go and experience the incredible effects of L.S.D. and all its accompanying implications in a natural environment of an ocean beach community, with the premier psychedelic therapists and heads of the time in attendance. But again the heat came down and in just 6 weeks Leary & crew were forced to leave Mexico because of the pressure from American authorities brought to bear on the Mexican government.

They next set up shop in a totally beautiful 64 room, several thousand acre mansion estate called Millbrook in upstate New York owned by Billy & Peggy Hitchcock, heirs to the Gulf Oil fortune and psychedelic voyagers. Here just a few hours from New York City, Leary renamed the IF-IF and called his new undertaking the Castalia Foundation in honor of a similar colony of spiritual adepts in Herman Hesse's *The Glass Bead Game*. The Millbrook Scene was one both of idyllic splendor and at times psychedelic frenzy. There was an ever arriving and departing entourage of guests, pilgrims, musicians, artists, filmmakers, & paying students who came to expand their minds and whose presence helped support the existence of Millbrook. Millbrook was without a doubt one of the happeningest places of its day.

In December 1965 Leary & his daughter were busted with a small amount of pot* crossing the Mexican border, and he received a 30 year, $30,000 sentence. While on appeal Leary returned to Millbrook to continue his psychedelic offensive, but a few months later more trouble came.

This time in the form of our old buddy G. Gordon Liddy, who at the time was the prosecutor of Duchess County, N.Y. The locals had been pressuring the sheriff to bust Millbrook for several months, and after Timothy came out of the house and purportedly passed around a small silver platter with neatly lined rows of hits of L.S.D. on it in front of an NBC news camera crew, this all got on the news and things just got worse. So in April 1966 Gordon Liddy & forces busted this psychedelic Wonderland, only to find nothing but a spot of pot and have the case thrown right out of court 'cause he forgot to read Uncle Tim his rights. But from then on the heat was turned up high until our psychedelic pioneers were once again forced to flee in the spring of '67.

By this time psychedelics were beginning to take root in America. L.S.D. had been made illegal October 6, 1966 but that did little to deter the seekers. There were psychedelic enclaves on both east & west coasts and the Summer of Love was just dawning. In Laguna Beach, California the

---

* Less than one ounce.

Brotherhood of Eternal Love was formed, a truly cosmic band of righteous dealer types whose goal was to spread the psychedelic message by spreading the psychedelics. Distributing Owsley's acid from the Haight, they also developed an extremely proficient Afghanistan hashish smuggling operation which was credited by the government with making 200 million dollars or so all told. At any rate it was with the Brotherhood which Leary next set up shop, along the beach, preaching the psychedelic bible as resident High Priest. Now if you thought Millbrook was a happening scene, this beat all. Mellow California hippies with Berkeley just up the coast a waze. The Brotherhood & the Psychedelic Movement continued to grow until state & federal agents began investigating their operation in 1971 and finally arrested over 40 people and seized over 1 and a half million doses of acid, 2 and a half tons of hash, 30 gallons of hash oil, & lots of pot and money.[1]

In March 1973 the Brotherhood was again ratted out by Billy Hitchcock, the owner of Millbrook. In late 1967 after Owsley was busted at his factory and given three years, it was Hitchcock who joined forces with the Brotherhood and put together the chemists & connections to make over ten million hits of orange sunshine. So people went to jail (Billy didn't) and the Brotherhood of Eternal Love still stands as legend for those who did their part and for those doing theirs today.

As for Leary, he was popped again for marijuana possession in Laguna Beach while living there. The amount involved was miniscule, but he was still facing a 30 year sentence from his bust at the Mexican border. When his trial came to date in February 1970 the particular climate of the times (just three months before 13 students were shot at Kent for dissenting) was such that Timothy Leary was made the martyr of the time, sentenced to 20 years in prison for his slight affair with Mary Jane & for being a "nuisance to society." Well, wasn't society a nuisance to him?

Nonetheless Leary would daringly escape from prison seven months later in a plan financed by the Brotherhood and carried out by the Weather Underground. Hiding out in safehouses & Indian reservations along the way, Leary issued a statement warning that not only was he free but he was armed and dangerous. This may have been a foolish jest on his part intended to please his rescuers, but did little to endear those Peace freaks who had cheered his escape.

Next thru negotiations by Abbie Hoffman, Leary & his wife Rosemary successfully slipped out of the country in disguise and fled to Algeria where Eldridge Cleaver & the Black Panthers had set up their government in exile after being forcibly driven from the U.S. by the law. At first Leary's escape and subsequent surfacing was a great propaganda coup for the

What a Long Strange Trip It's Been

Movement. The Acid King had not only formed an alliance with the radical Underground but with the Black Revolution to boot, all the while eluding the legions of law enforcement officials who were hot on his heels.

That soon turned out to be not quite the case. Leary & Cleaver worked from two completely different wavelengths- Leary into personal freedom and Cleaver into militaristic control. And to make things worse the F.B.I. & C.I.A. had infiltrated Cleaver's circle and ensured that the friction between the two continued. Leary it seems had brought 20,000 hits of acid with him and wanted to turn on most of Africa. Cleaver was not into this at all and announced that something was wrong with Leary's brain and had him put under house arrest.

Finally the Brotherhood of Eternal Love bailed him out for 25 grand and he & Rosemary fled to Switzerland where he was first jailed for six weeks, then let out in the care of a man of wealth and influence whom Tim called Goldfinger. With financial support from his benefactor plus the advance from the book he was writing (*Confessions of a Hope Fiend*) Leary spent 16 more months in Switzerland, traveling village to village staying until he had to move on. During this time due to the grind of life on the run, he & Rosemary split and her role was replaced by Joanna Harcourt Smith.

As Leary had been denied asylum three times by the Swiss government, he & Joanna decide to move on, but were snatched at the airport in Afghanistan and January 17, 1973 returned to L.A. where he was sentenced to five more years for escaping and sent to Folsom prison for 25 years.

While in jail Leary learned that both Joanna & Dennis Martino (his son-in-law's brother who also had been busted with them in Afghanistan and been in the Brotherhood) were not only having an affair, but had sold out and become government informers. Martino had helped bust 24 people and both he & Joanna constantly urged Leary to co-operate with his captors. Finally after 13 months he bargained his way towards freedom by beginning to sing. What Tim Leary told was old news for the most part, but he did give testimony which resulted in a lawyer serving 45 days in jail for once giving him a piece of hash.

So Leary's import to the fuzz was not so much as who he could help them bust, but how much distrust would be sown in the underground community when it was learned that the good Dr. Tim was squealing. And it not only did that, but for all he'd been thru and sacrificed it substantially damaged his L.S.D. credo & credentials at the time. Dennis Martino for his part was found dead in Spain- o.d. or so it looked- perhaps Karmic return.

For his part Leary was finally released from jail in September '76 and since then has toured the country as a stand up comic, as the proponent

A Hippy's History of the Sixties

of space migration, life extension, intelligence enhancement thru personal computers, and did a debate tour with Gordon Liddy. Since then his words & writings have accurately reflected the issues to which they're addressed, and Timothy Leary still remains one of the 10 most brilliant minds of the 20th Century.* He has, however, never regained nor honestly sought the stature which once crowned him as the Acid King. Which in a way is too bad.

That's perhaps the greatest lesson- never sell out no matter what the cost. For that's what happened to much of the Revolution. It was sold out by individuals and was co-opted by Madison Avenue....Kinda like Woodstock '94. How far and how fast the Movement advanced depended upon a number of things, the most essential being communication. The rock stars of the 60s should have bought one AM radio station per large city instead of spending all of their money on cocaine and such, and then we might be somewhere today. To stifle communication, to co-opt its mouthpiece was to stifle the Movement. Rolling Stone magazine is a perfect case in point. In the spring of 1968 Jann Wenner, head of Rolling Stone magazine, sold out to Xerox Corporation for a $100,000 "loan" in return for a pledge to discourage youth attendance at the 1968 Chicago counter convention and to help stem the "radical" politicization of the youth. Since then Rolling Stone moved from S.F. to N.Y. and became a slick, sold-out, bullshit music rag with high-priced Army ads and nothing much to offer but yuppie conformity. It was an early blow which definitely slowed things down alot.

But the worst sell out is selling other people out and sending them to jail. Too many people have been making too many deals and getting too many other people in trouble just to get themselves off the hook. You know what I mean. Right, Greg? . . . Eh, TAPPER?

You take the risk always, whether you're moving drugs, doin' politics, or any anti-establishment evolutionary activity. It's your trip, you know the hazards, and if you're still willing to stay on the line and fight for change, then you damned well always be ready to win, run, or fall. But never inform. No matter what. I don't care how long they put me away for- my life's for the cause or there's no cause at all. And remember...

Loose Lips Sink Ships.

---

* The other 9 will have to find themselves...

What a Long Strange Trip It's Been

So you talk about selling out...

How about Gracie Slick on those soap commercials. I mean maybe in '68 she wished everybody used Dial, but not today. Come on. At least she's still quick on the draw.

And Ringo Starr on the wine cooler commercials...if that's not masturbating on John Lennon's grave I don't know what is.

And Boy-Wonder Michael "I only beat off with my diamond glove on" Jackson. Ole Mr. Elephant Man himself. Jackson selling the Beatle's song "Revolution" to Nike shoes for a TV ad- these people got no sense of the Eternal or Karmic return.

And how about these New Age Channelers. What bullshit. These people might think they're acting as spiritual guides for others and doing a good deed, but all they're doing is fleecing the marks. Those gullibles in the New Age culture who pay money to get their egos stroked and find out what sort of Princess they were their last lifetime, should realize that none of that really matters and get on to the job of evolving themselves this time around. You're on the cutting edge of the New Age. Know it and use it. Don't abuse it. Or look for Messiahs lit up with Christmas lights. Or driving Rolls Royces. Alot of conning goes on in the Aquarian Age, and you can bet that if you're paying money, then you're tuned into the wrong channel.

If you fellow New Agers really want to do something- OM. By yourself or form OM circles. This is the real way to heal the world. Hold OM-ins and really see a change in material events in response to the focused energy, purpose & the age-old technique of employing vibratory intonation for planetary Peace & Healing. Just sit in a circle, and after a short prayer indicating intent & a short period of deep breathing to center, begin. Holding hands if you like, repeat the mantra OM nonstop for 20-30 minutes, maintaining a constant force of sound. Focus your voices into a single sound, and with your minds visualize the Earth bathed in a halo of shining Lite, sending healing energy to all and restoring the natural balance of Peace. Once you have started you will reach a point where the sound will carry on itself, the people acting merely as an instrument or channel for the tone coming thru them. At the end let the OMing slowly wind down to a stop. OMing can well hold Evil at bay & save the world.

At any rate, before the hounds of treachery & deception were unleashed upon the flower culture,
  in those days,
             Peace could be seen for the looking,
             Love could be had for the sharing,
             Heaven had come to Earth.

A Hippy's History of the Sixties

There was a certain feeling in the air,* and something was definitely happening. I could feel it all the way to Pennsylvania as a kid when the Jefferson Airplane's White Rabbit hit the airwaves and blew my mind for a short time until it was banned from the air. I mean banned...disappeared. The government was censoring all drug-related songs from the radio. No mind expansion allowed here.

I anxiously awaited the release of each new Airplane album, for they above others were telling it straight the way it was; in the mindframe of the emerging acid culture as it bumped heads with that which was but should be changed.

Spare change?

The establishment could spare no change at all. While the world around was veritably cumming in colours, it shunned the show and got all the rainbows it needed from the N.B.C. peacock.

The status quo had to be maintained even thru the turbulent winds about them.

Which was not easy.

---

* The Earth was charged up.

Chapter 19

With all this happening right out from under them and LBJ bowing out of the '68 Presidential race, the known unknowns behind the throne had to scramble fast to peruse a plan which would keep them in power. True to their nature it was assassination to which they turned once again.

Just four days after Johnson sung his swan song, Martin Luther King was murdered in Memphis by an assassin of the unknowns. This was not only instrumental in stemming the ascending tide of Black Power in America and halting the rise of a "Black Messiah" with which the F.B.I. & J. Edgar Hoover were so obsessed, but it set the stage for the most important assassination of them all- Robert Fitzgerald Kennedy.

For it was Bobby Kennedy who was the real Messiah- none of us who really knew this ever doubted it, and we watched as he was nailed before our very eyes. He was the best we had to offer, and the best I'd ever seen, with eyes fixed long and hard upon the horizon both then & now. He could have brought Peace to the entire world (...if anyone could).

Whatever excesses he displayed in his brother's administration he tempered with age and his own awakening.

Bobby took L.S.D., too, and reportedly was turning on U.N. diplomats on the side.[1] He led efforts to legalize L.S.D. research after his wife received successful therapy and in his words "it can be very, very helpful in our society if properly used." I've no doubt that the world would be a totally different place for the better had Robert Kennedy been elected President in 1968. And he would have, if he hadn't been blown away.

A master checkmate for the Darker Forces. (Enter Richard Nixon.) RFK's killing was a set-up too. After just winning the all-important California primary and giving his victory speech, he was led from the podium thru the kitchen pantry to where Sirhan Sirhan served as a diversionary gunman. In the confusion Kennedy was shot 4 times directly from the rear, the fatal wound being fired from just three inches from the back of the head above the ear. The true assassin was named Thane Eugene Ceasar, a last-minute security guard stand-in with mob connections who disappeared directly after the killing.

Sirhan himself was the fall guy, was tried & put away. Another case of the lone, crazed assassin. But not quite.

The assassination of Robert Kennedy was the result of years of research and hard work by the C.I.A. in the area of mind control and behavior

A Hippy's History of the Sixties

modification thru drugs & hypnosis, specifically hypnotically controlled assassins in Project Artichoke. Sirhan Sirhan was hypnotically programmed to assassinate Robert Kennedy by a Hollywood psychiatrist named William Joseph Bryan, Jr. Bryan worked extensively with the C.I.A. and in this case went as far as having Sirhan present at the ranch of a fundamentalist preacher named Jerry "The Walking Bible" Owen for weeks while being programmed. Owen was associated with Dr. Carl McIntyre., the right-wing fundamentalist who is in tight with the Texas oil crowd that helped bump JFK off. At the time of the killing Owens was waiting outside the back of the Ambassador Hotel in his pick-up truck and horse trailer to be used as the getaway vehicle if necessary. Bryan was also the Hollywood consultant to the movie "The Manchurian Candidate" about a brainwashed assassin programmed to kill the President.

Bryan also bragged of having programmed Arthur Bremer, the assassin who shot and paralyzed right-wing Presidential candidate George Wallace in the 1972 Presidential campaign to once again narrow the field for Richard Nixon.[2] It's interesting to note that Sirhan's immigration sponsors were a prominent Republican California couple who were active in Nixon's big campaigns and had known Tricky Dick at Whittier College.[3] The first I read years ago said that Dick and the woman had been college romantics. Tricky indeed.

The Mafia, too, was glad to see the passing of Robert Kennedy. Kennedy had been extremely hard on organized crime when he had been Attorney General, and the fact that his work helped throw Jimmy Hoffa in jail in 1967 did nothing to endear him to the mob.

He and his brother came up against the forces of Evil and they were both gunned down. They thought themselves invincible, or had to think so, to attempt the perilous job before them. Bravery in the service of Truth can have its costs, both John & Bobby knew this, but they accepted the fact that their lives might be part of the sacrifice. This is what real heroes are all about.

Acts of true heroism are rare. Like Jacqueline Kennedy. By far the most awesome display of love & courage I've seen by any woman was by Jacqueline Kennedy- from the second her husband John was shot, to her scrambling across the trunk grabbing his blown skulltop & putting it back on his head; to her refusing to change her bloodsoaked dress so the world could see what the bastards had done; to her vigil of awesome loneliness... a First Lady has never shone in the shadow of such dark wings which blotted out the sun as did she... it was her beauty which gave Camelot its song, and the walls grew ever cold with her leaving.

What a Long Strange Trip It's Been

So with the death of Robert Kennedy the dreams of the Left lay in shambles. But the forces were far from immobile. For the counterculture had grown up fast and knew how to march. With Robert Kennedy dead, it was up to the rank & file to put their bodies on the line & into the cogs of the machinery of the system in order to bring its atrocities to a halt.

Chapter 20

Students had been getting it together for a long time before they helped stop the war in Vietnam. The first modern western student revolt occurred in Germany in 1815, and today students all over the world are struggling for their future. Most recently in China in 1989 as many as 7,000 students demanding democratic reforms were massacered in Tienanmen Square in Beijing in a brutal display of evil. In the 1960's the Student Movement in America became a political force capable of influencing both domestic & foreign policy and thus history itself.

And it was the Civil Rights Movement which first awoke the social conscience of the American youth, which in itself shows you how radically different they were than the generations before them who sat idly by as the Black race in America remained enslaved.

Given the basic introduction to nonviolent dissent by Gandhi in 1949, it was Dr. Martin Luther King, Jr., who once again adopted the nonviolent approach to sensibly deal with the extreme state of oppression the Black Culture suffered in America in the mid-20th century.

King's efforts first appeared in connection with the Montgomery Bus Boycott, brought on when Rosa Parks, a Black Montgomery citizen, refused to give up her seat to a white person as city law required of nonwhites. The boycott lasted 381 days and resulted in total victory on December 13, 1956 when the U.S. Supreme Court declared segregated seating on Alabama buses illegal.

The struggle continued. In 1960 six Black college students ordered coffee at Woolworth's lunch counter which served whites only and bravely started a six-month sit-in until they got it.

They took it black.

In August 1963 over 250,000 people marched on Washington led by Martin Luther King, Jr. in an action whose impetus led Congress to pass the Civil Rights Voting Act of 1965. That's right. Black Americans were not given full voting rights in this country until 1965, and not until racism was forced out into the open.

Students gave great support to the Civil Rights Movement, and as they joined the cause and moved southward some would never return; murdered by the same white-robed hoodlums whose far-right frame of mind embraces racism, hatred, & killing and who had been lynching Blacks for over a hundred years.

What a Long Strange Trip It's Been

Those who did return put their newly learned organizational skills into action against the growing U.S. involvement in Indochina.

The college campuses became the educational forum & vocal mouthpiece for serious discussions and expressions of dissent concerning the escalating events in Southeast Asia, for the organization and mobilization of workers for Peace candidates, and for the presentation of the true ideals of democracy which the government was so necessarily trying to suppress in order to continue its unlawful practices both at home & abroad.

In March 1965 the first Teach-In was held at the University of Michigan, in which the focus of the entire academic community was turned upon the issue of Vietnam. Teach-Ins led to sit-ins the next year, as more & more opposition to the war crystallized among the college community. On November 15, 1969, the largest march to date on Washington, D.C. was held with over 600,000 people protesting the war.

Chapter 21

On campus organized dissent was most evident in the form of the S.D.S.- the Students for a Democratic Society. The S.D.S. was the largest organized mass-student politicized party of its time.

Formed in January 1960, the S.D.S. directly addressed the truly pressing issues of the day, and in 1962 issued the Port Huron Statement, which called for:

a completely new working of the nation & the way it relates to its workers;

a foreign policy other than militant anti-Communist ventures;

a taking away of the reigns of power from the Military-Industrial Complex;

giving first-off priority to the health & welfare of our own citizens;

and giving maximum attention to the issues of Peace & world disarmament.

In the next eight years the ranks of the S.D.S. would grow to over 100,000 members & 400 chapters nationwide. S.D.S. can be credited with building much of the support among students for the Civil Rights sit-ins in the South in the early 60's. S.D.S. led the first organized student resistance against the draft in 1965 and was the first to raise the question of the morality of university complicity with military research & recruitment.

Education, organization, & nonviolent protest were the main tools used by the S.D.S. and proved quite effective and politically acceptable in transmitting their point of view and widely expanding the opposition to the Vietnam War. These tactics were later used by such groups as the National Student Movement & the Student Mobilization movement to organize other marches & demonstrations against the war.

In a four year anti-R.O.T.C. campaign, 30 campus officer military corps were eliminated, 83 were made voluntary, and enrollment dropped 56%, not to mention the numerous R.O.T.C. buildings that were burned to the ground.

At their 1969 national convention in Chicago in response to the growing government violence against the Movement, more militant members of the S.D.S. formed themselves into a splinter group called the Weatherman Organization, named after a line in Bob Dylan's "Subterranean

What a Long Strange Trip It's Been

Homesick Blues":

"You don't need a weatherman to know which way the wind blows."

They would come to be known as the Weather Underground and would continue to be active long after the mainstream S.D.S., which had remained aboveground to build an illusive student-worker alliance, had pretty well disintegrated (by 1973). Their new tactics were formulated to bring the war home; to let the politicians know that if the war in Indochina was permitted to continue, then they'd have all hell to pay back here. Thus began the subterranean odyssey of the Weather Underground. Their strategy was to use the attention-getting device of symbolic bombings to further publicize the cause, and to threaten the government in terms of its own.

These bombings carried out by the Weatherman Organization were targeted against those complicitly involved in the slaughter of the people of Southeast Asia- R.O.T.C. buildings, draft centers, banks & appropriate corporate headquarters.

And slaughter it was. One out of every 300 people in Indochina was killed. One out of 12 wounded. And one out of five made a refugee.

In the schoolyear after the birth of the Weathermen, there was an average of six antiwar-related bombings a day, although the S.D.S. was in no way responsible for all or even the majority of bombings across the nation. Many attacks on R.O.T.C. buildings were acts of unaffiliated individuals striking their own blows for freedom or agent provocateurs.

One thing should be noted here. The bombings done by the New Left or radical left were aimed at the symbolic destruction of property and not toward the harming of human life. Not once did the antiwar movement pick up guns and really fight as they could have. Which says alot about their values and adherence to their own basic principles of nonviolence. The mass murderers in power are lucky that we threw pies in their faces instead of righteously blowing their shit away.

In only one instance did anyone die as a result of a bomb planted by the left, and that was in Madison, Wisconsin in August 1970 when a physics researcher working late at night was killed in the explosion of the Army Math Research Center. The Center made and housed the computer system directly involved in the co-ordination of bombing runs in Southeast Asia at the time. The system also updated the computers on board the B52s themselves to avoid N. Vietnamese anti-aircraft fire.

The bombing took place at 3:42 a.m. between semesters after the police had been repeatedly notified in advance yet issued no warning. This bombing was not an S.D.S. project, as they usually bombed in symbolic retaliation for acts of murder or aggression by the U.S. government against its own citizens or other countries of the world.

After the murder, for example, of the students at Kent & Jackson State in 1970, the National Guard Headquarters in Washington, D.C. was bombed. The Pentagon after the bombing of Hanoi and the mining of the harbors of North Vietnam in violation of International Law.

The U.S. Capitol following the invasion of Laos in 1971.

The 103rd Precinct of the New York City Police Department for the police killing of ten-year-old Clifford Grove in May 1973.

In all these no one lost their lives, yet the Weatherpeople themselves lost three members (Diana Oughton, Ted Gold, & Terry Robbins) when a bomb they were building in a N.Y.C. townhouse basement exploded in March 1970, killing themselves and completely destroying the building. Two women, Kathy Boudin & Cathlyn Wilkerson, survived the blast and came to be heard of later.

Nine months after the Townhouse Explosion a statement was released by the Weather Underground entitled "New Morning-Changing Weather" in which the cause of the accident and the resultant effects were candidly discussed. It seems the townhouse was the scene of the first antipersonnel bombs (intend to be used against people) made by the group, and as this was against many of the participant's philosophy there was extreme tension between members of the group- arguing, sleeplessness, inner conflicts; and all this led to an accident in assembly which was purely karmic in nature. The bombing brought the fact of death home to those remaining Weatherpeople, and they knew they had to return to & strictly adhere to their stated purpose of destruction of property only, and only in retaliation for murderous & coercive actions by our government against others.

The Weather Underground were true Robin Hood types, living and moving thru Amerika, evading capture by the most massive manhunt imaginable, publishing a book (*Prarie Fire*) & a movie (*Underground*), and continuing their socio-revolutionary activity with relative impunity.

The F.B.I. searched in vain for years for the Weather Refugees; illegally wiretapping, opening mail, and breaking into houses of the family & friends of the 19 Underground Politicos. They were a tight group-intelligent, dedicated, & impervious to infiltration. In many cases it was their very presence in the world which kept the police in line on nites they knew they could have kicked ass on some protestors but felt the Weathershadow lurking near, crouched in the dark, prepared for reprisal.

Their presence and role in the Revolution was significant in that the leaders of this country finally perceived that the deeper they got into the war in Vietnam, the deeper the opposition & rift in America would

What a Long Strange Trip It's Been

become, and it was the Weather Underground which brought this point home. The government well understands the language of violence & intimidation and in fact loves to speak in them, which is why you should never challenge the government directly on these grounds. But oftentimes it takes controlled militancy & righteous indignation to speak in a tone which the government will hear.

I don't advocate bombings or violence of any kind, but people do have to get vocal & unruly to a point before they're heard or taken seriously.

The Phillipines, for example.

When the people finally get fed up with the atrocities of their government and are personally willing to sacrifice their lives in order to change it, then the odds are drawn against the rulers and the sooner they abdicate or change policy to the will of the people, the less protracted the struggle will be. A struggle the government will ultimately lose. As in China.

So sometimes it is the perception of the threat of impending chaos which brings nonviolent change to pass. Only then can the government find some change to spare.

But violent revolution in America should never be attempted because killing is not where it's at, nor are guns, nor directed hatred. Education's where it's at. An armed insurrection would never work in this country for the government can merely contain any disturbance (campus, city, etc.) by pulling back, encircling the area, and if need be obliterate it with the countless choices of death machinery at their disposal.

So to be truly effective a movement must move somewhere within that gray area which lies between passive resistance & nonviolent direct action on one hand, and pre-revolution on the other. Not only spending the time to put pressure on elected representatives (letters, phone calls, petitions, voting, etc.) but also getting out in the streets en masse to let your voices be heard loud & clear. When those in power perceive a threat to their position, or life, or property, they will begin to swim with the tide or finally drown. History has maintained that fact ad infinitum.

As for the Weather Underground, they learned their lesson too. After years on the run capturing media attention in such classic fashion as helping Timothy Leary escape from prison in 1970 & their sheer invisibleness, some members (led by Kathy Boudin) abandoned their longtime principle of violence against property only and robbed an armored truck, killing two policemen & one guard and being caught in the process. Although the Weatherpeople had been tagged as violent revolutionaries this is not what they were about, and other underground members of the group unassociated with the robbery gave themselves up in protest to the killing. Those involved in the robbery were convicted and given lengthy jail terms (20-75 years) and many of the others who surfaced found the F.B.I. apparently no longer interested in prosecuting them.

Among those who surfaced in 1980 was Bernardine Dohrn, who was a core leader of the W.U. and had spent ten years underground. A 1967 law school graduate, she was fined $1,500 & put on three years probation, then went on to become a lawyer herself.

She was by far the most awesomely beautiful spirit to have led the Movement or to have ever graced the F.B.I.'s 10 Most Wanted list.

And in those days you had to count on the spirit of your image and image of your spirit to reach those aboveground & far away.

So the American New Left in its most violent form still abhorred the taking of human life or violence toward others. The most violent display of S.D.S. action appeared in October '69 when the Weathermen went on a four-day, street-clogging, window-smashing spree called the Days of Rage in Chicago & again in April in Washington, D.C. in order to stop the wheels of the machinery from operating as business as usual.

It was these actions and the resultant court charges of conspiracy & riot which initially prompted many members of the Weather Organization to go underground rather than to jail. In retrospect the Weathermen saw that such anarchistic actions, aside from venting frustration, won the hearts of no one, and needlessly exposed themselves to police violence, trials, jail, & crippling expenditures. So the Weathermen, quickly learning the futility of direct confrontation, went underground and adopted retaliatory bombings as their symbol of resistance.

But even in this, their most overt sign of discontent, the violence of the Weatherpeople was nothing in comparison to the violence planned and carried out against the New Left by the government itself.

V

Chapter 22

Which brings us to the real history of the 60's in America. The history of the repression of legitimate dissent, the repression of freedom.

The history of the Men in Black.

From what gaping chasm in the bowels of hell spewed forth these dark creatures & Agents of Satan we'll never know, but it's these vile Souls who are the hands of the assassins, the swift & silent messengers who deliver the blade of death in the deep of nite to those in righteous opposition to the throne.

That the government for years has had its own hit squad operating from elements of the F.B.I., C.I.A., D.E.A., Cuban exiles on the C.I.A. payroll, and at times assassins loaned by the mob is fact bigger than fiction.

They got the President and it's still a mystery in the history books.

It's the Men in Black who have maintained the cover up all these years....who have killed all these people. All what people? If they've done their job well no one will ever ask. But what about those people, some of whom you may never have heard of but were nonetheless X'd out by the Men in Black.

Karen Silkwood, for example. Killed for reporting faults in the nuclear power industry. Kerr McGee in particular.

Or Hale Boggs, for instance. You may never have heard of him but Hale Boggs was one of the major political powers of his time. At the time of his disappearance he was the House Majority Leader of the United States Congress. Boggs was also a member of the Warren Commission which investigated & successfully covered up the murder of President John Fitzgerald Kennedy.

It was Boggs who, April 22, 1971, scathingly attacked the F.B.I. for its massive secret police activities against the antiwar movement and who demanded Hoover's resignation in what was the first attack ever on J. Edgar by a leading politico.

That alone probably put the X on him.

But what Boggs was to find out later (perhaps about JFK, perhaps Watergate) would lead to his plane being lost in Alaska in October 1972, just three weeks before Nixon's second election win as President. Downed and never found, not a trace, despite a sub-substantial air search & all these years gone by.[1] Down the rabbithole with Amelia Earhart...

A Hippy's History of the Sixties

...hardly!
    With William Sullivan maybe. He's another one. Dead as a twinkie with his brains blown out. Now talk about a man in the know. Old Bill's the one. William Sullivan had a very interesting career. In 1966, after 20 years in the F.B.I., he became head of the Bureau's Domestic Intelligence Division. This gave him special duties, not the least of which was to neutralize the Civil Rights Movement. You see, J. Edgar Hoover was a racist extraordinaire, and if he could somehow weave those troublemaking blacks into his paranoid, Commie conspiracy dream, then they could be kept in their place even if racial prejudice was fastly moving out of vogue. Same as Nixon later tried with the Peace Movement. Label 'em Commies and that enables the Bureau to use any tactics it pleases to monitor & neutralize.
    In a 1963 memo Sullivan said about Rev. Martin Luther King:
    "We must mark him now if we have not done so before as the most dangerous Negro of the future in this nation from the standpoint of Communism, the Negro, & national security."[2] That the F.B.I. was out to destroy the leadership of the Civil Rights Movement there is no question, and that William Sullivan played a leading role in this is sheer history.
    First in 1963, he drew up a document to discredit King called "Communism & the Negro," and had it distributed to the White House and other government agencies. This document was so outrageous that Attorney General Robert Kennedy ordered its circulation to be immediately halted. Next a bit of real action. In January 1964 Sullivan's Domestic Intelligence Division bugged Dr. King's room in D.C. at the Willard Hotel (the first of several buggings & break-ins against King) and began photographic surveillance of the same.
    Once they got the good Reverend's bedsprings a-squeaking & a-squealing on tape and a few photos too, the F.B.I. prepared a little informational packet on Dr. King's extracurricular morality to be passed around to editors & journalists & lawmakers to turn them against the mighty King. The oldest ploy in the books. The Smoking Bedsprings. It was later to be the downfall of Wilbur Mills, Gary Hart, Jim Bakker & Jimmie Swaggart, but King was a lightning dynamo and a real man of God and could not be sabotaged that easily.
    In November 1964 Sullivan had a package delivered to Mrs. King containing the bedsprings tapes and a note threatening to make them public a month later when her husband was scheduled to receive the Nobel Peace Prize, and suggesting the good Dr. King trade suicide for public exposure. To no avail.
    The Bureau did get Marquette University to drop its plans to present

What a Long Strange Trip It's Been

Dr. King with an honorary degree. These were only some of the hundreds of attempts by the F.B.I. to harass & neutralize Dr. King which ceased only in success with his death.

It was under Sullivan that illegal break-ins or black bag jobs were adopted as standard Bureau operating procedure and it was Sullivan who directed the F.B.I.'s COINTELPRO operation against the Peace Movement. It was Sullivan who was the prime drive of the infamous Huston Plan which Richard Nixon ordered to illegally suppress antiwar dissent & who was Nixon's choice to head the plan. It was also Sullivan whom Nixon chose to head the Office of National Narcotics Intelligence, & Sullivan again who directed the Defense Industrial Security Command- the security & spy agency for the U.S. munitions makers created by old J. Edgar. What a guy.

Sullivan was to rise to be Assistant Director of the F.B.I., and at one time was in a position to succeed Hoover as Director, but he ran afoul of Hoover himself and that ended that. Seems he gave a speech refuting the F.B.I. line that Communism was the root of the current political unrest, and then in August '71 drafted a letter to Hoover outlining his criticism of some of the F.B.I.'s current activities. The next month Hoover ended Sullivan's 30 year career by changing the locks on his office door. But his job was not all that was to be terminated.

It seems years later there were Congressional hearings looking into the Kennedy & King assassinations and the lawlessness of the F.B.I. in the Hoover years, and the word was that "Crazy Bill Sullivan" as he was known for his gung ho encouragement of illegalities, was going to tell all he knew, which you can bet was plenty. But lo & behold, before ole Bill could give his testimony to the upcoming inquiry, he made the mistake of going hunting with some friends and had his head blown away in one of those unfortunate & nasty hunting accidents.[3] You know the kind.

So like I say, keep your eyes open and you can see what's going on. Like Mary Pinchot Meyer. Now here's a story. You'll find this best recounted in Timothy Leary's autobiography *Flashbacks*. Seems Mary Meyer (ex-wife of C.I.A. bigwig Cord Meyer) had met with Leary in the early 60's and asked him for some L.S.D. for a little project she had going on in D.C. Seems she & some Congressmen's wives had formed a small psychedelic cadre and were beginning to turn on as many prominent persons in power as they thought were ready. Mary told Leary that she wanted the stuff to turn on a very influential man in Washington (who just happened to be JFK himself). You see Mary Meyer was one of several close girlfriends (Judith Campbell Exner, Marilyn Monroe...) whom JFK gave the Presidential torking to on a regular go round. Marilyn was then passed on to Bobby, then killed by someone's hand (love's, her own, the Men in Black, perhaps we'll never know for sure...).

And Judith Exner has in years since, admitted to turning JFK on to pot in the White House at his request.[4] So it's sheer history that Kennedy had dosed with the best you can get, and that probably freaked out the C.I.A. even more about the guy.

So some months after JFK took his last motorcade, Mary Pinchot Meyer had her mind blown for the very last time. But not by Timothy's finest. Shot in the face and killed hit style in broad daylite along the canals in Georgetown.

The Men in Black.

Keeping secrets of state secret. Dead men tell no tales.

Elements of the United States government from the various Presidents, to the Attorney Generals, to the F.B.I., to the C.I.A., to the Army, to the dozens of other government & military intelligence agencies, to those who have pulled the triggers, have conspired and actively executed policies which were clearly criminal in their attempts to keep themselves in control and the emerging youth culture from taking on political form and power.

John Lennon, for example. The murder of John Lennon, like Robert Kennedy's before him, was the apparent successful result of the C.I.A.'s MK-ULTRA* mind control assassination program. Mark David Chapman exhibited all the outward tendencies of a hypnotically trained programmed killer. Unemotional, unremorseful, "...and when I saw Mr. Lennon I kept hearing this voice inside my head saying, Shoot him, shoot him, shoot him, shoot him, over & over and the voice wouldn't stop until I did." Then the dude sits down and starts reading *A Catcher in the Rye*- a pure ruse.

Lennon without a doubt had been targeted long ago by the Nixon Administration. The F.B.I. has over 26 pounds of documents in his file and to this day refuses to release them because of "national security" reasons. The Justice Department unsuccessfully tried to keep Lennon from staying in the States because of a pot bust years before in Britain, but he finally won his American residence in July of 1976. They were especially hot to get Lennon because he was one of the few people of his time (along with Bob Dylan) who could have walked down the street and singlehandedly led the Revolution, any time, any day. John & Yoko had started hanging out with Jerry Rubin & Abbie Hoffman, had done their infamous Bed-ins for Peace, and were getting deeper involved in the New Left political scene.

---

* Richard Helms was the prime driving force behind the early MK-ULTRA program.

What a Long Strange Trip It's Been

It was Lennon who thru his efforts & benefits got John Sinclair (leader of the White Panther Party & co-founder of the band MC5) out of jail after he'd been given a horrendous 10 years for possession of two joints of grass. Lennon had also planned to attend the counterdemonstration at the 1972 Republican Convention in Miami but due to massive police harrassment, surveillance, his fear of getting asssassinated by the government, and the probability of massive police violence against the demonstrators, Lennon refrained from going or calling the ranks of discontented youth to the debacle. In 1980 after years of solitude, Lennon cut a new disc & planned a world tour. So John's number came up on the list and the lone crazed assassin from nowhere was prepared to dispense with this enemy of the state. And did.

Mark David Chapman.

A religious boy who supposedly developed a festering hatred for Lennon after John had proclaimed the Beatles more popular than Jesus. But was there more to it than that?

It seems that Chapman had worked at a Haitian refugee camp in Ft. Chafee, Arkansas run by the World Vision Organization. World Vision works with refugees around the globe and published reports suggest it's in part a convenient worldwide cover for the recruitment & training of C.I.A. assassins to be used on targets wherever deemed necessary. It's World Vision along with Carl McIntyre's International Council of Christian Churches & others who moved into Jonestown after the Jim Jones death trip went down there, but this time its residents are Laotians who were mercenaries or opium growers for the C.I.A. (And, coincidentally enough, John Hinckley, Sr., Bush family friend and father of the ill-fated attempted assassin of Ronald Reagan, was a World Vision official at the time his son missed the mark. And, coincidentally enough, a double of Hinckley, Jr. who followed him across the country, wrote letters to Jody Foster, and was also arrested with a weapon intended he said to kill Reagan. This double was a fellow named Richardson who himself attended the International Council of Christian Churches' Bible Study in Florida.)[5]

But Mark Chapman didn't miss, and John Lennon lay dying in the gutter as another pillar of our culture was blown to dust.

In the last 25 years we have seen assassination become government policy, and elements of law enforcement agencies of this country on the highest levels complicit & guilty of the murder of the greatest leaders of our time. But that was only one tactic used in the massive effort to neutralize the Peace Movement & youth culture. Default by decapitation. And the only eyes left watching are the F.B.I.'s

A Hippy's History of the Sixties

Another fine example of the F.B.I. murdering someone is the case of actress Jean Seberg. Seberg was a famous actress of the 60's whose support for the New Left caused an intense harrassment campaign to be leveled against her in the press. When she became pregnant in 1970 the F.B.I. planted false stories in the press that the child's father was a Black revolutionary whom she supposedly slept with; but it was all a total lie.

The stress from this slander caused her to have a miscarriage and lose the baby, and resulted in her later being confined in mental hospitals and finally attempting suicide every year on the date of her child's death, until she was successful on the ninth anniversary in 1979.[6] F.B.I., nice guys, huh?

Chapter 23

The F.B.I.

The F.B.I. was Hoover's ballgame altogether. The political police force of America. Its acts of repression with regards to the civil rights of its own citizens are voluminous, well documented, & appalling. During the 20s, 30's, 40's, 50's, 60's & right up to today, the F.B.I. has been the internal security force of this country: monitoring, investigating, harrassing, menacing, & neutralizing many opponents of American foreign policy whose only crime was to be actively involved in the democratic process. It was Hoover's job to see that the power seat of the Military-Industrial Complex was not disturbed by organized political opposition from any direction.*

Hoover himself was a perverse type of person, driven with the same drive for power to offset his short-person insecurities that Napoleon had. Hoover looked exactly like a bulldog, and that well describes the way he ran the F.B.I. With an iron jaw, never hesitating to reprimand anyone who got in his way or out of line. If you were real bad he'd send you to Butte, Montana for a career move.

He also brought to the F.B.I. the racist traits for which it was finally charged with discrimination and acts of racism by a Federal judge in September of 1988.

Among the young his fame was one & the same with the vacuum cleaner of like name- Hoover sucked. The height of his political diplomacy was blackmail, & the depth murder. He gathered and kept dirt on Presidents, Congressmen, Supreme Court Justices, candidates, celebrities, and pulled it out or would threaten to whenever necessary. That is why Hoover stayed in power so long. Fifty years so long.

Hoover rose to power in 1919, when he was picked to lead the newly formed General Intelligence Division or Radical Division. In the next two years up to 10,000 suspected "radicals" were rounded up by Hoover's sweepers and jailed, beaten up, & hundreds deported. In 1924 Hoover was named full-time head of the Division, whose name was changed to the Federal Bureau of Investigation. So that's how Hoover got his start. Rounding people up in the nite. People like you & me.[1]

---

* His job it seems also allowed him to have a tax-free foundation established by ex-bootlegger Lewis Rosentiel with one million dollars in Schenley liquor stocks. Rosentiel was also a big contributor to Tricky Dick's campaign.

A Hippy's History of the Sixties

J. Edgar Hoover was movie gangster Edward G. Robinson come to life, and probably the closest thing America ever had to a dictator in his own little way. Until he died the F.B.I. was totally free from Congressional overview. After his death in 1974 the truth finally came out, even to the point of William Sullivan telling a newsman that Hoover had slipped into madness long before his death.

The greatest news about Hoover came in 1993 when both books & TV documentaries confirmed the long-known rumors that J. Edgar was queer & ran with a gang of the wild and weird. And the mob. Palling it up with leading Mafia figures of the day (Meyer Lansky and Frank Costello) he continued to ignore organized crime and deny its existence, as they blackmailed him with a photo of himself giving his long-time close aide Clyde Tyson a blowjob the F.B.I. way. And how about this, I quote the *New York Times,* "an acquaintance tells of being at a party thrown by Roy Cohn and seeing Hoover dressed in a black chiffon dress, very short with ruffles, and black lace stockings, high heels, and to top it off a black curly wig and black eyelashes." No wonder he was so good at blackmailing Presidents. The best book on Hoover's anal activities is entitled *Official and Confidential: The Secret Life of J. Edgar Hoover* by Anthony Summers, published by Putnam, 1993.

But by then it was too late. By then the Black Panther Party lay decimated in the streets and in their sleep, all planned & co-ordinated by the F.B.I. By then Martin Luther King lay dead in Memphis. By then four students lay dead at Kent State.

The F.B.I.'s main task during the 60's was to stifle dissent, foster violence, & cause trouble. Thru a network of informers, undercover agent provocateurs, and coordinated actions with local police, it took to its task with all the vigor & illegalities it required. In 1956 the F.B.I. began its Counter Intelligence Program (COINTELPRO) whose purpose was to neutralize the United States Communist Party, which in itself was an act against all the guaranteed freedoms of belief which this country was founded upon. So when the 60's came around the F.B.I. was all brushed up on its illegalities and thru COINTELPRO unleashed itself upon the Left in a myriad of ways, all designed in the end to preserve the status quo & bury the Underground. All in all the F.B.I. admits to some 2,340 approved COINTELPRO actions against the New Left.

Homes, offices, & cars were burglarized, phones tapped, mail opened, organizations infiltrated, violence incited, internal dissension fostered, and people murdered to name a few.

The Underground Press took a full frontal assault from the F.B.I. with the aim of breaking the vital communication links among the political young. Underground Press offices were bombed, their staffs harassed especially by local police, their advertisers advised not to continue their support, & their printers pressured not to print such scurrilous rags in the future. The C.I.A. worked hand in hand with this, dubbing its own efforts against the Left "Operation Chaos" (headed by none other than Richard Helms), and the Army was also used extensively to illegally monitor American citizens & disrupt the Underground Press.

Take the Liberation News Service, for example. Its members were followed, staff infiltrated, feuds fostered, and when that didn't work the F.B.I. tried to burn down its D.C. office with the staff upstairs sleeping.[2] The F.B.I. was successful in shutting down dozens upon dozens of Underground papers all over the country and in doing so illegally but effectively kept the Movement from spreading even farther than it did.

In an F.B.I. memo of July '68 entitled "Disruption of the New Left" and sent to their field offices in Atlanta, Baltimore, Boston, Buffalo, Charlotte, Chicago, Cincinnati, Cleveland, Detroit, Jackson, L.A., Memphis, Newark, New Orleans, New York, Philadelphia, Phoenix, Pittsburgh, Richmond, St. Louis, San Francisco & Washington D.C., 12 counterintelligence measures were outlined to be used against the New Left.[3]

Among these were preparation of a leaflet designed to counteract the influence of S.D.S. by showing "the most obnoxious pictures they could of local student leaders...the instigating of or taking advantage of personal conflicts between New Left leaders; the creating of impressions that certain New Left leaders are informants for the Bureau or other law enforcement agencies;...having activists arrested by local authorities on drug charges;" drawing up anonymous letters regarding individual's radical activities and sending them to their parents, neighbors, & parent's employers; the confusion & disruption of planned activities by misinformation that the events had been cancelled or postponed could be sent to various individuals;" the monitoring of "coffee houses;" exposing faculty members & graduate assistants involved in New Left politics as radicals to the press, Board of Regents, etc.

And this was only the beginning. As the memo stated in the end, the disruption of the New Left "must be approached with imagination & enthusiasm if it is to be successful." This even went as far as hiring a prostitute with V.D. to sleep with several activist leaders at a political gathering in order to further wreak social and political havoc later within the groups.

But again if violating all guaranteed constitutional rights didn't work, if all stops had to be pulled, murder was also covert Bureau policy.

And as usual, the Bureau's always covered; usually by the President they're currently spying for. Case in point is this very case. When the investigations were finally over concerning the F.B.I.'s illegal break-ins against dissidents, charges were brought against Bureau officials Mark Felt & Edward Miller for ordering these break-ins. The men were sentenced to jail but in 1981 were pardoned & commended by Ronald Reagan. And it was Reagan who once again loosened the rules against domestic spying which were implemented to keep such abuses from recurring. So you can bet the F.B.I.'s still at it, as can be seen in the revelations of their monitoring those groups in opposition to Reagan's Central American policies of the 80's.

But don't be intimidated, just aware. If you're politically active, expect surveillance; just live your life with sensible caution and be cool in all respects, *and watch what you say on the phone*! And stay away from guns and those crazies advocating acts of violence, 'cause 10 to 1 they're agent provocateurs trying to create violence to discredit the Left.

Case in point. In the early 70's a scumbag undercover agent named Ron Mohr infiltrated the Kent State branch of the Vietnam Vets Against the War and had a little plan. First he wanted to sell the Vets an AK-47 Chinese machine gun and a couple of rocket grenade launchers; then he wanted the Vets to knock off a couple of city police officers for the cause. Well, the Vets smelled a rat and had Mohr & his Communist-made weapons busted by the city police. Within ten hours, however, an agent from the Treasury Department had come in from D.C. to get Mohr out of jail because he was working for them, among others. The next morning the University announced that Mohr, whose cover had been blown, would be added to the parking enforcement department of the campus police...just the kind of guy you'd want around campus. Did the students take all this sitting down? Actually, yes. At twelve o'clock the main intersection near campus was blocked by scores of students sitting in the middle of the road protesting Mohr & the War. At any rate the Vets were lucky. For years on campuses across this nation agent provocateurs were used to incite violence & ensnare others in their plans. All to create the fear necessary in the populace at large to allow for the violent repression of those actively involved in change.

Another famous agent provocateur was Tommy Tongyai, known as Tommy the Traveler, who incited violence on campuses all over upstate New York; providing advice, explosives, building bombs and finally duping two students into an action which landed them in jail.[4]

Or how about F.B.I. informer Gary Thomas Rowe[5] who infiltrated the Ku Klux Klan and planned & participated in violent acts against Civil Rights workers- even murder. He shot a white woman, Civil Rights

What a Long Strange Trip It's Been

worker Viola Liuzzo, in 1965 after the Selma-to-Montgomery march, killing her and never being held accountable for it. Or how about F.B.I. informer #S179 being paid $200/month and doing what they told him to until his number was up. His name was Lee Harvey Oswald.[6]

So the proof of F.B.I. abuses are there, abundantly there, usually cloaked under the guise of investigating Peace groups for terrorism or links to Communist nations abroad. (Which are never found.) But in reality the F.B.I., as well as the C.I.A., (especially with its newly given powers by RWR to spy within the bounds of the United States on U.S. citizens) have been employed for decades as nothing short of a political police force- the Angels of Death for the New Left. But thru it all we've survived, or some of us, and the 80's showed clearly that the antinuclear, anti-apartheid, & antiwar forces were still going strong; peopled not only by the same people instrumental in change in the 60's but also by their children and a whole generation of kids who now so clearly see the madness of the world & the dire necessity for change.

So history will show that although a small group of urban revolutionaries did use symbolic violence to publicize their cause, it was nothing in comparison to the violence credited to and directed against the New Left by agents of the state.

This was clearly illustrated in the spring of 1993 when the World Trade Center was bombed allegedly by Muslim fundamentalist extremists. These extremists were taped by the F.B.I. for seven years with 7,000 reels of conversation totalling over 25,000 hours. Yet they didn't know what was up. Even when their inside F.B.I. informer taught the one group member how to drive a Ryder van two days before a Ryder van delivered the explosives to the parking garage beneath the World Trade Center (*Daily Camera*, Boulder, Colo., 5/11/93). The terrorists, who had been aided and abetted by the F.B.I., were given life sentences. To get these convictions, the prosecution used a supposed terrorist training film, said to have been found in the home of a defendant, as evidence, when the film was actually excerpts from the current film, *Death Before Dishonor*, from which they bleached the color and the truth.

Chapter 24

So if acute violence was not exactly where it was at within the Movement, let's try the Yippies. The Yippies were another ballgame altogether. Founded by Abbie Hoffman & Jerry Rubin (two longtime East & West Coast organizers) in a moment of stoned inspiration New Year's Day '68, Yippie was a word, an identity, a soon to be creeping disease in the minds of Middle America! Formed as the Youth International Party, they meant every word of it- especially the word party. Tho' to many they were not to be taken seriously (themselves included), they were masters in the crucial & dangerous profession of awakening the masses dressed in the guise of clown suits. The Yippies were the Marx Brothers of the political arena. They staged outrageous theatrical events for the sole purpose and success of capturing the hearts & minds of America thru the political theater of the absurd. And once public opinion was mobilized, then legislators & government policy would follow.

Undoubtedly they turned off as many people as they turned on, but those folks' minds had been turned off for years, and the minds they did reach were the ones that counted & marched. The Yippies were High Comedy in a moment of low tragedy...jesters mooning the King whose hands had been caught dripping with the blood of Asian babies.

Their antics were topped only by the next, and their instructional humor rocked the foundations of Amerika as strong as any Weatherman bomb.

Both Abbie & Jerry had been pranksters in their own right for years and now they teamed up as the Laurel & Hardy of the World Salvation League. Yippie!

Abbie's first big gig was at the New York Stock Exchange in the very heart of the capitalistic system. He & 15 fellow coverts pulled the coup d'etat of the day by joining a tour of the Exchange and while in the gallery, throwing 300 dollar bills down upon the heads of the stockbrokers, causing intense pandemonium and the temporary closing of the market as everyone left the financial handlings of billions of dollars to scramble for dollar bills.

On Valentine's Day '69 Abbie mailed out 3,000 joints (courtesy Jimi Hendrix) to TV news personalities and to people randomly selected from the phone book with instructions on how to smoke them and giving people a chance to decide for themselves what pot was all about, but also

What a Long Strange Trip It's Been

reminding them that possession of just that one joint could bring five years in prison.

In 1967 both Jerry & Abbie along with 3,000 others performed an exorcism on and attempted to raise the Pentagon, and its Satanically shaped connection with evil wasn't missed by those viewers at home.

As Abbie said, different visions created different tactics, and cultural disruption was the meat and potatoes of the Yippie antiwar strategy.

At any rate the outrageous became the contagious as each new act of guerrilla theater had its message and as more people became involved both as participants & observers, the sentiment against the war deepened. How about the time the Yips-Zips let the rats loose at the 51st Annual Republican Women's Luncheon and screwed up Pat Nixon's little tea party. Eek!

But of the many different Yippie events that I attended, my favorite of all occurred at the first Impeach Nixon march April 26, 1974 in D.C. There Bella Abzug (eternal brim above her brow) was the first to call for the balls of Richard Nixon. Bella's another great American patriot of her time who's been an inspiration to many thru the years.

It was a great day with balloons, & kids, & Yippies, & booths, & music, & speakers, and a Yippie float with the bobbing Elmer Fudd head of Gerald Ford mounted on an old Ford Edsel, with a picture of Nixon on it saying: "Would you buy a used Ford from this man?" Also present was a float of their own: two police photographers- a male & a female- pulled right up into the back of the rally in just the cab of a tractor-trailer rig, taking roll, after roll, after roll, after roll, after roll of film- at least 2-3 thousand shots the whole afternoon. They're always there, the government photographers, trying to intimidate you and document your actions and identify you so you can be kept track of in the future.

Anyway, this rental truck finally pulls up and out jumps a bunch of Yippies, stark raving naked, with nothing but Dick Nixon masks on.

It was great!

All these naked Nixons running thru the streets, scampering over the hoods of cars, balls & dicks a'flappin in the breeze, as the horrified D.C. police tried to get a grip on this one.

No way! It was purely Keystone Cops comedy, with the Yips leading the cops on a 20-block chase where they rounded the corner of an alleyway and all piled into their van which was sitting there waiting with the door up. As the last Yip got in the door went down, and the first wave of cops came running round the corner and smack into the closed door as the van took off; a total victory of Yip logistics by the Masters of Madness.

A Hippy's History of the Sixties

Sometimes Yip missions were solos, like pieing someone in the face...for in the face of ridiculousness fools are shown for what they are- vileness is revealed.

The Yip hit list has included such luminaries as Anita Bryant, scourge of gays (hit with a fruit pie), William Colby (former head of the C.I.A. & de facto murderer*), G. Gordon Liddy, Phyllis Schaffley, Billy Carter, & the Guru Maharagi, among countless others.

The first political pieing was done by Thomas Forcade, head of the Underground Press Syndicate, who after addressing Nixon's Presidential Commission on Pornography, dressed as a priest, completed his delivery with a pie in the face of the Commission's Chairman. Forcade was the only member of the Underground Press to gain access to the Senate & House Press Corps, was immensely intelligent & articulate, and was so active that police surveillance was a constant part of his life, especially after he turned ace smuggler & founder of High Times Magazine. Forcade alas took his own life somewhere along the line, but I hope somebody checked into that one too.

Or the time Abbie Hoffman & Gracie Slick from the Airplane made their infamous White House run. Grace, as it so happened, went to the same college as Tricia Nixon, so when Tricia threw a little tea with mom & dad for the alumni, Gracie got an invitation. So she decided not only to attend the tea with Abbie, but to dose the daylights out of the punchbowl and everyone there. In Gracie's words** "It was some of Owsley's finest. I had it in my purse & was going to put it under my fingernails & wave it over people's drinks as I talked to them. We were going to dose the kids, but first we were going to get Dick. We would have had his head bouncing off the walls like a ping-pong ball, but believe me we weren't going to let him go anywhere."

This was real. They would have strung these mad fools up forever for this one, yet they didn't care. They were there all the same ready to do their duty for their country.

The White House Acid Test.

As history retells, so many invitees arrived that their escorts were not allowed to attend, so Gracie raises hell at the door and Pat Nixon's press secretary catches sight of her see-thru blouse and refuses even to let her in. Then Abbie was recognized by a reporter even in his brylcreem best plus suit & tie. The jig was up. History missed an unexpected turn into the strange and unknown. Richard Milhous Nixon on L.S.D.

---

* Colby headed Operation Phoenix during the Vietnamese War which assassinated tens of thousands of Vietnamese citizens.
** Paraphrased from memory from a 1972 public radio interview I heard.

What a Long Strange Trip It's Been

He was strange enough when you were on L.S.D.

So, yeah, Abbie Hoffman was another true patriot of his time. And he took his knocks. Lots of busts. Busted up alot. Broken noses. Coke in noses. Caught in a coke bust in New York in 1974 (with Federal agents reportedly on both sides of the deal) Abbie then began a six-year underground odyssey traveling around the world and continuing his activism under assumed identities. His last project underground was an effort to save the St. Lawrence River from massive expansion & winter navigation. Then in 1980, true to style, Abbie turned himself in on ABC's 20/20 TV news shows, came aboveground and took Barbara WaWa on a tour of the town he'd been living in, then went off to face the charges.

Because of his primetime surrender and all the awards he received when he was masquerading as Barry Freed, environmentalist, Hoffman served some time (11 months) and did some community service but pretty much got off and continued to be active in major concerns. In April of 1987 he, ex-President Carter's daughter Amy, & 13 others won an important court case in Massachusets when they were acquitted on charges stemming from a protest of C.I.A. recruitment on campus. The case basically affirmed their right to commit a lesser crime (trespassing) to stop a larger crime (the C.I.A. killing civilians worldwide). This defense, called the lesser of evils defense, actually legitimized the moral right to protest government violence & lawlessness backing up the rights stated in the Preamble to the Constitution.

Hoffman went the Leary-Liddy route, touring the country debating Jerry Rubin, who in the late 70's copped out, sold out, got a job on Wall Street as a stockbroker & contended that it would be the Yuppies who will save the world. (Don't hold your breath.) In fact, Abbie quit holding his breath on April 12, 1989. Found dead at his cabin in New Hope, PA, he reportedly died of an overdose of phenobarbital and alcohol. Ruled a suicide by the coroner, this is highly debatable. He was not a quitter. When family members viewed the body, they were told he had died of a heart attack, yet there were visible bruises on both sides of his face & both hands were clenched in fists.* The coroner later ruled it a suicide once the body had been cremated and disposed of. If true, he died of a concern for the world, which is lacking in others. If anything kills us all, it will be Apathy. Abbie Hoffman was the greatest political activist & American patriot of the 20th century, & his Spirit lives on.

And the Yippies- they still continue today, a rag-tag band of cosmic comics, publishing their magazine *Overthrow* & *Zeinger* in fine tradition.

* As told to David Dellinger by Andrew Hoffman. (Retold to the author in a personal interview 7/9/94.)

A Hippy's History of the Sixties

The Yippies, for all of their misnomenclatures & jests with the straight press, are excellent investigative journalists and Yip books & publications have played an important role in the truth of this long, strange trip being told.

The Yippies caught much of the flak aimed at the New Left ranks (the Kennedys, King, & Kent State students catching it directly) for they like the S.D.S. were on the front lines at the Movement's vanguard.

But most of the heavy stuff was caught by the Black Panthers.

Chapter 25

The Black Panthers.

J. Edgar Hoover was out to exterminate the Panthers- he hated Blacks and like many of his kind thought that they should either be killed or given enough heroin to be politically impotent and to make them a big enough criminal threat to society as to require police attention.

There was finally such pressure & continual harrassment on the Panthers that by the end of 1969 their entire leadership was either dead, in jail, underground, or in exile.

Chairman Bobby Seale was in prison on a murder charge, as was Black Panther Defense Minister Huey Newton after being shot. Fred Hampton after being drugged by an F.B.I. informer had been murdered in his sleep in a predawn raid in Chicago as was Mark Clark. Bobby Hutton was killed, & Eldridge Cleaver had fled the country to Algeria to set up a Black Panther headquarters in exile rather than return to jail for parole violations.

By that time 28 Panthers had been killed by police in separate incidents around the country, and neutralization of the Black Panthers was near complete.

The Black Panthers represented a special danger to the forces in power because right from the start they adopted a militant stance, were not afraid to call a pig a pig,* and exercised their lawful Constitutional right to bear arms. In their eyes they were necessarily policing the police. This, however, just strengthened the government's conviction that if they were going to take any action against the Movement as a whole, the Panthers would have to be dealt with first.

So they dealt with them. Thru infiltration & extermination.

The fire & the scrutiny which the Black Panthers came under was overwhelming, and in time they turned their tactics from building takeovers and armed standoffs to educational & free lunch programs for the hungry Black children whom society had so abjectly ignored with downward gaze and closed hand for 100's of years.

But the Black Panther Party couldn't survive as an organization, and those who survived as individuals are still devoting their lives to change today.

---

* As Country Joe put it, not all cops are pigs but all Pigs are cops.

A Hippy's History of the Sixties

Bobby Seale, who in 1967 had led 30 Panthers armed with M1 rifles into the California State Capitol to declare their right to arm against police oppression, ended up as the director of a Philly youth program; while Eldridge Cleaver stayed on the run in Europe, became a chef, wrote a cookbook, designed a pair of pants for men with a pocket in the front for the penis, came back to the U.S. & gave himself up, did his time at community service, and emerged on the Berkeley political scene as a staunch anti-Communist Republican type, rebuking his revolutionary past.

Strange days indeed.

And Huey Newton last heard of, died in the streets. In August 1988 after serving a 60-day sentence for parole violation, Newton refused to leave San Quentin in protest of the continued 16 yr. incarceration of fellow Black Panther Geronimo Pratt, one of America's foremost political prisoners. They finally made Newton leave but not before another spark was ignited by a fire they'd thought was out long ago. Unfortunately this flame was snuffed out in an early morning shooting in Newton's neighborhood in 1990, leading to many suspicions.

Probably the greatest Panther today is Stokely Carmichael, who once headed the instrumentally important Student Nonviolent Coordinating Committee, & ended up living in Guinea Africa leading the All African People's Revolutionary Party and bumping heads with the military government in power there. Carmichael never sold out, and like those of the 60's who didn't, has paid his dues being true.

The Black Panthers are a prime example of the fact that you cannot come up against this government with a gun in your hand and win. Or sometimes even walk away. If they don't gun you down in your sleep, they'll frame you for a murder you didn't commit & put you in jail for life, as is Black Panther Geronimo Pratt in San Quentin. A Black militia, or even a Black political party whose members exercised their right to own & bear arms could not be tolerated in the America of the 60's.

(Just as a Black President could not be tolerated in the America of the 80's.)

Chapter 26

The Black Panthers in terms of blood & spirit sacrificed more than any other continental U.S. resistance group except the Native American Indian Movement. They've been up against the same government oppression & genocide for almost 500 years- and are still fighting.

You talk about the Holocaust- well, Hitler ain't got nothin' on us, babe...cultural genocide the American Way. Let's be real.

Nations, whole nations living on this continent in harmony with the Earth, to be forcefully replaced by a bunch of greed-driven, alcohol soaked, murdering thieves is not necessarily a step in the right direction.

The very fact that we have almost totally polluted the land with pesticides, the air with lead & fumes (Americans consume over 8 tons of lead daily in the air they breathe, mostly in the cities) & the water with hideous toxic chemicals doesn't leave much to be said.

Let alone the fact that we have created a "defense" system which will radiate the entire world if activated, does not reflect well upon our stolen role as the caretakers of this land. And that we suffer from diseases from the poisons we cultivate, this speaks for itself & should be recognized as a sign to change direction.

Are we any more happy, healthy, or righteous than they? I say nay to all three.

When the white man first arrived in North America there were 500 different languages being spoken on the continent by the native inhabitants here. The Iroquois Indians (a matrilineal society in which the women held the tribal power) had a federation which enjoyed a 200-year Golden Age of Peace. Thomas Jefferson in his notes on the State of Virginia, illustrates the eloquence of Indian spokespersons, reprinting a speech by a Mingo chief, categorizing it as better than any oration in either Greek or European history. So the myth of the ignorant savage was just that- a myth used to justify abusive treatment against an indigenous people in order to steal their land and resources because theft against subhuman species, not to mention enslavement, was A-O.K. with the white man's God.

That the Native American was not particularly articulate in the vocabulary of profiteering, land ownership, & treachery, they were soon to learn that these newly arrived people had a mindset which precluded Peace and harmonic co-existence, and were driven by an inner greed which if left unchecked could grow to such proportions as to destroy their entire existence with its polluted entrails. And it did.

King Phillip, the Wampanoag's leader who rescued the Pilgrim's on Thanksgiving, caught the drift and joined the neighboring tribal nations together in order to drive the settlers out. They attacked 52 of the 90 colonial New England towns but were defeated in 1676 by superior firepower & the usual touches of treachery.[1]

Technology played a huge part in subduing the original inhabitants of this land so wrongly called the "New World."

When Christopher Columbus first landed in Haiti he left an army behind to oversee the mining of gold by the locals. Upon returning he found that his troops had been slaughtered by the island inhabitants who didn't get off on indentured servitude. He then began a systematic extermination & enslavement of the people he so wrongly called Indians. In the 20 years after Columbus "discovered" them, there were less than 14,000 natives left on his plantations compared to the 300,000 who had been alive & living there when he arrrived. And look at Haiti today.

Genocide.

It takes many forms including the killing of over 3 million Fillipinos from 1898-1920 by an American mercenary military outfit called the Phillipine Scouts, who along with the U.S. Army & Marines, lost some 44,000 men themselves.[2]

Genocide as a means of colonial expansion, carried out thru a technological edge held by the invading forces. Us.

The technological superiority of the rifle, revolver, railroad, & telegraph combined to become overpowering tools in the hands of the white expansionist who saw killing the Indians and stealing their land and mineral wealth as their Manifest Destiny. The atrocities committed against the Indians were both senseless & brutal. Smallpox-infested blankets were given to tribes as gifts, this being the early forerunner of germ warfare. Makes you wonder about AIDS.

Buffaloes, a main support and staple necessary for the Indian's survival in the wilderness, were completely slaughtered as if in jest.

By the 1600's, bounties had been put on Indian's heads, so that in the colonies if you killed or scalped a native resident then you could collect $50-100 for the scalp. This was a huge sum in those days and did little to encourage Peace & goodwill toward the native populace.

And Indians today, 500 years later, as a culture and a people are in a state of devastation. The degree of poverty is the worst in the nation. The infant mortality rate is the highest in the nation, three times higher than any other group. The suicide rate is ten times the national average, the conditions of alcoholism, hunger, & disease are appalling, & the life

What a Long Strange Trip It's Been

expectancy is the lowest in America- 43 years.

So with other winds stirring, the American Indian Movement had a rebirth in the 1960's & 70's and engaged in such symbolic resistance as occupying the abandoned prison of Alcatraz in San Francisco Bay, and in February 1973, occupying the town of Wounded Knee, at the Pine Ridge Indian Reservation in South Dakota. Wounded Knee was the site of the last clash of Federal Troops with Indians in 1890, resulting in the massacre of 237 men, women, & children by the 7th Cavalry.

Once again in 1973 the U.S. government responded with a preponderance of force bringing in armored personnel carriers, .50-calibre machine guns & troops with M-16 rifles. All against a sovereign nation occupying its own ground with rifles, shotguns and some old Buicks & pickup trucks.

As with the Black Panthers, the F.B.I. proceeded to murder individual Indian activists & neutralize others with lengthy jail sentences for government-instigated shoot-outs on Indian land.

Leonard Peltier, the most prominent political prisoner in America today, is still falsely in jail on murder charges. America owes him his freedom.

Russell Means is another person whose vision, leadership & defiance has been instrumental in the struggle for the rights of the Native Americans.

The same with John Trudell, whose leadership in the struggle led to the murder of his wife, children, and mother-in-law.

Such recognition of injustice was achieved thru their efforts and others that many tribes have sued the U.S. or state governments for repayment of stolen lands and have been successful in winning substantial monetary & land settlements. But the U.S. government is still today engaged in attempts to once again rip off sacred Indian land in the Black Hills and elsewhere for the uranium & minerals underneath.

At Big Mountain, Arizona, they've even gone to the point of instigating trouble among tribes, then relocating them off their mineral rich lands to settle the dispute and make way for development. This is being done with our tax dollars. Its about time we stop fucking with the Native American people, call off our genocidal goons & give them enough space and resources to reclaim their national heritage and run their own affairs. The best thing we could do for this country would be to give it back to the Indians and let them keep the $24 at that.

Chapter 27

So the New Left Movement was made up of alot of different groups, all oppressed or in the fight to stop oppression. The Civil Rights Movement, S.D.S., Yippies, Black Panthers, the Native Americans, nonaligned students, musicians, artists, Quakers, liberal labor unions & just plain folks joined to rein in the trampling hooves of runaway militaristic capitalism.

When events drew them together they were one, but always knew what it was like to be alone & have your back up against an alley wall with a nitestick in your ribs.

It was not without personal danger that people moved into the streets, but it was a time when people had decided that murder in the name of America was wrong, and they were willing to risk harm to themselves to express their dissent with government policy.

Nothing illustrates this better than the act of Norm Morrison, who in November of '65 following the example of dissident Buddhist monks in South Vietnam, doused himself with gasoline & lit himself on fire on the steps of the Capitol in protest to our involvement in Indochina.

Another illustration is the case in 1987 of Vietnam Vet Brian Wilson who in protest to our involvement in Nicaragua kneeled in front of a Navy train carrying munitions to Central America and refused to move as the train intentionally ran him over, cutting both his legs off & crushing part of his skull.

It was the willingness of these people who formed together to press for change which enacted the mechanisms within the body politic which dictated to the existing politicians that if the politicians didn't change the policy, the people would change the politicians. So it was a long struggle fought on a myriad of fronts (still being fought) with many battles lost & won.

Chapter 28

So it's to some of those individual battles we'll now turn, with Mr. Peabody's hand on the Way-Back Machine. Back to those events of history which widely reflect the degree of velocity with which change was summoned to appear, and the ferocity with which the status quo replied.

Eventually resistance was everywhere, but initially it was most evident in the Frisco Bay area. In September 1964 at the University of California at Berkeley came one of the first and most important of these events- the Free Speech Movement. Spawned by the University's refusal to allow antiwar information tables at the entrance to campus, this ban was defied and led to the arrest of one student and the subsequent surrounding of the police car he was in, an all-nite stand-off, & a negotiated release with charges dropped. Four months later, however, charges were brought against four students in the matter which led to the occupation of the Administration building, where Mario Savio, the spokesperson for the Free Speech Movement, talked of the University & the War Machine:

"It becomes odious, so we must put our bodies against the gears against the wheels...and maybe make the machine stop until we are free." Eight hundred fourteen people were arrested, a student strike ensued, and the faculty voted that speech should not be censored or restricted on campus. The tables went back and a victory of sorts was won but the War dragged on.

Years later when we were still involved in Vietnam, Berkeley would be host to another kind of confrontation. In April of 1969 in a university-owned lot which had been vacant and barren for some time, residents and students began construction of a user-built, user-maintained park which came to be known as People's Park. In less than a month a warm & colourful community effort had transformed the useless into the beautiful. Swingsets, trees, grass, flowers, benches, sculptures all graced the park as people came to share music & conversation & food & energy in the midst of their achievement.

The University had other ideas, however. Ignoring an earlier recommendation by the Committee on Housing & Environment, the University announced a week after the park was born that it had plans to build an intramural soccer field on the site. Two weeks later 250 city & state police cleared the park and an eight-foot steel fence was constructed to keep people out. Later in the day 6,000 people marched peaceably to the guarded park site to sing & chant, and when police moved into the crowd to shut off a fire hydrant which had been opened, they met resistance and began firing tear gas to disperse those gathered.

In the chaos which followed tear gas & rocks were exchanged between the police & demonstrators, then a squad of sheriff's deputies moved down the street and began shooting at people with their shotguns loaded with birdshot. When that ran out they began shooting people with 00 buckshot, seriously wounding many people & killing James Rector, who had been shot on a rooftop & died four days later in the hospital. All in all 128 people had been injured & 50 arrested. A point had been made that day. That the American university system was willing to have students & people physically assaulted and even killed if need be to protect its ego and property interests. And events in the coming days would underscore this point.

The day after James Rector died a faculty vigil was held on campus, and when the thousands of people tried to leave they were blockaded by National Guardsmen. They were then gassed and doused copiously with clouds of CS tear gas which was sprayed crop-duster style by an Army helicopter hovering over the campus. The gassing was so bad that it not only had U. of C. students wretching their guts out on the ground, but also spread to nearby schools, a hospital, and into the surrounding community, making children, the hospitalized, & nearby residents extremely ill. The next day 500 more persons were arrested, and on & on.

A University referendum on People's Park showed 13,000 of the 15,000 who voted supported the Park, and the city itself asked the college to lease the land to the city to be used as a park. But the University of California Regents voted to turn People's Park into a parking lot. The park was subsequently ripped apart by the police- trees, bushes, flowers, all the positive visions which had been planted- ruthlessly destroyed. Which clearly told you where the University was at.

As Joni Mitchell said, "They paved Paradise and put up a parking lot." All in an effort to stop people from getting together. Just as the original idea of the University buying the land in the first place- to remove the low-cost housing available to potential "subversive" elements around the University & Bay area, and thus supposedly drowning their ideas out. Another effort at control. Today, the park survives as a park, but the fight continues as the University now wants to build dorms on the site.

A very similar situation had occurred a year earlier at Columbia University in New York City. Columbia borders Harlem, and in the seven years previous to this had purchased 150 buildings in the neighboring

What a Long Strange Trip It's Been

community and had 10,000 or so folks evicted. Then, in 1968, as the S.D.S. was already protesting their ties with the Pentagon thru the Institute for Defense Analysis, Columbia announced that it was going to build an 11 story gymnasium on public land:* Morningside Park which lay between Columbia & Harlem.

The Blacks in Harlem, in turn, would get to use their own little part of the gym but have to come in thru the back door. This didn't set well with the students or the locals. On April 23rd a group led by Mark Rudd and other students from S.D.S. & the Student Afro-American Society took over two buildings on campus, one of them being the President's office in which they found files documenting University complicity in war-related projects. Other buildings were to follow.

Six days later the University President ordered the police to retake the buildings, and true to fashion they stormed the buildings before dawn & literally kicked the shit out of as many people as they could, arresting 700 people & injuring 150. This was another instance of well-documented police brutality which was a common scene on the front lines. In response the students staged a strike which shut down Columbia, forcing it to close for the entire semester. (The book & movie *The Strawberry Statement* provide an excellent look at the Columbia riots. The soundtrack alone is worth it.) Harvard too would be shut down in April of '69.

At the height of the antiwar movement, virtually every campus across the United States and many high schools had experienced demonstrations, strikes, & sit-ins as an expression of student dissent with the way things were going.

And the response to this was often brutal.

---

* It had been public up until then, but the University bought it for $1. Where else could you get such a land deal, 'cept maybe Manhattan.

Chapter 29

By far the biggest display of police brutality was at the Democratic Convention in Chicago in 1968. Here the shit hit the fan.

Set only months after the shattering assassinations of Martin Luther King and Robert Kennedy, the Democratic Convention was a showdown of Good & Evil. It was the Democrats who had pounded Vietnam so unmercifully under Johnson, and with McCarthy knocking the wind out of LBJ at New Hampshire and Kennedy shot & out of the race, at starting time it was pretty much Eugene McCarthy and Hubert Humphrey (LBJ's V.P.) heading into the gate.

Humphrey was your typical liberal (insubstantial on the front lines) whose best face forward was not too stable a picture reception indeed. He belonged with Hugh Downs hosting a game show somewhere. He always reminded me of the old fat laughing lady rocking back & forth in the fun house window at the amusement park as a kid. But amusing he wasn't.

His direct complicity with the Johnson Administration's genocidal policies make him nonetheless a war criminal also. He'd spent his share of time on the Red Scare bandwagon in the early days, once introducing a bill which would have made it a crime punishable with five years in prison for being a member of the Communist Party. I would have thought that just being a member would have been punishment enough, but not old Hubert. And now he wanted to be King. The legions of Peace cringed at the thought.

So into this uncertain arena came the Yippies, like lambs to slaughter, calling for a Festival of Life to replace the Festival of Death taking place the next ring over.

Mayor Daley (the ultimate archetype of the corrupt, big city boss, kinda the J. Edgar Hoover of the Chicago gestapo) had no time for a bunch of protestors with their music, poetry, dope, & revisionist optimism. This was _his_ town & _his_ convention and a bunch of long-haired vermin were not going to spoil his finest moment. Faced with an ensuing parade of crazies who purportedly were planning to spike the city water supply with a purple sex drug called Lace and perhaps abscond the delegates wives- no way!

The Yippies & other protestors from the National Mobilization to End the War were denied permits to march or sleep in the parks, leaving perhaps 8,000 people with no place to go. When they stayed in the parks they were raided at nite by the police and tear gassed, beaten & maced. From the first nite the police had nothing in mind but to see as much blood flow as they possibly could. Everyone in the parks, in the streets, and on the sidewalks were fair game- clergymen, old ladies, reporters. Especially reporters.

And when them damned kids from the McCarthy Organization started dropping urine-filled baggies onto the cops' heads below in response to the horror they saw going on, well they charged right up to their hotel headquarters & kicked the shit out of them too!

Mayor Daley had ensured that no live television coverage could be transmitted anywhere but inside the convention hall itself, thus blacking out the reality of the massive police brutality which was going on outside. And brutal it was. The Chicago police force & the National Guard were so viciously overenthusiastic in their indiscriminate use of violence that the President's National Commission on the Causes & Prevention of Violence issued a report on the situation, calling the actions of the enforcement officers nothing short of a police riot.

The television cameras were out in the melee anyway, and as they recorded the evenings events, thousands of antiwar protestors chanted

"the Whole World is Watching,
the Whole World is Watching
the Whole World is Watching,"

as more blood flowed in the streets. And indeed the whole world was.

Although the scenes filmed could not be broadcast live, they were rushed to the convention center where they were developed and shown on national television, as the networks cut into the Democrats' nominating process to show them. The scenes shocked & horrified both those at home and those inside the convention hall.

Senator Abraham Ribicoff, when giving the nominating speech for last-minute Peace candidate George McGovern, said, "With George McGovern as President, we would not have such Gestapo tactics in the streets of Chicago." Mayor Daley freaked! Sitting in his seat from which he was doing his best to orchestrate the entire convention, he was seen on TV redfaced & shaking uncontrollably with anger, his fist waving at Ribicoff as his mouth could be seen to shout at the podium calling Ribicoff a "Jew son-of-a-bitch" and "a lousy motherfucker!"[1] Honest Abe stared right back at him & replied, "How hard it is to accept the truth," which really pissed Daley off. And this was all on TV. I saw it! Who says the Revolution will not be televised?

So amidst the disturbances both inside & outside the convention, the forces of Peace still tried to rally in hopes of gaining sway over the political forces at large. To no avail. Hubert Humphrey, with his party & labor connections won the nomination, although Julian Bond, a brilliant 28-year-old Black politician from Georgia, was among those nominated, and although he was technically too young to run, was probably the best for the job ahead of McGovern & McCarthy.

The Yippies candidate, a pig named Pigasus, couldn't make the convention because he had been abducted at a press conference early in the show by the Chicago police & disappeared.

Today's pig, tomorrow's bacon?

Who knows.

In the aftermath of the Chicago seige* which left one person dead (Dean Johnson, a 17-year-old Native American from Souix City), scores injured, & almost 700 arrested, Mayor Daley did what he could to put a better face on events. A one-hour film was assembled with a phony soundtrack and was aired on the 142 TV stations nationwide so that people could hear & see for themselves the verbal provocation which started the whole bloody mess....right!^{2}

With this propaganda out it was easier than ever to blame America's troubles not on the war, but on the "Commie youth" at home, and both Humphrey and especially Nixon played on people's fears & prejudices in order to try to get elected.

The Yippies meanwhile found themselves put on trial with some other activists to be held responsible for the entire Chicago debacle and the events which transpired in what came to be known as the Chicago Conspircy Trial or the Trial of the Chicago 8. The eight were Abbie Hoffman, Jerry Rubin, Rennie Davis, David Dellinger, Tom Hayden, Lee Weiner, John Froines, & Bobby Seale and were charged with conspiracy to riot and crossing state lines to incite a riot.**

The trial started as a kangaroo court and ended up as a full-blown zoo. This was the biggest spotlite the Yippies had ever had, and for a while it looked like Vaudeville was back. Abbie & Jerry coming into court taking off their coats to reveal judge's robes beneath; then when ordered to remove those they complied with Jerry sporting a big red Santa Claus suit under that.

The trial was a spectacle of the absurd, Yip art, an open display of repression & more. All came to sing or speak or read poetry, or rant against the murderous system which was the cause of the protest to start, the cause

---

* The best book I've seen on Chicago '68 is *Miami and the Seige of Chicago* by Norman Mailer.

** This was called the Rap Brown Law as it was first used against H. Rap Brown, a Black activist.

What a Long Strange Trip It's Been

& dispenser of the carte-blanche violence so efficiently dispensed, & now was the judger of those recipients of that abuse. On the stand came Allen Ginsberg, Country Joe McDonald, Phil Ochs, Judy Collins & a host of others, each themselves an amoebic cell of the New America; a windborne spirit of sorts swiftly led by the silent footsteps of the quickly passing shadows in the nite sky. What was on trial was Woodstock Nation, and freedom was not allowed. This is perfectly illustrated by the action of Judge Hoffman in ordering Bobby Seale bound & gagged by court marshals when he continually objected to being denied the right to defend himself after the court refused to postpone his participation in the trial until his lawyer got out of the hospital. But every time they gagged him he came to his own defense, and they gagged him tighter & tighter, but each time he struggled free or could still be heard beneath his bonds. Finally the judge separated Bobby Seale from the proceedings of the Chicago Conspiracy Trial altogether, and he was tried separately. From then on the trial was pure pandemonium.

When it was all over the defendants had accumulated months & months & months of jail time for contempt of court, and five of the seven were found guilty of inciting riots (with Abbie himself getting five years)- convictions that were later overturned. And justly so.

Chapter 30

Regardless of Nixon's best efforts by 1970 the Movement was still growing, even branching out. By this time there were some 3,000 communes across the U.S. and this ideal of living in concert with the Earth helped greatly in manifesting the Environmental Movement into form. Its birth signaled both the recognition and admittance of how we were poisoning the world & ourselves with it and the need to clean up our act.

On April 15, 1970, the first Earth Day was held, and across the nation at schools and campuses; lectures, discussions, & presentations were held to bring about a greater awareness of the delicate balances within our environment and the current plight of the Earth. Since then major steps have been taken in many areas to reduce pollution (recycling, solar power, etc.) but in no way are enough resources being allocated to deal realistically with the pollution by automobiles & industry. We are suffocating in our own human-made fumes and industrial excrement and told it's the price we must pay for progress. Well, if it ain't healthy, it ain't progress.

This same feeling is what spawned such organizations as Greenpeace and Earth First! whose members consider it their duty to monkeywrench the operations of those profiteers who spew their wretched cancer-causing poisons out into the world so voluminously & nonchalantly. As if it doesn't matter. Well, it does matter and it is killing us whether people even care or not. The environmental threat which is a direct result of the industrial revolution and modern technology can best be seen in the Earth's current bouts with drought due to the greenhouse effect & in the recent nuclear/industrial catastrophies: Three Mile Island in the U.S. (in which over 50% of the reactor core melted down and the resultant cancer rate has been seven times the norm) & the disaster at Chernobyl in the U.S.S.R. which sent clouds of radiation drifting and falling round the globe; the murderous gas leak at Union Carbide's chemical plant in Bhopal, India, which killed some 2,000 people & injured many more; the depletion of the ozone layer in the atmosphere linked with the growing hole in the ozone layer over Antarctica; Exxon's Alaskan oil spill; & the saturation of our fruits & vegetables with deadly pesticides which cause neurological problems, liver problems, cancer and who knows what else. And now these fools are preserving our food by irradiating it with radioactive wastes (Cesium 137) left over from nuclear bomb production which in itself represents the greatest environmental threat imaginable.

What a Long Strange Trip It's Been

The fact that the world is only 30 minutes away from total nuclear destruction at any given time is not a comfortable thought.

This is technology at its maddest. Even considering the radiation in the atmosphere from past & present, above & undergound nuclear testing around the world plus Chernobyl, there's little comfort there either.

We are a very sick people & planet, mostly for what we've done in the last 50 years, mostly the last 30. And will get even sicker unless we clean up both the planet & our individual selves. The facts of health are there, it's no mystery; good health is no longer a birthright but something which must be strived for & maintained. And that's the realization that came from the 60's, and Earth Day, & Acid- that the Garden is no longer a healthy garden and needs our help as much as we need a poison-free environment and food and water if we are to survive as a species; physically, mentally, & spiritually.

Overall one of the nicest manifestations of the environmental movement was the saving of the whales. For years & years & years people in the U.S. and around the world worked to bring a halt to commercial whaling and the senseless slaughter of these most magnificent creatures. And they did. Japan, Iceland, & Russia are the main culprits who still whale in numbers, who, like others, whale for supposedly "scientific" purposes; but for the vast part whaling is off, and the whales have and will survive, perhaps longer than we ourselves. They still have to contend with an ocean full of garbage, once again reflecting the human mentality that the ocean seas are a great place to dispose of huge amounts of human, chemical, & radioactive wastes. From sea to shining sea.

It's a matter of consciousness and that takes time, but time is short, & tho' we've come a longway in our environmental awareness in the last 20 years, only a point 20 years hence will tell if we've succeeded in moving soon enough. And how about the merciless killing of the baby seals? Clubbing their brains out in the snow so some rich bitch can hide her flab lines in a fur coat has no justification whatsoever. A note of thanks & praise here for Bridgette Bardot & Cleveland Amory for their concern and activism on behalf of the little animals.

Even more immediate and equally important as, say, the water on this planet, are the global rainforests which are being destroyed at a voracious rate* depleting the planets largest source of oxygen just to grow cattle for American's fast food hamburgers & oranges for their breakfast. Try breathing an orange in 30 years & see how far that will get you. Seriously. Thankfully people are becoming more aware and are responding to this

---

* 100 acres a minute, 86,000 square miles a year, destroying 17,500 species of plants & animals a year.

problem, but much remains to be done. As with the acid rain problem which is killing tens of thousands of trees due to industrial pollution.

We've been dancing toward Oblivion and the whole Earth's on an edge-teetering seat, each & every one included, and our only salvation is ourselves. And that perhaps is not a very comforting thought either.

The times call for a radical change in stewardship.

We must take better care of ourselves & our planet. Quality of life. A very important concept. Don't settle for a world that's going to kill you. And that was a big change of thought for the time.

By this time also the Women's Liberation Movement had re-emerged stronger & more organized that ever, and strides were begun toward equal pay, equal jobs, & equal rights which were taken en masse in the streets and in the mindset of society. The National Organization of Women was formed, the Equal Rights Amendment revived, and the collective struggle against prejudice and sexism struck out on its long, long road which still winds on today.

But while the Movement was growing and expanding it's vision outward in the world, it was not immune from its own inner devastations. Drugs took their toll. The killer drugs- speed, downers, heroin, booze, & finally cocaine. Jimi Hendrix, Janis Joplin, Jim Morrison, Brian Jones, Al Wilson, Pigpen, Lenny Bruce. All dead. Overpublicity and the flooding of the streets with speed and the accompanying violence it brought totally destroyed the fabric of Haight Ashbury as rape, rip off, & murder haunted the halcyon scene.* There was the breakup of the Beatles, due to creative & management differences, and before that the Altamont Speedway Concert, with the Rolling Stones, in which Mick Jagger's sympathy for the Devil finally turned around and bit him & the Souls of everyone there.**

And then there was Charlie Manson. Did he lay a number on our national psyche or what? ...Hard to get a ride hitchhiking after Charlie passed thru. And in the midst of such defeat we had to always remind ourselves that it was violence we were standing against, must filter out from their society to ours. Violence. Pure, unadulterated violence; Grade A violence; Clockwork Orange violence; spoon fed to a nation nite after nite & day after day from the mysterious little box in the corner which hypnotizes whole cities of people and floods their conscious and subconscious with radiation & murder & mayhem over & over & over again until

---

* In the case of the huge influx of speed into the Haight there has been the question of government involvement for obvious reasons. Speed was the easiest way to destroy the scene.

** Energy follows thought and you shouldn't mess around with the Darker Forces.

they're conditioned to believe in violence as a viable solution in life. No wonder we've got such a problem with violence in this country. By far our society is the most violent peaceful society in the world. We've got the murder rate record for the Nth year running & violence-prone might describe a disturbingly growing segment of our population. TV's lowered the acceptable threshold of violence, and today people don't think twice about going out and blowing someone away for nothing, a situation which was extremely different when I was a kid. To say this is good or healthy would hardly be correct. Are we as a society so pitifully uncreative, unimaginative, & socially irresponsible that we cannot devise television entertainment whose plots do not perpetually involve violence & guns? Violence begets violence. Again we're digging our own grave.

TV's bad shit, Harlan will tell you that, & it'll leave you with a serious case of mindburn. I leave it alone almost strictly (the news, old movies, etc.) but TV and MTV* for that matter is almost totally trash, & yes, it will make you stupid. Just as stupid as they're trying to make you. Just as stupid as Laverne & Shirley. "And now, my friends," as the Shadow, or Green Lantern, or Felix the Cat, or another hero from the past, our friend the White Rabbit, might say, "is not the time for stupidity."

But with the revelations of the Pentagon Papers, the rise of the Back to Earth, Environmental, & Women's Movements & the continuing nagging moral atrocity in Vietnam, young people in 1970 were observantly neither stupid nor passive, and with time had come greater organization & committed dissent. So by then Richard Nixon had seen that his best efforts to stop the Movement had not been good enough. Which brings us to Kent.

---

* More twisted sex & violence & commercialism galore.

Chapter 31

Of all of the demonstrations, confrontations, & airings of dissent in those days, it is one which is remembered in the deep reaches of horrific memory which most tells the truth of the times.
Kent State.   May 4, 1970.   4 dead in Ohio.
The antiwar forces were growing too strong in this country and something had to be done, or with the '72 election the Boys in Black would no longer be in power. Whereas infiltration, incarceration, & extermination had slowed the Movement down (especially the assassination of Robert Kennedy and also Martin Luther King, Jr., who was forging an alliance between the Antiwar Movement & the Black populace in order to stop the war), the Movement was still alive and signs of resistance were abundant, no more so than within the ranks of students & those of the age to be drafted.

The military draft had been one of the main symbols of directed resistance against the war since it started. Burning one's draft card became the major sign of opposition for those who found themselves unwillingly being pressed into the armed services. The idea that your government could start a war in some far-off country for capital gain, then involuntarily appropriate your person as an expendable outlay in the quest for that profit, and then expect you to kill other human beings to accomplish such a dubious & morally repugnant undertaking in the first place, didn't set well with many young Americans. Slavery, hatred, murder, violence, & blind obedience were not on their agenda for this time around. No matter who wanted them to do their killing for them. In response Congress passed a law making it a crime of five years in jail & a $5,000 fine to destroy one's draft card. They still went up in smoke. While thousands of draft resisters went to jail, went underground, or migrated to Sweden or Canada* rather than participate in such madness. For this they were called cowards but many times the real cowards joined the National Guard where they could dodge the draft yet not have to take an uncomfortable moral stand against the war. They in turn were the forces which the government used to forcibly quell dissent when Americans gathered en masse to protest the murderous policies being carried out in their name.

---

* Canada has since signed an agreement with the United States stating that in future wars draft resisters from the U.S. can no longer seek political asylum there. The fascism spreads.

What a Long Strange Trip It's Been

One ploy of the Nixon gang was to create in late 1969 a lottery system for the draft, so that going to war became a big life or death contest, and if you got a high number you won and wouldn't be drafted. And many of those who lucked out and were no longer in danger of being drafted themselves just copped out and ceased their antiwar activities, just as Nixon had hoped they would. The people in power are masters of psychological manipulation of the masses; you should always remember that.

But you can't fool all of the people all of the time so the administration knew it would take stronger measures to stop dissent in its tracks. And stronger measures meant greater oppression of the citizens in opposition to the war.

To handle the immense amount of resistance which would meet his planned invasion of Cambodia and to use whatever force might be necessary to do this would require some preparation. For months Nixon had framed his rhetoric fostering a bad image & false reality of the characters of those folks within the antiwar movement and had been feeding it to the American people. "Bums," he called them, and our beloved Vice-President Spiro Agnew called them "Nazis, worse than brown shirts...." To Dick & Spiro patriotism was passively supporting your country's attempt to exterminate a whole people, who by all rights we had no business messing with anyhow.

Then the shit hit the fan.

On April 30, 1970 Richard M. Nixon announced that a huge force of South Vietnamese troops with American support had invaded Cambodia, a legally neutral country, in search for North Vietnamese military headquarters said to be there. Nixon said that this was a limited effort designed to shorten the war, but in fact just expanded the war even more. This was the last blow to the psyche of the American youth- the last lie they would listen to. Enough was enough.

They saw perhaps the time had come for the people to alter or abolish this murderous horde which ruled the land under an obscene sham they called government. The students took to the streets. In abject frustration a nationwide student strike began to form, and rallies & antiwar demonstrations were held on campuses across the country. One-third of the nation's students boycotted classes and it was few universities if any which didn't feel some effect from Nixon's move.

The same was true at Kent State. At noon the next day there was a rally to protest the Cambodian invasion and a copy of the United States Constitution was buried as well. That nite, Friday nite, as many students went home for the weekend, others went downtown to the bars.

In the ensuing hours chaos would mount; first as a motorcycle gang built a fire in the streets, then as people gathered round, a motorist attempted to run them down, then a beer bottle was thrown at a police car, & then an anti-Nixon window smashing spree began which brought out the police. They in turn cleared the bars out forcing even more people out into the street, kicked some butt, & when things cooled down, went home.

At this point the Mayor was still totally freaked out, so he set a town curfew & then called the Governor's office telling them that S.D.S. students had taken over a part of Kent, which was not the case at all. The National Guard was put on standby alert and a lieutenant sent to survey the scene.

After things were quiet the entire next day Mayor Satrom decided to call in the troops anyhow, and the National Guard was ordered to the town of Kent. This was a major mistake, as the Guard units which were called in were 40 miles away and for the two weeks previous to this had been involved in a mean truckers' strike in Cleveland, had been shot at, were exhausted, & had been expecting to go home. Instead they were sent to Kent to quell the backlash of Nixon's Genghis Khan foreign policy.

Once in town the Guard's legal duty with regard to the campus was that unless martial law was declared by the Governor, which it wasn't, its only role was to be supportive of the civilian law enforcement agencies there. This meant that the University police, the county Sheriff's Department, & the Ohio Highway Patrol (which was the most professionally trained of them all) had priority command over the Guard. Or should have. This, however, was not to be the case.

On campus there was an evening rally of about 1,000 students and afterwards a small group marched to the R.O.T.C. building and torched it. Firemen arrived, met some resistance in putting the fire out, did their thing, and left. Police arrived, found the fire out, & they left too.

Later, however, just as the Guard was arriving in town, the fire rekindled* into a spectacular scene as ammunition inside the building exploded and lit up the nite. The Guard moved immediately up to the campus, which they occupied and took over without a legal right to do so or the legal consent of the University.

From then on the military mind set took charge. That nite the Guard set out to "clear the area" with tear gas & fixed bayonets and ended up stabbing several students, one of whom was not only stabbed in the leg but received an eight-inch bayonet slash across the face. The next morning, May 3rd, the campus was like an occupied war zone with troops, jeeps, & armored personnel carriers all over the place, guns in prominent display.

---

* Whether on its own, by a demonstrator or agent provocateur, it is unknown.

What a Long Strange Trip It's Been

At this point had any rational human being been in or anywhere near control or in a position of power, the Kent massacre might never have occurred. But Governor James Rhoades took control, refused to close the University, and proceeded to set the stage for coming events. Rhoades, who was as vulgar & crude a politician as LBJ and just as mean as Nixon, knew just what had to be done. He was running for State Senator and with two days until the primary election and himself trailing behind, he decided to make his stand at Kent and politicize on the law & order issue.*

Taking his cues from speeches made by Nixon & Agnew with regard to the antiwar movement, Governor Rhoades called a press conference with the leaders of the Guard and gave a speech which was broadcast both to the voters at large and, more importantly, to the National Guardsmen in their barracks. In part Rhoades said about the protestors:

"We're going to use every weapon of the law enforcement agencies of Ohio to drive them out of Kent. They're worse than the brown shirts & Communist element & also the nightriders & vigilantes. They're the worst type of people we harbor in America.... It's over with in Ohio.... I think we're up against the strongest, well-trained militant revolutionary group that has ever assembled in America.... We're going to eradicate the problem, we're not going to treat the symptoms. No one is safe in Portage County. It is just that simple."

Added to this, Major General Sylvester Del Corso commented on the degree with which they might respond: "As the Ohio law says, use any force that's necessary even to the point of shooting. We don't want to get into that but the law says we can if necessary."[1] But things were not that simple, nor was stopping the continued use of acute violence by the Guard.

That evening there was a sit-in at the gates of K.S.U. and the students asked to speak with the President of the University & the Mayor about having the armed guard removed from the campus. The President's underlings rejected such a meeting and the Mayor promised to show but didn't. The R.S.V.P. was picked up by the National Guard, however, who once again exerted undue control by illegally placing a ban on gatherings and changing the Mayor's curfew on campus from 1 a.m. to imposing an immediate curfew on all students.

The Guard read the riot act which gave the students five minutes to disperse then with tear gas and fixed bayonets they once again attacked-bayonetting at least seven students, some seriously, two of which had to

---

* After all it was only three days before that a demonstrator at Ohio University had been shot and the Ohio electorate seemed to respond well to that.

be taken to the hospital. This scene went on for hours, with this surreal reality becoming even more ominous as the whirl of a helicopter & the rays of its sweeping searchlite bounced off clouds of tear gas in something reminiscent of Vietnam or the scene of the Martian invasion in the movie of H.G. Wells's *War of the Worlds*.

Needless to say all of this did nothing but frustrate the students even more. Not only was their country slaughtering hundreds of thousands of people abroad, but now its own citizens were being forcefully denied their freedom of assembly & dissent by armed agents of the state. But their biggest lesson was yet to come.

The following day on Monday, May 4th, a noontime rally was held which had been scheduled at the rally on Friday. The gathering was perfectly legal* & peaceful and was attended by much of the student body. In spite of all the violence by the Guard, classes were still on, and many of the students returning from the weekend found a dangerous situation in their midst, and no one from within the administration was willing to deal with it. So the students gathered together hoping to work something out amongst themselves and bring some unity to the situation.

That morning, however, a meeting was held between the Mayor, President White of the University, and representatives of the Ohio Highway Patrol & the National Guard in which it was decided (purportedly by the Guard) that the noon rally should not be permitted for some reason. This decision came after President White had decided not to ask the Guard to leave the campus, even tho' the potential for violence to the students had clearly been demonstrated in the previous days. So in the midst of the abrogation of all true sense and authority, the Guard were sent out to break up the rally while President White waltzed off to lunch. And while he sat at the Brown Derby eating some slaughtered cow, his continued ineptitude & failure to command a situation which he was responsible for, led in turn to the slaughter of four students whose education and well-being was his job.

It seems that everyone was so worked up by other people's rhetoric about teaching those students a lesson in law & order, everyone so easily sucked into the hate mode, that no one actually considered the danger to the students or cared. It was this unspoken mentality from the President of the United States on down that if, "God forbid, a few students were shot it'd cool their heels and make them think twice about demonstrating" that

---

* The rally was perfectly legal. The campus was not under martial law, a state of emergency had not been called by the Governor, so the only legal guidelines in effect were the Mayor's State of Civil Emergency which specifically allowed for students to lawfully assemble and peacefully demonstrate on campus.

was in command. With any luck it might become standard operating procedure which would certainly be useful in curbing dissent.

The Guard approached the rally which was peaceful and ordered the crowd to disperse immediately, but the students knew they were legally there and stuck. The Guard then read the riot act and prepared to move in. The crowd in return told the guard to fuck off and a few rocks were thrown toward the retreating jeep which had advanced and read the act. With tear gas, fixed bayonets, & rifles loaded the Guard advanced upon the crowd and as a few students tossed some cannisters of tear gas back at the Guard, most fled up the hill, around Taylor Hall and began dispersing across campus.

Although their initial objective had been accomplished (clearing the commons & dispersing the assembly) the Guardsmen continued marching across the campus until they boxed themselves into a practice football field which was surrounded on three sides by a fence. Noting they could go no further they then turned, kneeled, & aimed their rifles at the dozen or so students in the parking lot at the other end of the field who had been yelling at them and throwing some rocks their way. (As the distance was a good 150' the rocks were falling short.)

At this point, for whatever reason, one of the Guardsmen raised his pistol into the air and fired a shot. From here the Guard proceeded to march back out of the field and up the hill toward where they had come. As they moved up, a small group of the Guard held to the back keeping an eye on the students in the parking lot. As the Guardsmen reached the crest of Taylor Hill, those in the back wheeled in concert and fired at the students still in the parking lot. What followed was a 13 second barrage of gunfire which was to leave four students dead and 9 wounded.

In the aftermath of the shooting the Guard would claim that they fired because their lives were in danger by a charging mob which was only 4-5 yards away. Photographic evidence and the subsequent F.B.I. report would prove this to be a total fabrication. The students who were shot and killed- Jeffery Miller, Allison Krause, William Schroeder & Sandra Scheur- were 265', 343', 382', & 390' respectively from the guard when they were gunned down on that May afternoon. That's over the length of a football field away! The closest students shot were 70 & 100' away, but all the rest were between 200 & 730' away. Photographic evidence shows in fact that the Guard were in no danger at all, and that the shooting of certain students by certain Guardsmen appeared to be an intentional and premeditated act. The students shot at had been those taunting the Guard the most as they had been in the area of the practice field. The closest student shot was 70' away and had been giving the Guard the finger and was subsequently shot in the balls by Sergeant Lawrence Shafer who, it is said, bragged about shooting Jeffery Miller also. The fact that the National Guard would not let ambulances get to the students for 20 minutes after they got there while students lay bleeding to death shows the exact disposition of the Guard that day. The disposition of cold-blooded killers.

As to who if anyone gave the order to fire, the National Guard officer in command, General Del Corso, gave no such order, but he did lie to investigating agencies about the charging mob when photos show him at the front of the Guard leading them on and not under attack from any side. The photos do show an apparent huddle on the practice field by the same Guardsmen who were the ones who wheeled & fired. All told, 28 Guardsmen are listed as firing their weapons that day and to their credit some of them aimed away from the students. Others were human enough not to fire at all. It's a miracle that more people weren't killed, as at least 30 bullet holes were later found in cars in the parking lot.

One of the biggest mysteries of all is the exact role played by undercover agent Terry Norman that day. Norman was an F.B.I., campus police undercover agent who for three-and-a-half years had spied upon & photographed campus activists while posing as a part-time student and freelance photographer. Immediately prior to the shootings Norman was running to the side of the Guardsmen when he pulled a pistol from his coat, began waving it wildly around in the air, reportedly struck a student over the head, & some say fired four shots. Several civilians chased Norman from Taylor Hall to the main Guard formation and to Sgt. Delaney, the Guardsman to whom Norman surrendered his .38 caliber pistol. Delaney claims that Norman's gun had been fired, & Norman was overheard by an NBC newsman saying that he did in fact shoot. Later the campus police would deny that the gun had been fired, and to get him out of the picture, Terry Norman was transferred to D.C. to be a nark.

In none of the subsequent investigations or judicial proceedings was Terry Norman ever questioned concerning his actions. Which leaves some major questions unanswered. Did Terry Norman in fact fire his gun? If he did was it in panic reaction after he realized the students were on to him, or was it premeditated, perhaps part of his job to trigger an incident that might leave a few students and, hopefully, the antiwar movement dead in its tracks? Did the Guard fire in response to Norman's initial firing or were they coincidental incidents?

Again, with Norman being hustled quickly out of the scene, all we have to go on is photographic evidence, which shows certain Guardsmen very intently wheeling & firing at certain targets and not in the direction of Norman at all. So no matter what intent was present, justification was not, and events show that on May 4, 1970, agents of the state murdered four students for their opposition to the war. Which well paralleled the needs of the ruling class.

And the whole affair was packaged to Middle America as an altogether different set of events. A wild and unruly mob of hippy Communists who were attacking the Guard on all sides with bricks & bottles. The Guard's lives were in danger & they'd run out of tear gas. All lies.

Richard M. Nixon, ultimately responsible for these killings and the rest of the vast slaughter in Vietnam under his rule, was to be quoted the next day: "When dissent turns to violence it invites tragedy," thus laying the blame on the dead students. In other words, they deserved it.

The only violence on the student's part had been the throwing of stones at the Guard and the burning of the R.O.T.C. building. Neither of these are acts which justiy shooting, especially if it's unknown just who torched the building. Regardless, its burning symbolized the abject frustration of the young people with their government, and the government's response in stifling their dissention thru taking their lives speaks for itself. There's no silence like dead silence.

Ronald Reagan was a bit more poetic concerning student unrest, saying, "If it takes a bloodbath, let's get it over with now!"[2] And he meant it.

The attempts by those people in power to polarize the masses continued and materialized in such forms as a huge rally of construction workers or hardhats in New York City, which took to the streets a week after Kent marching with their American flag and beating up on longhairs along the way. All this to show their support for the good job our boys were doing in Vietnam and with killing the antiwar critics at home.

But after Kent, protest continued; indeed, the killings acted as a focal point for even further demonstrations against a government with a soul so black that it was killing its own children.

But this was not the first time that dissenting students had been shot & killed in America, nor would it be the last. In 1968 three students were killed when police opened fire on demonstrators who were protesting racial segregation at a bowling alley in Orangeville, South Carolina. In North Carolina a year later police would kill demonstrator Willy Grimes at the North Carolina Agricultural & Technical Institute, and that same year blind student James Rector was killed at the People's Park demo. In February 1970 an Isla Vista College student died in a confrontation with police* in which the Bank of America was burned to the ground. And ten

---

* The cop first said he dropped his gun & it went off but later said he sighted in on the kid for practice & his trigger finger slipped.

A Hippy's History of the Sixties

days after Kent, police opened up on protestors in Jackson, Mississippi, killing two, wounding 12, & riddling one hall with almost 400 bullet holes. And two other students were killed at Southern University in Baton Rouge, Louisiana, & one in Santa Fe.

It was open season on students in America, as Justice became a blindfolded whore whose favors could be bought by pieces of eight robbed from dead men's eyes.

As for what went on at Kent and as far as the judicial system goes, cover-up was once again the word of the day with all the necessary agencies of government playing along. First Richard Nixon formed the Scranton Commission to investigate the goings on there. Although the Commission termed the shootings unwarranted, unjustifiable, & inexcusable it did not especially pursue the course of truth nor did it even take testimony from Governor Rhoades or the Guardsmen involved. And even though members of the Commission including its head William Scranton felt that a grand jury should be convened for the sake of justice, the President viewed things with different eye. It was a blind eye & with its blinking RMN washed his hands of the Kent affair refusing to order a Federal Grand Jury to investigate the incident.

In October 1970 the Ohio Grand Jury- a true redneck-necktie party kinda group if there ever was one- decided to straighten this whole mess out and indicted 24 students & one professor and held them responsible for the murders on May 4th. The Guard had no charges brought against them, and only one Guardsman was called to testify. Of it all two people plea bargained when the trial first started, then things got so ridiculous that charges were dropped against the remaining 23 for lack of evidence. This supported both the F.B.I. report & the Justice Department investigation that none of the students shot were in a position to pose even a remote danger to the Guard at the time of the firing.

Even tho', Attorney General John Mitchell decided against convening a Federal Grand Jury to seek justice in the matter. In response students from Kent State gathered 50,000 signatures on a petition calling for a grand jury investigation, and presented these to the Nixon White House. In response to this Attorney General Kleindienst, who had replaced Mitchell when he was indicted for Watergate and who himself had committed perjury by lying at his Congressional confirmation hearing, held to Mitchell's decision to bury the matter.

It was not until May of 1973 that the U.S. Department of Justice reopened the Kent investigation and in December a grand jury was sworn in. This turn of events was totally due to the integrity of Elliot Richardson. He followed Kleindienst as Attorney General when Kleindienst was

What a Long Strange Trip It's Been

caught breaking the law and saw to it that justice was pursued in this matter. Richardson would further exhibit his moral quality when he resigned as Attorney General rather than follow Nixon's orders to fire Watergate Special Prosecutor Archibald Cox when he was closing in on Tricky Dick.

Finally on January 4, 1979, after almost nine years of frustration, governmental cover-up, & legal battles, the parents of the dead and wounded students agreed on a $675,000 out of court settlement which included a vague statement of regret from the National Guard. Out of this the parents of the dead students only received $15,000 each. This is the closest thing to justice in America and in Ohio we could come, and it's a bleeding shame.

The University's position on this, meanwhile, is equally shameful. Not only were they the ones who threw the students to the wolves in the first place, but they continually tried to sweep the whole thing under the rug. And in a move both calculated & callous, and amid significant demonstrations, the University constructed a gymnasium complex on the site of the shootings to further obscure history. And almost two decades after the shootings there has yet to be a memorial built on the campus of K.S.U. for the students. The one sculpture by noted sculptor George Segal, which was a designated gift to the University for memorial purposes, was rejected for it realistically portrayed the biblical scene of Abraham holding his knife over his son Isaac ready to kill him. But that was too much to the point for the University whose negligence in this whole matter has been reprehensible if not complicitly murderous. It's no mistake that at Kent State they've for so long been unable to come up with the money for a memorial, yet the University's new fashion museum was worth whatever the millions they threw into it. Finally, by 1989, the university had approved the construction of a memorial. A little too little, a little too late.

Which shows you the price we paid for going against Richard Nixon, his insidious policies, and trying to stop a war. Intense alienation and hatred by Middle America to the point that the government could shoot students and get away with it.

Chapter 32

The killings at Kent State would certainly never have occurred had Richard Nixon not been elected in 1968.

The violence would not have manifested itself. And violence is the answer to our twice-asked question: how such a son-of-a-bitch as Richard Nixon came to power. By the process of elimination you might say and by depending on his well-hewn ability to manipulate the American people thru the technique of playing on their fearful & prejudicial natures. That, and the fact that his campaign was turned over to the Madison Avenue crowd- slick ad men & public relations firms and millions, tens of millions of dollars were spent to package the "New Nixon" and sell this image to the American voting public. The book, *The Selling of the President '68*, by Joe McGinness gives a good look at their effort to successfully market Nixon.

And the fact that they even had to do this shows you what a bad image people had in their minds of Richard Nixon. And with good reason. His campaign tactics even far before Watergate had been ones of lies, smears, illegal campaign funds, & dirty tricks. One fine illustration is the infamous "Checkers" case of 1952. During his first run as Vice-President with General Eisenhower, it was revealed that seventy some California executives had contributed to a secret fund for Nixon's personal use. Nixon then went on TV to explain all this and pulled off one of the best snow jobs ever seen. He made his financial plight sound even worse than Jimmy & Tammy Bakker did when they said they were down to their last 50 thou, had to sell the Mercedes, and please send cash. Even worse than Ferdinand & Imelda Marcos* when they fled to Hawaii after being driven from Manila.

And damned Dick went on about Pat and her thrifty Republican cloth coat and how he needed this illegal money just to get by, and then came the tear jerker. Nixon lashed out at his opponents by bringing his cocker spaniel Checkers into the scene, saying that she was also a gift and to give her back would break his little kid's heart so he wasn't going to give the dog back or for that matter any of the money back either.[1] And enough people bought this drivel that he stayed on with Ike, got elected V.P. in '52, re-elected in '56 and lost the Presidential election to John Kennedy in 1960. So after losing the 1962 California gubernatorial election Nixon retired

---

* The woman with 10,000 toes and a bullet-proof bra!

from politics with his infamous line: "You won't have Dick Nixon to kick around anymore."* But that wasn't exactly true.

He returned in 1968 like a ghoul from the dead to play his evil little role in American history. We should have learned something from gypsy lore & driven a stake thru his heart the first time he died politically. And it should certainly not have been overlooked again.

Nixon & his chosen V.P. Spiro Agnew were masters of hate & polarization and knew if they could succeed in convincing the American public that all antiwar protestors were dirty, violent bums then they could not only continue to do what they wanted with the war, but could wipe out the opposition as well.

That's where all the agent provocateurs came in. Going around speaking violence, passing out explosives, setting people up to do things they wouldn't have done on their own, blowing things up, and in the resultant publicity & arrests convince the American public that there were radicals in every closet just waiting to jump out and slit their throats. Plus the increased government violence acutely directed against targets of the New Left and their resultant militant response and inclination to arm for self defense was seemingly futher proof that danger was at hand and gave the government a supposed valid license to kill and not be questioned.

By dubbing their constituency the "Silent Majority," Nixon & Agnew insured that those good middle Americans who so believed in law & order would not chance being lumped with these longhaired, cutthroat heathens, by coming to their aid or by raising embarassing inquiries about the war; that they would remain silent with all those other fine folks whose morality was based on their being the supposed majority. This was the forerunner of the so called Moral Majority who supported the likes of Ronald Reagan (Mr. 666), Oral Roberts (God's own extortionist), Jimmy ("I wouldn't leave him alone with my kid") Swaggart, Pat (Mr. Korean War) Robinson, Jerry Outhouse Falwell, & Jim & Tammy Fae Bakker (the pancake pitbulls of TV envangelism). Heaven forbid! Spiritual vampires one and all.

It's this group psychology of go along with the majority and don't make waves which the government so desperately needed to perpetuate in order to intimidate the nation into looking the other way as our young men, also steeped deep in this philosophy, went about systematically destroying a country smaller than South Dakota. And those who spoke against the war were not good Americans, were unpatriotic, & in effect

---

* When JFK heard this line he said, "Nobody could talk like that and be normal." He thought Nixon was mentally unsound, or in his words "sick, sick, sick!"[2]

were the enemy too. At least in the government's mind. And what a paranoid mind set that was.

So the lines were drawn and it was Richard Nixon who can be most credited with widening the division which was tearing the very fabric of this country apart.

It was Nixon who was the one.

It was Nixon who promised to heal and only picked the edges of the half-formed scab & pulled it from the bleeding hide of the national psyche.

And that was just exactly what he was supposed to do.

That's why in 1968 for the people in power Nixon was the one. He was maneuvered into position because he could do the job and could be counted on. Nixon was their boy. He hated the right people and had the keen ability to broadcast that hatred into the masses in such a way as was necessary at the time. Polarization, hatred, divide & conquer. Richard Nixon-style.

He was an old hand at intimidation and playing on people's fears. His rise to power was initially due to his role in the era of the so called McCarthy Communist Witchhunts, which ruined the careers & lives of thousands of right-on people in the 50's. True to form, McCarthy died hopelessly insane in a sanatorium, which really tells ya what this Commie-hating craze which was to become government policy was all about. But Nixon lived on. Nixon knew how to badger, corner, & where to strike for the kill; and in his position as President this made him the most dangerous man in the world.

Once he felt that he had the middle Americans psychologically muzzled, he then went to work assembling the mechanisms of a police state and putting them into motion. He gathered around him those men who shared his thirst for power and hatred of those who threatened it. With Spiro Agnew as V.P., John Mitchell as Attorney General, with J. Edgar Hoover still head of the F.B.I., and the likes of the slick S.S.-types John Dean, John Ehrlichman, & H.R. Haldeman to do his bidding, near open warfare was declared on the New Left, which would include more acts of violence & criminal deeds than any elements of the antiwar movement ever dreamed of, perpetrated, or carried out.

Nixon was out to get the opposition in whatever form it appeared- militants, pacifists, Democrats, journalists- all were considered enemies. And of course different groups required different tactics, whatever method proved expedient was the rule. The Black Panthers could merely be wiped out, whereas the Justice Department's policy was one of prosecuting the leaders of the antiwar movement in hopes of disabling the Movement. Wild schemes were hatched, legalities dispensed with, agents dispatched.

What a Long Strange Trip It's Been

It began five months into his first term, when in response to leaks in the press, he illegally ordered the phones of 17 persons (13 government employees & four newspeople) tapped. These phones were monitored from the spring of '69 to the spring of '71 & turned up nothing.

That summer, he asked his White House aides to draw up an "Enemies List" to be used by the Internal Revenue Service and others for investigation, surveillance, harrassment, & political neutralization. Shortly therafter the I.R.S. set up its "Activist Organizations' Group" to ostensibly analyze individuals & organizations promoting "extreme views and philosophies." Renamed the Special Service Group in 1970, it gathered information on 4,300 citizens & 1,000 organizations in its first year alone, and did the bidding when the White House sent hundreds of names of political opponents to be monitored. This went on for three more years, until it was abolished in 1973, but it's been subsequently revealed that the I.R.S. had drawn up and kept an enemies list of their own & you can bet today those slimedogs are probably doing the same.

...Slime dogs? I only call them that because of their viscious little police force which has gone around terrorizing & assaulting U.S. citizens for years who owed the government back tax money. These agents would come to instantly repossess your car, & if you gave even the hint of resistance beat the living crap right out of you. And love it. I don't know where the government continually finds the thugs to fill the ranks of their enforcement agencies, but some people just love to use violence on those weaker than themselves. It's the old power-control personality types; fascism never works without them. I don't think this is quite what our founding fathers had in mind. Things were actually so bad that they finally passed an I.R.S. reform bill in 1988 which among other things, disallowed the practice of promotions based upon the amount of goods an employee repossessed and also stopped immediate repossessions by providing for a 30-day notification period before repossession. But then they were working for Nixon. And Nixon was certainly not going to stop there.

In the summer of 1970 he ordered the development of a "domestic intelligence plan" with which illegal & unconstitutional means were to be used to gather information on antiwar dissidents. This included surveillance of personal mail, breaking & entering, and the monitoring of foreign phone calls to and from the U.S. Known as the Huston Plan after its architect, White House aide Tom Huston, it was to orchestrate the F.B.I., the C.I.A., the Justice Department & the National Security Council and unleash them on the New Left. J. Edgar Hoover, however, refused to go along with the plan as it would mean giving up agency power and operational tasks to other organizations. Within a week after its creation, the proper agencies were notified that the President had rescinded his approval of the plan, and it was supposedly never implemented, or at least not in the scope originally intended. This didn't mean that the F.B.I. didn't take them up on the breaking & entering aspect of the plan in their intelligence gathering efforts. You would have thought the F.B.I. field offices were a training school for petty crooks with all the black bag jobs that were going on.

In lieu of the Huston Plan, Nixon created the Interagency Evaluation Committee with the likes of John Dean, John Ehrlichman, & H.R. Haldeman* presiding and though we have no public knowledge of what these jokers were up to, it was only a prelude of things to come.

But it was the publication of the Pentagon Papers which really blew Tricky Dick out and pushed him over the edge. This time in June of 1971 he set up his own illegal secret police force & covert operations squad at the White House. Housed in the White House basement, this squad was called the Plumbers in reference to their job of plugging leaks. The Plumbers, true to form, were made up of a whole collection of right-wing screwballs. G. Gordon Liddy, perhaps the screwiest and strangest of them all. Liddy got on the squad cause he had busted Leary at Millbrook years earlier. E. Howard Hunt, who had been with the C.I.A. for 25 years & knew his stuff. He was, in fact, the first Chief of Operations of the C.I.A.'s Domestic Operations Division from 1962-66, which is really intersting seeing how the C.I.A. is prohibited by its charter from operating domestically or inside the United States. He had proved his worth at Dealey Plaza. (I wonder if Liddy was jealous that he wasn't in on the action there....) Liddy & Associates also broke into J. Edgar Hoover's house when he was giving Nixon some heavy grief during Watergate, and put poison on his toiletries which would kill him and look like a heart attack. The report to the Ervin Committee, however, said that before Hoover had a chance to use his solid stick deodorant that he had a heart attack and died in early May of 1972.[3]

James McCord, also with the C.I.A. for over 24 years & the F.B.I. seven years, came to the Plumbers from the position of chief of security of the Committee to Re-elect the President. And then there was Egil Krogh, Jr., the head of the team and someone whom to describe as a pain in the ass would be a poor description of the bloody, festering hemorrhoid he was to the process of democracy.

---

* Ehrlichman & Haldeman were the Goering & Goebbels of the Nixon set, that is, close to their Fuhrer.

What a Long Strange Trip It's Been

Not to mention John Mitchell who had been the chief of Governor Ronald Reagan's police operation "Garden Plot" to quell dissent in California by harassing activists and setting them up and also meeting them with the stiffest resistance in the streets.

And with Ehrlichman at the helm barking orders from the stateroom of Captain Milhous Queeg, they set out to James Bond the opposition & ensure that Nixon would win the election in '72 & the New Left would be buried. Or so they hoped.

First Liddy & Hunt were dispatched to case the office of Daniel Ellsberg's psychiatrist. This they did fully equipped with disguises & a spy camera illegally provided by the C.I.A. which was hidden in a pouch of tobacco. Ellsberg was the Defense Department analyst who had leaked the Pentagon Papers which were interagency papers from within the Pentagon concerning the true nature and operation of the Vietnam War. These papers gave many revelations to the American public- mainly that they were continually lied to by several President's concerning the conduct of the war, and also the fact that our entrance into the war was a total fraud on LBJ's part.

A week after they cased the place Liddy & Hunt met with three Cuban Americans (some of Hunt's buddies from the Bay of Pigs fiasco) and after receiving instructions, these three broke into Dr. Fielding's psychiatry office in hopes of getting some information to discredit Ellsberg with. When they turned nothing up, Nixon himself would meet with the judge of the Pentagon Papers case at Nixon's California White House and have John Ehrlichman offer him the job of F.B.I. directorship after he was "finished" with the Ellsberg case. A clear bribe attempt, indeed, and although some judges would have disqualified themselves from the case after such an improper approach, it was not until the court had been informed of the Fielding break-in & other government misconduct in the case that the judge declared a mistrial and set the defendants Daniel Ellsberg & Anthony Russo free.

But this was not to slow the Plumbers down any. From here they embarked on a wild barrage of dirty tricks & illegalities, all designed to undermine the opposing political party and the American political process. For the dirty tricks department the White House hired Donald Segretti,* another festering hemorrhoid par excellance, who conducted

---

* Segretti was hired by Dwight Chapin, Nixon's appointment secretary & was paid $45,000 for his work by Nixon's lawyer Herb Kalmbach. Kalmbach was in charge of illegally raising funds- usually by shaking down big corporations in return for favors by the administration or by promising ambassadorships to people in exchange for $100,000 campaign contributions. He's also the one who paid out $220,000 to keep the Watergate defendants quiet.

his undercover sabotage campaign in at least 10 and perhaps as many as 38 states across the nation. Political sabotage aimed primarily at the leading Democratic candidates which took a variety of forms.

Edmund Muskie was the initial target, as he was the biggest perceived threat to a Nixon re-election. The first move they made was to infiltrate his staff with two spies acting as a chauffeur & secretary. Their reports went directly back to the Oval Office. Next Muskie stationery was used by Segretti to fabricate letters charging Hubert Humphrey & Henry Jackson with sexual misconduct and being drunks while it went on to accuse Shirley Chisholm, a Black congresswoman and serious Presidential contender, of being nuts.

Next a letter accusing Senator Muskie of making derogatory remarks against French Canadian Americans caused a big stir in the New Hampshire primary and some published remarks about his wife prompted Muskie to hold an outdoor press conference in which he tried to refute those charges, but he only appeared to the TV nation as an emotionally hyped-up babbling putz. Totally not in control. Years later I read that Muskie had been unknowingly dosed with a hallucinogenic agent right before his speech & just lost it.[4] This is not as wild as it sounds, as this was the same plan the Nixon gang had to pull on columnist Jack Anderson before one of his radio broadcasts. Just a dosed microphone stand, or something slipped in his drink* would do the trick. Seeing the speech myself I could totally believe this. After his speech Muskie was pretty much out of the race and the Nixon henchmen then turned to the others. More letters, more dirty tricks, more disunity among the Democrats.

In December 1971 Gordon Liddy was made General-counsel to Nixon's Committee to Re-elect the President, or C.R.E.E.P. as it was aptly known. Here Liddy's job was to foment even greater plans to disrupt the Democrats' campaign & especially their convention. In Attorney General Mitchell's office with Mitchell present, he outlined his plans which included electronic surveillance, mugging, & kidnapping the leaders of the legal demonstrations, using prostitutes to get the Democratic candidates in compromising photos for blackmailing purposes, plus he also mentioned plans to bomb the Brookings Institute in order to retrieve the stolen Pentagon Papers.[5] These plans were scaled down twice, with some

---

* In an Associated Press story, August 17, 1973, former C.I.A. official Miles Copeland is reported to have said that "senior Agency officials are convinced Senator Edmund Muskie's damaging breakdown during the presidential campaign last year was caused by convicted Watergate conspirator E. Howard Hunt or his henchman spiking his drink with a sophisticated form of L.S.D."

What a Long Strange Trip It's Been

of them implemented & some not,* but they were only a few of the many different actions being considered.

Along those same lines brings us to an October 1971 press conference in which Louis Tackwood, a veteran agent for the Los Angeles Police in the Criminal Conspiracy section, told about secret inside plans to disrupt & bomb the '72 political conventions. According to Tackwood, the F.B.I. and members of the L.A. police's antisubversive unit had formed together into what they called "Squad 19," and on orders from two men from D.C. with C.I.A. contacts named White & Martin (Hunt & James McCord's code names) Squad 19 was to infiltrate the protestors outside the convention halls and start street fights with the police. At the same time their agents inside were to set off explosions which would not only kill a few delegates but which would outrage the public and supposedly allow Richard Nixon to cancel the elections and to detain all political activists & foes of the war under special emergency powers.[6] This sounds a bit extreme but it coincides with Nixon's request for the Rand Corporation to do a secret study on the feasability of cancelling the 1972 elections in the wake of radical attacks & protests. But before anyone could bomb anything the Watergate burglars were caught and that changed a lot of things.

---

* The Brookings Institute bombing would have been carried out but was cancelled at the last moment by John Dean who flew across the country to call it off.

Chapter 33

The Watergate break-in of June 17, 1972, was to serve a couple of different purposes. One was to replace a tap they had placed there on their first visit a few weeks earlier, and another was to find damaging information on Democratic Party chairman Larry O'Brien. (O'Brien rose to power by way of a $50,000 payment to Hubert Humphrey with which O'Brien left the services of Howard Hughes, the reclusive billionaire, and became a Humphrey aide.) What the Plumbers were after was to find out how much O'Brien knew of a secret $100,000 payment made to Nixon by Hughes in return for some favorable antitrust action concerning some of Hughes' interests. It was their intention to blackmail O'Brien into silence if the case required.

The money was channeled thru Bebe Rebozo, Nixon's best friend and equally shady character. Rebozo the clown would later perjure himself concerning what he did with the money according to Nixon's other main money man & personal lawyer, Herb Kalmbach.[1]

Prosecutors concluded Rebozo used some of the money to pay Nixon's private bills, and also, Kalmbach charged, Rebozo gave Nixon's two brothers some ($3,000 & $5,000) & his secretary Rosemary Woods some too. With all that illegal money around it was easy to be generous.

Using a complicated maze of bank accounts thru his own lawyer's name, he channeled $50,000 of campaign contributions to his buddy Dick for his personal use, and when Pat's 60th birthday rolled around, again used campaign money to purchase a pair of diamond earrings for Pat from Dick. Bebe threw in the first $5,000 from the slushfund, then Rosemary Woods threw in $90 (?), then Dick threw in the last $560. Wonder what her beloved got her for Christmas- a box of popcorn?

At any rate the Hughes loan was not exactly kosher, especially since it coincided with two government rulings favorable to Hughes giving him the go-ahead to acquire Air West airlines & another Las Vegas Hotel. But this was old hat for Howard & Dick. In December 1956 Dick got in the same sort of trouble while Vice-President for soliciting a loan from Hughes for his brother Donald. The loan was for $205,000 made by the Hughes Tool Company and shortly thereafter the I.R.S. reversed itself and gave the Howard Hughes Medical Foundation tax-exmpt status. This saved old Howard a bundle, (a cool million the first day) as all his stock for Hughes Aircraft was held by the Foundation. Nixon talked his way out of the first loan deal at the time, and with the help of a little plumbing hoped to cover up the second loan. But the Plumbers got caught redhanded breaking into the Democratic Headquarters by security guard Frank Willis, one of the unsung heroes of our time.

Now the scene starts to get weird. It's June 1972, less than 5 months away from the Presidential election, & Nixon's boys get caught in the opposition's office with their pants down. What to do?

At first denials were issued that James McCord, Bernard Baker, Frank Sturgis & the two Cubans (all of whom were past or present operatives for the C.I.A.) had any connection with the White House or the Committee to Re-elect the President (CREEP). But connections were being made. McCord (who himself had worked for 24 years for the C.I.A.) was known to work on security matters for CREEP. Howard Hunt's name was found in the address books of two of the burglars, thus providing a direct link to the White House where he was an aide to Charles Colson, White House Counsel to the President and a real mean S.O.B. who would also do some time for the Watergate affair. Things did not look good- the Washington Post and other papers were hot on the trail and beginning to piece things together.

In a classic move to cover-up & obstruct justice, Nixon, Ehrlichman, Haldeman, Dean, & Mitchell all scrambled to do what they could those first few weeks after Watergate. The ball had been dropped and tho' at first the team tried to pick it up & run with it, before long they would find themselves just plain running. But first things first.

It was immediately necessary to 1) keep the burglars' mouths shut, 2) get a grip on the F.B.I. investigation which had already uncovered C.I.A. involvement, 3) stonewall the public, & 4) make sure the trial didn't start till after the '72 elections four and a half months away. The last was easiest of all. The Justice Department announced that the trial would be postponed until January 8, 1973. That would certainly stonewall the public at least until after the election.

As for the others the F.B.I. was tracing a check found on one of the burglars which led directly to CREEP & some other monies which were from illegal campaign contributions that had been laundered thru Mexican banks and used to finance the break-in. Nixon agreed to the plan of having the director or deputy director of the C.I.A. call F.B.I. head Patrick Gray* and tell him that the F.B.I. was uncovering some C.I.A.

---

* J. Edgar Hoover had died just a few months before, ending an era of F.B.I. lawlessness under his command. He managed to stay in power so long by blackmailing Presidents with their own dirt. Some say Nixon got him. Who knows, but whatever the case he's in bulldog heaven now.

A Hippy's History of the Sixties

operations that are best left secret and as Bob Haldeman put it, to "stay the hell out of it!" At first Pat Gray resisted attempts to obstruct the F.B.I. investigation, but in the end he too became entangled in the web of Watergate by giving John Dean 82 Bureau reports and burning some "politically sensitive" material which had come from Howard Hunt's safe.*

As far as keeping the Watergate defendants quiet, money and the promise of clemency would probably do there. Within two weeks after the break-in, funds had been set up and a method of delivery devised. (The burglars' lawyer Anthony Ulasewicz would pass on the cash given him by Nixon's personal lawyer Herb Kalmbach.) Ulasewicz's first payoff to the defendants was on July 7th and continued until September 19th when the burglars all pleaded not guilty and were released on bond.

But strategy required that all the defendants plead guilty, accept their sentences, and at a later date be pardoned by Nixon.

Dorothy Hunt (Howard's wife, who also was helping deliver orders and payoffs to the defendants) told James McCord on November 30th, just weeks after Nixon had been re-elected, that they would receive no more money "unless you fellows agree to plead guilty & take Executive Clemency...and you keep your mouths shut."

But it seems that someone wanted Dorothy to keep her mouth shut also. Just eight days later she would die in a plane crash with so many oddities attached that it could hardly be but sabotage. Who knows what mistake she made to be killed? Perhaps it was an example for her husband to keep his mouth shut, or perhaps something she said over the phone about being fed up with this whole mess- we may never know. But killed she was. On December 8, 1972, at Chicago's Midway Airport, United Flight 553 crashed upon landing, killing Dorothy Hunt and 42 others, some related to the Watergate investigation. On Mrs. Hunt's body was found $10,000 in $100 bills bound for Watergate defendants. Also allegedly on board the plane was another $40,000 in payoff money, $2 million in securities also carried by her, & some documents linking Attorney General Mitchell to an illegal stock payoff.

These materials were seen by a Justice Department informant who later started his own personal investigation of the crash. 'Cause something was fishy.

In fact a lot of things were fishy. Immediately after the crash the place was crawling with 50 F.B.I. agents who took over the on-site investigation.

---

* Including some phoney cablegrams Nixon had Hunt forge to make it look like JFK had ordered the assassination of South Vietnam's President Diem in 1963. Nixon... what a thug.

What a Long Strange Trip It's Been

The day after the crash Egil Krogh, Jr., who later went to jail for his part in the Watergate number, became the Under Secretary of the Department of Transportation, thus becoming instantly in charge of the National Transportion Safety Board's investigation of the crash. Dwight Chapin, Nixon's secretary who hired the dirty trickster Donald Segretti and later also went to jail for it, was then moved from his job at the White House and became an official for United Airlines, in fact, *the* official who was United's contact rep with the crash investigators. How convenient cover-up &, in appearance, even murder can be when it's done from the top. Even Charles Colson who directed the Ellsberg break-in from the White House was extremely suspicious of the death of Mrs. Hunt and tried to get the investigation of the crash reopened to no avail.[2]

So Dorothy went as a warning. What Howard thought is unclear, but it seems he got the message. He took his money & shut up. What was feared, of course, was that he'd spill the beans concerning the assassination of President Kennedy, the C.I.A.'s role in it, the Bay of Pigs veterans role in it, the whole works.

This can be seen in the taped meeting on June 23, 1972 between Haldeman & Nixon just six days after the Watergate break-in, in which they're discussing bringing in the head of the C.I.A., Richard Helms, & his deputy, Vernon Walters, and instructing them to tell the head of the F.B.I. to cool their investigation of Watergate for it was the C.I.A.'s job which they didn't want uncovered. But Nixon's rationale for why Helms would do this relates back to the Kennedy assassination which Nixon refers to as the "Bay of Pigs thing:"[3]

Here's the transcript of some of their conversations that day:

Haldeman - And the proposal would be that Ehrlichman and I call them in and say, ah-

Nixon - Allright, fine. How do you call him in? I mean, you just— well, we protected Helms from one hell of a lot of things.

Haldeman - That's what Ehrlichman says.

Nixon - Of course, this Hunt, that will uncover a lot of things. You open that scab, there's a hell of a lot of things, and we just feel that it would be very detrimental to have this thing go any further. This involves these Cubans, Hunt, and a lot of hanky-pank that we have nothing to do with ourselves.

Nixon - When you get (Helms & Walters) in...say, look, the problem is that this will open the whole, whole Bay of Pigs thing...and the President believes that it is going to open the whole Bay of Pigs thing again.

Nixon - O.K., just say very bad to have this fellow, Hunt, ah, he knows too damned much if, he was involved, the Cuba thing, it would be a fiasco.

It would make the C.I.A. look bad, it's going to make Hunt look bad, and likely to blow the whole Bay of Pigs thing, which we think would be very unfortunate, both for the C.I.A. and the country at this time.*

Yes, it probably would have been very unfortunate for the C.I.A. & Nixon if the American people had learned the truth of the JFK assassination in 1972... or in 1963. But they didn't & wouldn't, and so cover up begat cover up and the truth of Watergate was also successfully delayed, at least until after Richard M. Nixon would win re-election November 7, 1972.

---

* In an article entitled "Nixon Takes Another Oath" in the June 1979 issue of *Overthrow*, A.J. Weberman agrees that the "Secret of the Bay of Pigs" was code for the JFK bumpoff. He reports that even H.R. Haldeman stated: "The Bay of Pigs really meant the Kennedy assassination." Also brought up was the fact that Richard Nixon was in Dallas on November 22, 1963, although I've read elsewhere he had told F.B.I. investigators that he had left the night before. What's the dif? If he was there, he was there.

Chapter 34

And what of George McGovern, the man who lost to Richard Nixon, whose campaign headquarters after two unsuccessful break-in attempts was next on the list to be burgled after Watergate? Had the truth come out in time, it would have been a totally different election.

The McGovern candidacy was a political phenomenon; grassroots, built with heart, with tens of thousands of young people united in cause. The McGovern campaign shook up the very foundations of the Democratic Party. With party rules restructured to truly give the youth and minorities a voice in the political process. For the first time in ages it was truly a people's party and policy was no longer made in smoke-filled back rooms by big city bosses. McGovern was intelligent, compassionate, verbally articulate,* and out to stop the war. And so were we. It was the only time except before Bobby Kennedy was blown away that I had any real hope for the fate of the country based on the calibre of the individuals running for President. Except for Ron Dellums, Berkeley's veteran Congressman who's been with us all the way.

McGovern had grown up at Chicago '68 too & knew not only what we were up against, but knew the imperative of winning. When McGovern took the Wisconsin Primary in the spring of '72, it began a drive which finished with his becoming nominated the Democratic Presidential candidate at the convention.

The McGovern campaign's success was due to its youthful zeal and effort put into the race, and also in part to Nixon's gang for knocking Ed Muskie out of the running at the start. But once McGovern got the nomination he made several blunders which hurt him greatly. First, he voiced an unpopular tax proposal unclearly thought out; next he chose a Vice-Presidential candidate to run with, Thomas Eagleton, who had been hospitalized for psychiatric problems years earlier & failed to tell him. When the news came out Eagleton resigned as McGovern's running mate but the political damage was done. McGovern's subsequent search for another running mate finally landed Sargent Shriver, JFK's brother-in-law who had directed the Peace Corps, but only after being turned down by about seven others thus causing him further political embarassment.

---

* His State of the Union Address in the January 1972 issue of Rolling Stone is one of the greatest speeches I've ever heard or read.

All in all, tho', these mistakes were miniscule in comparison to the real issues at stake. The election was called the clearest choice of the century, and that it was indeed. But it was not just a matter of morals or right or wrong here. For we were dealing with the American voting public who for years had been led around like a bunch of sheep and blinded to all sensitiveness, all the while spending hours upon hours a nite in front of a stupid, glaring, radiation box getting programmed to be normal & buy Ivory Soap.

But Richard Nixon had been hoodwinking these political amoeba for years, so this was nothing new to him. In fact, having McGovern as the opposition (or Eugene McCarthy, for that matter) would be the best of all worlds for Nixon. For he, remember, was the media master of the politics of polarization, and here he went to work. First, he scared all these seemingly mental midgets into thinking that McGovern was going to cut defense spending so bad that the Salvation Army would be our only standing army left. TV ads for Nixon showed rows & rows of toy tin soldiers suddenly swept away by the blur of a hand and a message to frighten the viewer concerning McGovern defense cuts.

And in another one of Dick's clever little psychological ploys (like the draft lottery) he & Henry Kissinger announced that they had a "secret plan to end the war" and that if they weren't re-elected to power it would fail, thus putting the immediate burden of peace on the shoulders of the American public. McGovern, of course, would have brought peace anyway, but Nixon visibly obscured that fact. His secret plan, by the way, was to bomb the fuck out of North Vietnam, especially the city of Hanoi for 13 days over Christmas (real Christian-like, eh?) in one of the most viscious individual acts against humanity to date. Kissinger & Alexander Haig were also reprehensibly responsible here. And then Nixon promised them 4.3 billion dollars to rebuild their country plus complete withdrawal of American forces if they would sign a peace treaty. The North Vietnamese looked at the stakes, agreed they were favorable terms, & the Paris Peace Accords were signed in Jan. 1973 thus "officially" ending the Vietnam War. So with Watergate yet to unravel, Richard M. Nixon coerced the American public into re-electing him, then coerced the Vietnamese into a treaty which he had no intention of living up to.

McGovern meanwhile was struggling against unfavorable press coverage and Nixon's ability to manipulate people's fears & hatreds. He was betting that people could finally see that the Emperor wore no clothes...but he was wrong. And he lost. The biggest state by state loss in American history and I would agree. Instead of the Peace & healing which this country so badly needed, it only got further torn apart

What a Long Strange Trip It's Been

as Richard M. Nixon ripped his talons deep into the fabric of America in an attempt to stay in power, as Watergate stalked him the whole of his second term.

Chapter 35

On January 8, 1973, the day after Nixon's second inauguration, the Watergate criminal trial began with Judge Sirica* presiding and Howard Hunt, G. Gordon Liddy, James McCord, Frank Sturgis, & the Cubans- Barker, Gonzalez & Martinez- all before the court. The trial was set to last 16 days & by the trial's end Sturgis, Barker, Gonzalez, & Martinez had pleaded guilty to all counts against them, Howard Hunt to charges of wire tapping, conspiracy, & burglary, and McCord & Liddy were found guilty on all counts. Not a word had been said by the defendants connecting the White House with the break-in. They had taken their money and kept their mouths shut.

But in the next couple of months as time got close to sentencing, things began to fall apart. Hunt demanded $120,000 immediately,** one million dollars eventually- plus executive clemency or he threatened to implicate Ehrlichman in the espionage activities. Liddy was playing the cool cucumber in jail and it looked as if Sturgis & the Cubans would keep playing along. But then there was McCord who seemed to be playing his own ballgame altogether. He was warned that this could cost the President, but I think he knew this already.

Nixon on the other hand was still scrambling to keep the ball in play. On March 21, 1973, just three days before the defendants were sentenced, the President and his aide John Dean met to discuss events. The conversation was taped.

Dean - Well, first of all there is the problem of the continued blackmail which will not only go on now, but it will go on while these people are in prison, & it will compound the obstruction of justice situation. It will cost money...

Nixon - How much money do you need?

Dean - I would say these people are going to cost a million dollars over the next two years.

Nixon - We could get that. On the money, if you need the money you could get that. I know where it could be gotten. It's not easy, but it could be done. But the question is who the hell would handle it?[1]

So King Richard King Rat continued to preside over the cover-up, but

---

* Judge Sirica played a hero's part in a role which required nothing less.
** $75,000 of which was delivered that night.

alas it was too late.

Two days before this James McCord had sent a letter to Judge Sirica telling him a couple of interesting things. Not only had the defendants been given money to keep quiet, plead guilty & perjure themselves, but there were figures higher up on the political ladder who were involved in the Watergate affair.

Four days later "Maximum John" Sirica handed out sentences for the burglary of the Democratic Headquarters at the Watergate Hotel. They were, of course, the maximum: Howard Hunt 35 years; G. Gordon Liddy 6¾ - 20 years; Frank Sturgis & the others 40 years. James McCord's sentencing was postponed but he eventually got 1 - 5 years, but later Judge Sirica reduced his sentence to four months in jail in appreciation of him coming clean.

Five days after he sent his initial letter, McCord really started talking. He told investigators that both Dean & Magruder had been in on Watergate. Then he told the Ervin Committee that Attorney General John Mitchell had known of the break-in before the fact. Two weeks later he was to finger the then-deceased Dorothy Hunt as the bag woman. The next blow came three weeks later as White House involvement with the Ellsberg break-in became known, and within the week Haldeman, Ehrlichman, Dean & Kleindienst had been forced to resign, as well as Patrick Gray head of the F.B.I.

At one time there was a move to make John Mitchell the fall guy and make it look like he had ordered and carried out the job without the knowledge of anyone higher up. This would later come to be known as the Ollie North-Twinkie Defense, but it didn't cut any cake at the time. It really pissed John's wife Martha off tho', & she began calling reporters in the middle of the nite telling them that Nixon was a crook & what was really going on. She got to be such a threat that the Secret Service had to beat her up, inject her to knock her out, kidnap her and take her to California to keep her quiet. She's another one like Jack Ruby who died suddenly with cancer and whose death was extremely convenient and, in retrospect, highly suspicious.

Chapter 36

So the castle stones were crumbling and still sitting in the palace was King Richard, his trusty doberman Spiro, & new to the team to replace Haldeman was Alexander "Policestate" Haig. Now if he thought Liddy was a nut- and Nixon did: "Is it Liddy? Is that the fellow? He must be a little nuts. I mean he just isn't screwed on right, is he? Is that the problem?"* then he should have seen Haig coming. Haig's a power monger extraordinaire who actually took charge of the Watergate White House for the last 15 months of Nixon's reign. He's best remembered for his appearance on national television as Secretary of State after President Reagan was wounded by John Hinckley and telling everyone that everything was alright now that he was in command. Was that scarey or what? This surprised a lot of people at the time, especially Vice-President who ever he was, George somebody. Watch out for Al, in some circles he's considered dangerous.

By that time political bombshells were falling all around the White House, and the hottest of them all came on July 16, 1973 at the televised Senate Watergate Committee Hearings in which Alexander Butterfield, the deputy assistant to the President, revealed to the world that President Nixon had the Secret Service tape record all of his meetings & conversations on the phone and in his office since 1970.

This was the turning point of the whole affair. From here on in Richard Nixon would fight tooth & nail to keep these tapes from becoming public and legal evidence. But once the Committee learned that there was material evidence which would reveal who knew what about Watergate and when- including the President- well, they weren't about to let it slip out of their grasp.

Meanwhile, trouble continued at 1600 Pennsylvania Avenue. On October 10th, Spiro was the next to fall. Found guilty of a charge of tax evasion, Agnew was fined $10,000 and put on probation with no jail term. This all stemmed from bribes & payoffs he'd been getting from 1967 when he was Governor of Maryland until seven months after the Watergate break-in. In an interview for his then unpublished book, *Go Quietly, Or Else*, Agnew said that a memo for him from Nixon delivered to his top aide by Haig reported that Nixon no longer wanted Agnew in office and

---

* Tape of June 23, 1972, between Nixon & Haldeman.

What a Long Strange Trip It's Been

implied that he might be murdered if he didn't step down. Gerald Ford (lots of folks thought he played football too many times without his helmet) was then nominated to take Agnew's place and was sworn in as Vice-President on December 6, 1973. Ford was the right person for the job, as he was an early participant in the Watergate cover up. In a White House taped meeting (September 15, 1972) President Nixon suggested to John Dean that House Minority leader Ford could "work something out" to block an investigation by Rep. Wright Patman's House Banking and Currency Committee. "This is the big play," said Nixon. "He has to know it came from the top." Ford then met with 15 Republicans on the committee and these members were later instrumental in blocking this investigation into the Watergate "funny money."[1]

But throwing Spiro to the wolves (and rightly so) did little to placate Lady Justice's palate. Only ten days after Spiro hit the wayside the heat was once again on high at the White House. In another wild, last-minute defensive block, Richard Milhous Nixon ordered Special Prosecutor Archibald Cox to be fired and his position abolished immediately. Cox was demanding access to Presidential tapes and Dick freaked out. Elliot Richardson, then Attorney General, refused Nixon's order and resigned rather than carry it out as did his assistant William Ruckelshaus. The person who did carry out Nixon's order (which one month later was ruled illegal in federal court) was Robert Bork, who would later gain fame for being rejected by this country in his bid to become a Supreme Court Justice under Reagan. It seems that among other things Bork believes that Americans have no fundamental right to privacy, which seems pretty strange to me.

Chapter 37

At any rate the walls were falling- Mitchell, Dean, Haldeman Ehrlichman, Gray, Agnew- gone!

Just Gerry & Dick & Uncle Al...

In November '73 more bad news. Not only political trouble with half* the country and George McGovern calling for his impeachment, but legal trouble as well. Ashland Oil, Braniff Airlines, & Gulf Oil all admitted to making hundreds of thousands of dollars in illegal campaign contributions to the Nixon re-election campaign. But this was merely standard operating procedure for the Nixon gang.

Extortion & bribery.

Herb Kalmbach, Nixon's personal lawyer, was sent around to get the big bucks from the corporations (I.T.T, for example) which had government lawsuits or antitrust actions pending against them. Over $20 million was raised secretly and illegally from such corporations as American Airlines, 3M, Phillips Petroleum, & Goodyear to name a few. All at the real expense of ourselves & the environment. But now it was all coming out.

And what's worse the battle for the tapes was still raging full-tilt boogie, and with Cox being fired from an obviously guilty hand, Nixon had to do something to look good. So he turned over several tapes which Judge Sirica had wanted.

It appeared however that some of the tapes had been tampered with, including two tapes which were apparently re-recorded over. One tape had an 18½ minute gap which was between Nixon & Haldeman just three days after the break-in. True to form Nixon's personal secretary Rosemary Woods would testify that she'd erased the tape accidentally by hitting the wrong switch while talking on the phone, but nobody really bought that one. Things ground on.

In December the General Accounting Office charged the Nixon re-election campaign with hiding payments to political spies; $35,000 to spies in the McGovern campaign alone. If this wasn't subverting the democratic process I don't know what is. Deliberate infiltration & political sabotage.

By January 1974 there were 13 full-time White House lawyers working on Watergate-related matters to keep Richard Nixon in office & out of jail.

On March 19, 1974, the Democratic Party won a $775,000 out of court settlement against the Committee to Reelect the Prez for the Watergate

---

* Bunches at least.

What a Long Strange Trip It's Been

burglary. April 30th, in another misthrown block, Richard Nixon tried his best to stay afloat. Once again he went on TV and lied, lied, lied to the American public in a television speech in which he released 1300 pages of transcripts taken from the Watergate tapes. But these transcripts were heavily edited, censored, & altered, deleting criminal evidence and the regular vulgarities & racist terms which Richard Nixon used daily among his closest confidants.

The transcripts in no way satisfied the requests by the investigative bodies for the tapes themselves, which is where the real truth lay. By May Nixon's state was so pathetically eroded that the call for impeachment grew louder & louder.

In June, in one of the greatest miscarriages of justice in America, Richard Kleindienst- former Attorney General of the United States- pleaded guilty to one federal misdemeanor charge, was given a suspended sentence of one month & a $100 fine, and avoided conspiracy, extortion, & perjury charges in connection with his lying at his confirmation hearings about his dropping an I.T.T. antitrust suit. This was so absurd that two of Jaworski's lawyers & the head of the Watergate investigation resigned at such a judicial mockery. At his hearing the judge called him "a man of the highest integrity who has been & still is universally respected and admired." Must be some other universe he was talking about.

All that's kind of overshadowed by the fact that he was the first Attorney General in the history of America convicted of a crime, and he was the highest law officer in the land when he purposely lied to Congress. Or how about his role in Watergate on the tape of March 21, 1973, when John Dean's talking about parole for the Watergate burglars and he says, "Kleindienst has now got control of the Parole Board, and he said to tell me we could pull paroles off now where we couldn't before."[1] Kleindienst would also face trial in 1981 on charges of perjury in connection with his testimony concerning a 7 million dollar insurance scam involving a Teamster Union Health and Welfare Fund, his role in the appointment of a mobster to administer the contract, and his role in two attempts to siphon off the money. He could probably only have hoped at this point that he was a better lawyer than liar.

But back to Tricky Dick. By the end of July 1974 the Supreme Court ruled that he had to fork over the 64 tapes he was withholding. Then on July 27th, the House Judiciary Committee began drawing up articles of impeachment against President Nixon, and two days later had three complete articles of impeachment prepared concerning his conduct in office. The First Article dealt mainly with his making false or misleading

A Hippy's History of the Sixties

statements to the law, to the public, and ordering others to do likewise; thus, obstructing justice by interfering with the F.B.I., C.I.A., & other investigative bodies. This included the payment of hush money to the original Watergate defendants and aiding his aides in avoiding criminal liability for the things they had done in his service.

The Second Article of Impeachment dealt with the criminal misuse of the I.R.S. & F.B.I. by the President, his establishment of a secret police force within the White House, and his unlawful surveillance of American citizens and other illegal operations.

Article III basically said that Nixon's actions had been contrary to and subversive of constitutional government and that he had not faithfully executed his duties according to his oath of office and the public trust.

On August 5th the last blow to the corporeal political body of Richard Milhous Nixon was delivered by Al Haig. Having learned of some damning tapes which Nixon had just found and refused to turn over, he knew the time was now. These were the tapes in which Nixon ordered Haldeman to block the investigation of Watergate and which first revealed Richard Nixon as an active participant in a cover-up of the facts. Haig accompanied by two Presidential lawyers, met with Nixon and told him that if he didn't hand over the tapes to Judge Sirica then they and the whole White House legal staff would quit pronto.

So Dick came clean- sort of. He released the tapes and in the understatement of the century admitted that some of the things on the tapes were at variance with what he'd previously said occurred. After this, whatever support he had before in this country went right down the drain.*

The tapes spoke for themselves.

Three days later, most likely after Al Haig assured Nixon that the deal had been made and Gerald Ford would indeed pardon him if he resigned, Richard Nixon did just that. On August 8, 1974 on national television with jumpin' Gerry in the batter's box, Richard Nixon delivered his resignation to the American people effective the next day, and don't think that America didn't party hardy that nite. That nite as he gazed out of the White House window thousands of people in the streets chanted "Jail to the Chief." This really bummed Dick out once he realized they weren't saying "Hail to the Chief." This feeling was compounded shortly thereafter when the Mayflower moving vans rolled up to the White House to load 'em up & move 'em out, but lo, they were only responding to a Yippie prank call. ...And the next day he was gone.

---

* And his staunch Congressional supporter Republican Hugh Scott with him.

What a Long Strange Trip It's Been

Which of course left Gerald Ford as the big cheese. And true to his word, one month later Gerald Ford pardoned Nixon of any and all crimes he committed during his years as President.* And they were quite a few. Nixon could have been impeached for a lot of other things also, mainly the secret & illegal bombing war in Cambodia and his habitual love of shaking down corporations for illegal campaign contributions in return for resultant favors. He's one of the biggest criminal extorters ever to hold political office, and that's saying a lot. So Richard Nixon brought all the qualities of a cheap, petty crook to the White House and then got off scott free: with government pension money, money for office expenses, the works.**

They should have given him life- his life. He was one of the greatest mass murderers in the history of the modern world- second only to Adolph Hitler and Joseph Stalin.

That's what Richard Nixon was-   lest we forget.

---

* Ford has repeatedly said he never made a deal to pardon Nixon in order to get him to resign, but we all knew Richard Nixon a little better than that. Ford's lied in the past and Nixon's too sharp to even chance going to jail. Wonder how he likes Hell?

** And as far as this post-Watergate Richard Nixon elder statesman bullshit goes... you gotta be kidding! This nurd regurgitating reality and then giving us some revisionist history of the times... Nixon was the one they marched out to convince everyone in the 80's that the Vietnam War was a just cause for America and that they truly could have won with a little more effort; thus trying to soften the American public up for another bloody military incursion into Central America. Fuck you, Dick. History's got you by the balls and Truth crowns you as what you really were.

The lingering malaise and evil spell of Richard Nixon persisted even into the 90s when in January of 1993 a Senate subcommittee investigating the 2,264 American POW/MIAs left in Vietnam revised portions of its report critical of Richard Nixon & Henry Kissinger's blatant abondonment of these soldiers along with any chance of getting them back by refusing to pay Vietnam the war reparations agreed upon. Knowing the report was about to be released, Kissinger and his lawyer read a draft of the findings and were successful in "having some of the documents conclusions changed." This just shows the pure callousness of Nixon and Kissinger is still alive It is rumored that many of those left behind were involved in the government's illegal S.E. Asian heroin trade so they strung them out to die (*New York Times*, 1/11/93). This malaise would be somewhat relieved when Richard M. Nixon died a few months later. I say we dig him up and kick him around one more time.

Chapter 38

And who did Gerry Ford pick to succeed him as Vice-President? Well, not Al Haig. It was Nelson Rockefeller, a true man of fortune. Now we're getting close to the people who really run this country- the Rockefellers. Old Nelson had been around political circles for a long time. His biggest moment was in September 1971 when as Governor of New York he refused to negotiate with prisoners who had taken hostages & occupied part of the Attica State Prison. Instead, he sent in the riot squads with guns ablazing & in the subsequent slaughter, 44 prisoners & 10 hostages were needlessly killed by police.

The perfect man for the job.

As for the Rockefeller fortune, estimated at between 6-10 billion dollars at the time, here's some of the corporations they controlled at least back then in '74-75: Standard Oil, I.B.M., A.T. & T., American Express, Eastern Airlines, Pan American Airlines, Chase Manhattan Bank, Chemical Bank, Metropolitan Life, Allied Chemical, Mobil Oil, Borden, & CBS. Not only are the Rockefellers one of the very richest families in Babylon, but they controlled both 20% of all U.S. industry and 20% of all U.S. banking interests at the time Rocky was made V.P.[1] But their control extends much farther than that. Thanks to two Rockefeller organizations, the Council on Foreign Relations & more recently the Trilateral Commission,[2] the Rockefellers have been able to keep quite a grip on the direction of American foreign & domestic policy thru the years. Both of these organizations seek to school and co-opt future leaders in government, business, & the military and maneuver them into positions of power within the framework of the U.S. government and thus ensure the continued implementation of Rockefeller foreign policy to protect the economic interests of "their" world.

But the Trilateral Commission goes further than this country. The Trilateral Commission, in fact, is made up of members of the military, government, industry, & media in North America, Western Europe and Japan. Thus, global economic and political manipulations are easier than ever when it's all in a small circle of friends. Under Carter, for example, there were 18 major administration posts filled by the Trilateralists. This included Fritz Cardboard Mondale as V.P. (Mr. Vanilla Pudding), Cyrus Vance as Secretary of State, Michael Blumenthal as Secretary of Treasury, Harold Brown as Secretary of Defense &

What a Long Strange Trip It's Been

Zbigniew Brzezinski as National Security Adviser. In fact it was Brzezinski who was chosen the first director of the Trilateral Commission in its inception in 1973.[3]

So lest there be any doubt about who runs this country, it's the Rockefellers and their political puppets backed by the military and law enforcement agents of the state who make and execute foreign & domestic policy to their (the corporate) benefit.

You see, we are only peasants in their world. The world really belongs to them. For now. So, yes, these are the people who control most of America, along with their rich family counterparts, the Du Ponts, the Mellons, those fine families who raped the earth & the working people at the turn of the century for their fortunes. The most perfect example of this is the Federal Reserve System and its controllers made up of international bankers. Enacted in 1913 by an act of fraud, it has raped the nation since of trillions of our own dollars by setting falsely inflated interest rates and by issuing paper for gold. Recent research turned up in part by Project 93 (now known as Power, Box 492200, Redding CA 96049) reveals that the Sixteenth Amendment creating the Internal Revenue Service was voted in favor of by only two states, yet was publicly declared to have been "apparently" ratified by the necessary 36 states by then-Secretary of State Filander Knox. These lies enabled 300 of the world's richest families and banks to control the money of America- to pilfer the gold that once stood behind the money & even the metal in the coins. This is the reason the richest nation on earth is so poor. Thomas Jefferson warned of this happening and that if the gold standard was abandoned, the banks would "bleed the people dry till their children were homeless." Sound like America today? This coupled with the fact that the IRS income tax is a voluntary tax & was originally enacted to tax only those whose profits were derived from the sale of alcohol, tobacco, & firearms shows you how much arm twisting & pocket picking has been going on. In fact, the "national debt" is nothing more than an imaginary phoney debt owed to private banks. All brought to you courtesy of the Rothschilds and the Rockefellers, those same fine folks who have been buying presidents for decades and are currently busy forming their One World Order... Watch out! But the only Rockefeller to get near the Presidency was Nelson & then as Ford's V.P.

Ford's Presidency was pretty much uneventful,* except that he kept falling down stairs and people kept trying to shoot him- Sarah Jane Moore,

---

* Like the times. As Jane Fonda once said in a speech at Kent, "The 70s were like wading thru marshmallows."

longtime F.B.I. informant, & Squeaky Fromme, one of Charlie Manson's girls.

Perhaps the most interesting thing which occurred during the Ford years was the kidnapping of Patty Hearst. This was a strange one, indeed. On February 4, 1974, Patricia Campbell Hearst, daughter of one of the real Mr. Bigs and established families of Capitalist America, was kidnapped by members of the Symbionese Liberation Army (S.L.A.).

The exact truth may never publicly be known, but the possibilities are as follows. Either the Symbionese Liberation Army was the first true armed revolutionary force to declare total war on U.S. imperialism (assassination & kidnapping included) or it was another government project against the Left which went awry. But whichever way it went down it was scarey in its implications.

The January 22, 1976 issue of The (Metropolitan Detroit & Greater Michigan) Sun contained a lead article which charged that the S.L.A. was the creation of a combination of government agencies including the C.I.A. & the California Department of Corrections. It reported S.L.A. leader Donald DeFreeze as a longtime police informer & agent provocateur who was allowed to escape prison in order to arm and associate violence & terror with politically leftist groups.

The S.L.A. had been formed within the prison system at a time when a new and radical politicization of the prison populace was reflective of the large numbers of prisoners there for purely political reasons- Black Panthers, draft resisters, drug offenders, etc. Also, the greater awareness in the Bay Area as to the oppressive conditions which constituted the prison system led to significant outside support among local politicos who began educational, cultural, & political programs to change both the system and the conditions which existed there.

On January 13, 1970 at Soledad Prison south of San Francisco, a prison fight which started between two inmates was brought to a swift conclusion when a white guard in a tower first shot one of those involved then shot two inmates who came to his aid. The guard then refused to permit any medical attention until after the inmates had died. All three were Black, & when the district attorney called the killings justifiable homicides a few days later, the prison movement on the inside immediately turned violent. An hour later a white prison guard was beaten and thrown three floors to his death in what was to be the first death of a guard in the prison's history.

Three inmates, including George Jackson (one of the most brilliant & articulate persons to have lived), were held for the murder. Meanwhile, plans were made on the outside by a group of radicals, collegiates, &

attorneys to break into the Marin County Courthouse with an armed force, free the inmates there, and release Jackson and his two co-defendants. Also in on the planning was one James Carr who not only was George Jackson's friend in prison, but also was plotting his death into the escape attempt to create a martyr and thus let himself be the new boss. The usual power politics of deceit. Another interesting point is that Carr's brother-in-law who was always around at the time was none other than Louis Tackwood, undercover agent from the Los Angeles Police Criminal Conspiracy Division who filed continual reports of the activities and escape plans of the group. Tackwood, as you recall, was the agent who held the press conference exposing the L.A. Criminal Conspiracy Division, and the F.B.I.'s plan to violently disrupt the '72 Presidential conventions and blame it on the Left.

But before any plans were carried out George Jackson's younger brother (Jonathon, age 17) jumped the gun and raided the courthouse himself, armed some inmates, taped a sawed-off shotgun around a judge's neck, and was killed along with the judge & two inmates when their escaping van was riddled with bullets.

A year and two weeks later, George Jackson was killed in an apparent escape attempt which left three guards & two other inmates dead. The prison at San Quenton refused to allow any outside investigation, and whether Jackson was set up or not isn't known, but the official version of the incident was immediately branded untrue by the inmates at San Quentin themselves.

But from all this turbulence and the ideals of radical groups like Venceremos working within the prisons, came the basic strategy and momentum from which the S.L.A. spun off and began its own crusade of urban guerrilla warfare.

The first public move of the Symbionese Liberation Army was the shooting murder of Oakland Schools Superintendent Marcus Foster and the wounding of his aide on November 6, 1973. The next day the S.L.A. claimed responsibility and warned that members of the school board would be next for supporting new proposals for police on campus and student identity cards. A week later these programs were canned.

Among the professed goals of the S.L.A. was "to unite all oppressed people into a fighting force and destroy the capitalist state; to place controls of all the institutions and industries of each nation into the hands of its people; to take control of all state land and that of the capitalist class and to give the land back to the people; to totally destroy the rent system of exploitation; to create a system where our aged are cared for with respect, love, and kindness; to give back to people their human and

Constitutional rights; to destroy the prison system."

In the communique they stated "We of the S.L.A. DO NOT under the rights of human beings submit to the murder, oppression and exploitation of our children and people and do under the rights granted to the people under the Declaration of Independence of the United States, do now by the rights of our children and people and Force of Arms and with every drop of our blood Declare Revolutionary War against The Fascist Capitalist Class, and all their agents of murder, oppression, and exploitation." Serious stuff, indeed. Not that they didn't have a point, but guns just aren't the way to go.

Their next move was to adopt one of the stated strategies of James Carr who himself had plotted the murder & escape of George Jackson, been a hit man for Panther informers, and was blown away by a Black Panther strongman after Jackson's death and Carr's later release from jail.

At any point Carr's one plan of action for the forces of the Second American Revolution was to kidnap the children of rich and influential people for substantial ransoms & publicity coverage. It's this idea the S.L.A. picked up when they picked up Patty Hearst.

Patty Hearst- well traveled, a 19-year-old Berkeley C.U. student whose daddy owned the Hearst Publishing Empire and who lived with her boyfriend Steve Weed and a pound of pot when she was abducted February 4, 1974 by the S.L.A.

First off the S.L.A. demanded $70 worth of food to be given to every local impoverished & old person before they would talk about releasing Patty.

Well, bunches of food was given out in chaotic fashion in an organization which coincidentally (?) was co-run by one Sara Jane Moore, longtime F.B.I. informant & future failed assassin of President Gerald Ford. Another 4 million dollars was set aside for more food to be given away with Patty's release.

Then things got stranger.

On April 2, 1974 the S.L.A. sent a bunch of roses and a communique that Patty's time & place of release would be announced the next day. The next day, however, a tape was released by the S.L.A. in which Patty proclaimed that she had joined the S.L.A., turned revolutionary, and taken the name Tania. Two weeks later the S.L.A. robbed a bank in which Patty participated and two people were shot.

On May 16, 1974 two S.L.A. members were caught for shoplifting at a sporting goods store and Tania blasted a round of automatic rifle fire across the top of the store from a van across the street, thus obtaining their release and get away. The next day, the police surrounded a house with

What a Long Strange Trip It's Been

S.L.A. leader Donald DeFreeze and five other members in it, and in the ensuing shootout & bombing by police the house burned to the ground killing all either by bullets or by smoke & flame.

Tania, however, was not among the dead. She had no doubts, however, that the F.B.I. was out to kill her. Thus she began a year & a half odyssey in which initially she was driven across country by sports writer Jack Scott who dug playing revolutionary and planned to write a book on it all, & then she hid out for a while in a farm house in Pennsylvania. Then she later returned to the San Francisco area and hung out with S.L.A. members Bill & Emily Harris, and sympathizers Wendy Yoshimura and Steve & Kathy Soliaho. On April 21, 1975 Patty helped rob another bank in Carmichael, California in which a woman was killed and $15,000 taken.

Finally on September 17, 1975 Patty Hearst and the other members of the S.L.A. were caught living just one mile from the F.B.I. office and arrested peacefully. This was due in part to both leads and luck; but Jack Scott fucked up when he told his alcoholic brother Walter who was an overseas assassin for our government about his part in the Hearst thing, and old Walter tipped off the F.B.I. anonymously, then spilled his guts for the price of a bottle or whatever a man sells his soul to the Devil for.

When Tania arrived at the police station in handcuffs she gave the raised fist salute to photographers and on the police report listed her occupation as urban guerrilla. They bugged her cell, put in a female prisoner with her to get her talking and incriminating herself, and were prepared to lock her away as a real lesson to "terrorists."

But then Big Daddy Warbucks Randy Hearst entered the scene and sent word to Patty that if she didn't straighten up and play little Miss Goody two-shoes, put on her Sunday dress & renounce her whole revolutionary foray, then she'd spend her next 10 years or so in jail and never get any of his money or any of her grandfather's.[4]

So she went right along, saying she was brainwashed and never did any of the actions on her own, just so she wouldn't become another one of America's caged oddities like Charlie Manson. But in the process she sold out. She bought the Ivory Soap. Even tho' revolutionary violence is in no way in, standing up for the Cause is, and she sold out the big time, married her bodyguard, had babies, & got right back into the blue blood swing of things.

But the question still remains as to whether Donald DeFreeze who escaped prison to form the S.L.A. and started the whole show with another escapee was a police agent or not. Our old buddy Louis Tackwood, who got sick of being a police spy & quit the biz, later collaborated with a couple of authors investigating the matter and they charged that DeFreeze was indeed a police agent with the Los Angeles Police Department at the time when Tackwood was employed as the same. So whatever the case the S.L.A. experience once again proved that violence is not where it's at, nor are the people running around promoting it, who are either cops or good people to stay away from. Those types tend to have short lifespans.

But other than the S.L.A. and the attempts on his life, things were pretty quiet in the Ford years. Not much happening around the White House. But that all ended when Jimmy Carter won the Presidential race in 1976.

VI

Chapter 39

A peanut farmer from Georgia, Carter was something else. Although he too was a member of the Trilateral Commission,* Carter was a really decent person, decent in the terms that Johnson, Nixon, Ford, & Reagan weren't. Jimmy Carter quoted Bob Dylan in speeches and got his boost in Presidential politics by financial fundraising from Capricorn Records & the Allman Brothers blues band.[1] Much of the Carter gang did drugs including Hamilton Jordan, Carter's personal aide, and Peter Bourne, his personal physician who apparently snorted cocaine a few times too many in public** and the word got out. Carter's big mistake was after he was elected they tried to legalize both marijuana & cocaine at the same time. His coke-heads were too anxious and instead of recommending the decriminalization of marijuana first, and then perhaps to consider other substances, the report drawn up for the administration recommended the immediate decriminalization of pot & toot- a step that America was certainly not ready for then and I doubt ready for now, as far as cocaine goes. (Cocaine, phew! A hungry ghost that'll eat your Soul.) Pot of course should never have been illegal in the first place.

So that having failed Carter can be remembered for bringing some rationale to our military policy, stating that we were not the policeman of the world nor should we interfere with the internal governing of other countries. Under Carter U.S. aid was cut off to countries who practiced human rights violations and the C.I.A. came under new rules of order. In fact Carter fired 800 agents who had been involved in past distasteful covert operations. But atrocities in Central America continued. Under Reagan, both of these policies would be reversed, except, of course, the atrocities.

One of the other dramatic incidents of the Carter years was the taking of 52 American hostages at the American Embassy in Teheran, Iran. The hostages were taken after the fall of the Shah of Iran who had ruled Iran (as had his father before him) since 1954 when the C.I.A. put him in power. The Shah was a brutal dictator, much like the governments of the

---

* As too in the next election was 1980 election-year political maverick John Anderson who supposedly was in that race as a people's alternative to Carter & Reagan, but once again it seems wore the uniform of the Rockefeller ball team.

** Actually, at a National Organization for the Reform of Marijuana Laws party. It was Keith Stroup, former head of NORML, who reportedly narked on Bourne.

A Hippy's History of the Sixties

Phillipines, South Korea, Taiwan, & Chile which we were also maintaining at the time. Which is to say that under Carter U.S. atrocities worldwide were scaled down, perhaps, but not curtailed. The hostages were held for 444 days and released the morning of Ronald Reagan's inauguration as President, and at least one former White House aide, Barbara Honeggor, among others, claims a deal was made with the Iranians by the Reagan camp (and Richard Allen of the Carter camp) not to let Carter negotiate the hostages' release before the elections. Bani-Sadr, former president of Iran, claims that George Bush personally sealed the deal with the Iranians, by some reports at a secret meeting in Paris in October of 1980. Also, it would appear that Carter's military rescue attempt to free the hostages before the election was sabotaged from the inside and had to be abandoned due to a suspicious series of accidents & breakdowns. It would appear to be more than coincidence that Ollie North, Richard Secord, and Albert Hakim, who all later played such a close role with Bush and Reagan in smuggling arms to Iran, were integral operational units of Carter's failed Desert One rescue attempt.[2] Although a House panel concluded in 1993 that there was no "credible" evidence of the October Surprise, the specter of truth still persists over this corpse of history. ...This and many more.

Chapter 40

Ronald Reagan. Everybody's grandfather, the Teflon President, Mr. 666, the Anti-Christ. In 1980 Carter lost to Ronald Reagan and his running mate George what's his name, and thus the Reagan Regime began. Reagan's trip made Nixon look like Goldilocks...or would have. With mirror-like characters portraying similar roles: Nixon-Reagan; Agnew-Bush; Mitchell-Meese; Kill 'em dead Helms-Wild Bill Casey.

Reagan was an actor and that's about all he was, and a bad one at that, but good enough to fool most. Reagan's every move was scripted and his intellectual ability strained to the point of most of the time ducking reporters' questions by pretending the helicopter he was going to or from was too loud to hear over. He played the role old & bumbling, but that's exactly how he had to play it to get away with the things he did and not get impeached or jailed. He was notorious for falling asleep during briefings and his "short attention span" was well known. But he knew exactly what he was doing as he and his like ethical deviants Casey, Meese, Bush, & North circumvented both Congressional and Constitutional law.

His election marked the beginning of another administration of unbelievable sleaze and inborn fascist tendencies. Although the numbers certainly rose since then, at one time* there were 242 major Reagan administration members who had been accused by the law of unethical or illegal conduct since Ronald Reagan had taken office, making it the most corrupt administration in American history. The likes of Anne Burford, who headed the Environmental Protection Agency, & Rita Lavelle who were both forced to resign and face charges in connection with improprieties at the E.P.A., for example. Of course, Congress never pursued or very little was ever said about the 10 million dollars of E.P.A. funds which were missing at the time. Or how about Reagan's best buddies Michael Alcoholic Deaver & Lyn Nofziger who were found guilty of illegally using their influence with the President to swing deals for their clients. Nofziger's conviction was later overturned on appeal.

Criminality was the norm. This is clearly illustrated in the Carter spy memo case in which members of the Reagan camp illegally obtained briefing papers which Jimmy Carter was using in preparation for the Carter-Reagan debates of campaign '80. It was Bill Casey who set things

---

* By Spring of '88

up and got the papers for the Reagan-Bush campaign. This was made public in 1984 by a House subcommittee. Casey had by then been made head of the C.I.A. but was still not brought to task when this was brought to light.

Ronnie himself played a little undercover role in the old days it seems, something akin to an Auschwitz door monitor or the likes. Being the great patriot he was, he & his first wife, Jane Wyman, snitched out fellow actors in Hollywood to the F.B.I. who they thought were Commies. They ratted on two groups within the Screen Actors Guild for following "the Communist Party Line," & when he was elected president of the guild in 1947, the House UnAmerican Activities Committee began investigating the Communist influence in Hollywood the same year. Of course, all this was more red-scare hysteria concocted to politically neutralize liberal elements within America by creating an Enemy and portraying liberals as sympathizers. It gave people someone to hate and take revenge on by watching the government screw them. Lots of people had their lives and careers ruined by lies & innuendo, and Reagan was a part of all of this. Just an easy way to climb to the top. Humphrey Bogart once led a march on D.C. against the harrassment of actors by the government witchhunts and I'm sure his view of Richard Nixon's & Ronald Reagan's role in those days was pretty dim.

Then there's honest Ed Meese, a Porky Pig look alike if God ever intended one. Just imagine ole Ed in a straw hat going "Ba dit, ba dit, ba dit, ba dit- That's all, Folks!" Now aint that scarey. What's even more scarey is the fact that this guy was the Attorney General of the United States and had advocated such things as workplace surveillance of what he called problem areas, "such as locker rooms, parking lots, shipping & mailroom areas, and nearby taverns if necessary," in an effort to expose recreational drug users. This is the same Ed Meese who also advocated overturning the Miranda decision in which the Supreme Court ruled that all suspects held by the police are allowed to have a lawyer present before they're questioned & they must be informed of that right. That's so you don't get railroaded into jail & never let out.

Meese himself is not exactly outside the criminal category as the General Accounting Office concluded that Meese violated a federal ethics law by ommitting financial assets which were a conflict of interest at the time to the government position he held. There were many questions raised concerning federal jobs going to individuals who had made unreported loans to Meese. And poor Ed, on at least 52 occassions in front of Congressinal questioners, couldn't recall a darn thing about all that business. But his bad memory is legendary- this is the guy who sat in his

What a Long Strange Trip It's Been

office while seven versions or so of a speech that Reagan was to give to the American public to stonewall them on the Iran arms sales deal was drawn up right before him by McFarlane & the rest, a process which was clearly an obstruction of justice taking place before his very eyes. Then he later tells the Congressional committees that, indeed, he was in the room at the time, but he wasn't listening to what was going on. Right, for hours on end! Meese had been with Reagan since the early days, and certainly his role in the Iran-Contra affair & other activities deserved unemployment if not jail.

But Meese was just doing his job, as everybody was just doing their job. For once again the mechanisms of a police state were being assembled and slowly put into place. To do this it would take some orchestration but things were in motion. First, legal rights of Americans had to be taken away, and this was the Supreme Court's department. There were many rulings during Reagan's era which did just that. In 1984 the Court ruled that illegally obtained evidence by police could be used at trials if the police thought they were legally obtaining it at the time. Well, if the police don't know they're illegally obtaining evidence, they shouldn't be obtaining anything at all. In 1985 the Court noted that students in public schools were not protected under the 4th Amendment to the Constitution from warrantless searches of themselves or their belongings, meaning high school students have no rights of privacy and can be searched by school officials when they've not even broken a law. Take note of this, kids... Also in 1985 the Court ruled that suspects could be detained indefinitely even when there was insufficient evidence for arrest.

In 1986 with regard to the Miranda decision the Supreme Court declared that police could lie to a lawyer telling them their client wouldn't be questioned until morning, not tell the suspect their lawyer even called, question that person that nite, and all this questionably obtained information could be used in court. In 1991, the Miranda Act was further eroded as the court also oversaw assaults on established rights against search and seizure, on abortion rights & the immoral and bitter absolution of Ollie North. Also, in 1991 and 1994, the resignations of the last true liberals on the Supreme Court, Thurgood Marshall and Harry Blackmun, threatened to further setback the Court in its stand to uphold civil liberties. Clinton's nominee, Steven Breyer, was the main architect of the drug war's most Draconian law- the maximum/minimum sentencing guidelines opposed by almost everyone in the judicial system and which has resulted in the jailings of people for 20 & 30 years for minor offenses.

In 1987 the Supreme Court destroyed the basic principle of innocent until proven guilty & withdrew the fundamental Constitutional concept of the right to bail by making a ruling that permits detention without bail, which supports the Bail Reform Act of 1984 in which a person may be denied bail if the police feel they may committ a crime if released. This decision is a pretty wide one, however, and in the first four years since its inception almost 3,000 people have been jailed without trials. The majority opinion of the Supreme Court was written by Chief Justice William Rehnquist, who's an old hand at helping take people's civil rights away from them. During the Nixon era Rehnquist was Assistant Attorney General to John Mitchell and helped direct the arrests of antiwar protestors in D.C. He also wrote a memo in 1969 in which he proposed Army surveillance of civilian antiwar protestors and the detailed use of the military in civil disturbances. But at his Senate confirmation inquiry to be made Chief Justice, Rehnquist alleged that he had no recollection of his role in the matter. I would think that one of the qualifications for people in political office from now on in is that they have a good memory. As far as Nixon's memory of Rehnquist goes, this can best be seen in his conversation of July 18, 1974, a few months before Rehnquist was appointed to the Supreme Court, in which Nixon called him a clown & termed him "Renchburg."[1]

The confirmation of Supreme Court Justice Clarence "Long Dong" Thomas in 1991, after strong testimony accusing him of long-term & blatant sexual harassment, reflected the basest & most horrendous levels with which the petticoat of Lady Justice had been drug thru the mud & lifted to accommodate admittedly substantial but nonetheless substandard meat.

At any rate Rehnquist's early legal report on citizen detainment became the foundation of Ronald Reagan's Secret Directive 52 which allows for the establishment of concentration camps to detain liberal trade unionists & Peace activists in case of national emergency. This is exactly what Ollie North & company had in mind and were trying to implement.

What they were going for basically was the military invasion of Nicaragua and the jailing of the American Peace Movement all at the same time (these plans were called Operation Nighttrain and Rex 84).[2] Here's what went on. In 1984 Marine Lieutenant Colonel Oliver North helped draft a plan which would impose martial law under such circumstances as nuclear war, widespread internal dissent, or national opposition to a United States military incursion abroad. This secret plan called for suspending the Constitution, the taking over of state & local governments by military commanders, declaring martial law, and turning the government over to the Federal Emergency Management Agency, an obscure agency which he was liaison to in his role at the National Security Agency.

What a Long Strange Trip It's Been

It was apparent during Reagan's entire reign that the American people were not into his dirty little war in Nicaragua, but the People in Power wanted Nicaragua back in their pocket as soon as possible, and certainly by the '88 elections, just in case something happened and one of their boys didn't get in. It was one thing to invade Grenada where we had some U.S. students in very remote danger, another to break international law on a big scale & bomb Libya in flawed retaliation for a terrorist bombing in West Germany which the Syrians carried out. But both of these actions Ronald Reagan accomplished with little opposition by manipulating nationalism and the anger-hatred of the Amercian public. Nicaragua had been useful to us in the past, namely as a major military base from which invasions were launched like the Bay of Pigs, the latest U.S. invasions into the Dominican Republic in 1965 & '72, and the overthrow of the El Salvadoran government whenever democracy threatened to appear there.

It should be noted that in the Grenada invasion the U.S. press was denied coverage access by the U.S. military in an effort to keep the public uninformed about events and to control the reporting. This was a first, but intentionally a soon-to-be standard operating procedure. But invading Nicaragua was something which the American public would not take sitting down. Memories of Vietnam were too vivid in their minds to allow such atrocities to happen again; while conversely the American military leaders desperately needed to purge their limp egos from Indochina in the green hills of Central America. And as the American-paid Contra force was getting nowhere, the only way to invade Nicaragua with American forces over the objections of the American people would be to go for it and deal with the people in the streets. Which they might have done had it not been for the Iran-contra affair.

Chapter 41

Irangate- how it all began. Actually the whole arms to Iran for hostages for profits to be used for the Contras was nothing but standard operating procedure by the same group of people who'd been doing the same thing around the world for 20 years or so. The selling of guns & drugs by the C.I.A. and its shadowy worldwide network is fact and has been documented by many excellent books such as *The Politics of Heroin in Southeast Asia* by Alferd McCoy. A key reason for our involvement in Indochina was the C.I.A.'s desire to control the opium trade there, and much of the cocaine & heroin smuggled into the U.S. today is done by past & present operatives of the C.I.A. The money from the drugs goes into the pockets of those running the operation and back into the funding of illegal C.I.A. secret wars & projects around the globe. These days much of the C.I.A.'s drugs have been run thru the Central American Contra supply network; coming from Columbian druglords and being smuggled thru C.I.A. operative John Hull's Costa Rican ranch and flown to the U.S. on C.I.A. transport planes to be bought & distributed in the U.S. In '89 Hull was arrested by Costa Rica on drug & gun smuggling charges.

But back then the drugs came from Asia. For almost ten years up until 1975 the C.I.A. was smuggling Laotian opium & its end product heroin into the U.S. and the proceeds funnelled to train assassins to kill some 100,000 "suspected Communist sympathizers" in that country.

That's standard C.I.A. operating procedure too. Move into a country, identify a Communist enemy within, create hate, arm the right, suppress the left, all opponents to the C.I.A.-backed government are jailed or killed, and the country & its natural resources are ripe pickings for the Agency and American corporate entities as long as their puppet government can remain in power thru the torture & coercion of its own people.

This is not to say that the Communists are not experts at the very same thing, that's the point. Both our government and the Commies have been equally guilty in their fascist and totalitarian methods of control which they've practiced both at home & abroad for decades. These methods include lying, brainwashing, stealing, murder, genocide, coercion, & the wrongful incarceration of millions of people whose only crime is that they want to be free.

Vietnam is Afghanistan is Nicaragua. And that's not to say that it's right. But it is to say that it is.

What a Long Strange Trip It's Been

Iran, Guatemala, Nicaragua, The Phillippines, El Salvador, Chile, Haiti, South Vietnam, South Korea, Taiwan, Panama.

In each of these countries the C.I.A. has been responsible for installing & maintaining unpopular, undemocratic, repressive regimes which continually brutalize & murder their own people the entire time they are in power.

In Iran the C.I.A. brought to power the Shah of Iran and the long and sordid road of human abuses & repression was begun. Iran was a typical C.I.A. target operation. A nation with oil. Oil which had just been nationalized, and that could not be allowed to happen. But as usual after so many years the natives got restless and more suppressive aid was needed. During the Nixon years Henry Kissinger was in effect the stalwart of administration support of the murderous Iranian regime. Henry was always seen hob knobbing with the Shah, giving him a private helicopter this time, a bit of advice that time. Meanwhile, as the Shah's military and political grip began to slip,* Richard Helms, head of the C.I.A., was made U.S. Ambassador to Iran, and sent to Tehran to assist the Shah in repressing the people. About this time also, Theodore Shackley who was C.I.A. station chief in Laos and had directed the C.I.A.'s assassination programs in Cuba, Laos, Vietnam, & Chile, also moved to Tehran to help the Shah's secret police identify & assassinate political opponents. Yet with all this help the Shah still fell.

It's Shackley, by the way, along with the likes of John Singlaub (head of the World Anti-Communist League), Richard Secord, & others who allegedly make up the core of the "Secret Team," the shadowy network of current & former military & C.I.A. personnel who run cocaine and enact a foreign policy of their own making. Shackley was the deputy director of worldwide covert operations for C.I.A. when George Bush was C.I.A. head. In fact Shackley, Singlaub, & Secord all worked together in conducting programs in Southeast Asia that killed at least 160,000 Indochinese noncombatant civilians. Richard Helms as C.I.A. head was in on this too. Helms has more blood on his hands than will ever flow thru his body.

Helms was maneuvered into position of heading all the C.I.A.'s covert operations after the Bay of Pigs failure, a time when President Kennedy thought not too kindly of the C.I.A. and was putting into motion steps to severely curb the C.I.A.'s power. National Security Action Memoranda #55, 56, & 57 were specifically drawn up to limit the size, number, & scope of future covert operations and were personally signed by the President.

---

* Kissinger's grip itself was known to slip at times it seems. According to Charles Colson on the Today Show, December 8, 1973, Nixon had said of Kissinger, "You know, Henry is really unstable at times."

A Hippy's History of the Sixties

This is why top elements of the C.I.A. so willingly co-ordinated the JFK bumpoff. If Helms was in on that one it might be hard to say, but it was in reference to some heavy shadiness that prompted Nixon to say on that tape to Haldeman, "Well, we protected Helms from one hell of a lot of things..."* Helms was head of the C.I.A. by that time. A quick move to the top in a profession where back-stabbing to get ahead meant just that. And if the job required a little obstruction of justice like burning some tapes in 1973 which related to the Agency's dealings with Howard Hunt, then that was O.K. too. Or lying to Congress & the American people about the C.I.A.'s role in overthrowing Salvador Allende's freely elected government of Chile and other assassinations and abuses.

Originally the C.I.A. was created by the National Security Act of 1947. In its initial inception it was not intended as a fountainhead of covert operations around the world, but as its power grew thru the 50's it was soon able to chart its own course, and by the 1960's established its own infrastructure which planned, directed, and executed the multitude of secret team assignments and C.I.A. operations both here & abroad which were clearly in violation of not only international & U.S. laws, but also the sovereign principles which this country was founded upon.[1] But let's not let little things like moral turpitude delay the eager. Gun running, drug running,** assassination, financing right wing dictatorships, training & equipping death squads, and teaching police forces the most effective techniques of torture & repression- that's what the C.I.A. is all about. All for the good of their own right wing bid to control the world for the benefit of Corporate America. All financed by our tax dollars & smuggling. Examples abound.

The death squads in El Salvador are a case in point. For over 25 years the C.I.A. and members of the U.S. State Department and military (Green Berets) financed, organized, trained, equipped, & assisted in the formation of intelligence, interrogation, indoctrination, and assassination squads who not only were paid by C.I.A. funds but also killed on the C.I.A.'s orders and on targets selected and cased by the C.I.A. Colonel Caranza, then director of the Treasury Police, was a major organizer and operator of the Death Squad network, and was also being paid $90,000 a year by the C.I.A. (for six years). Treasury Police and members of the National Guard & National Police trained in the U.S. in such techniques as surveillance & interrogatory torture and promptly put their new-found skills to use upon the folks back home.

---

* Tape of June 23, 1972.
** The death drugs, heroin & cocaine.

What a Long Strange Trip It's Been

Here's what one ex-torturer of the Treasury Police had to say about the methods learned from the C.I.A.. It seems when they pick up political suspects for questioning, the standard torture routine goes something like this: if the person won't talk after a time of psychological torture, then the physical torture begins. First the prisoner is handcuffed naked to a bedframe in a small, cold, dark cell filled with the urine & excrement of its former tenants and kept awake for a week. Then the subject is either severely beaten, burnt by cigarettes, or has his skin sliced off, and if that doesn't work he's taken to a toilet full of feces and has his head submerged for 30 second intervals. Beyond that, there's electro-shock administered in soundproof rooms with wires attached to their genitals and between their teeth as the prisoners stand in water or sit on iron.[2]

Tortured prisoners are generally killed- it's an extermination process complete with castration of male subjects and the dumping of the body in an alley with a death squad sign claiming responsibility. This is what our tax dollars are and have been doing. The El Salvador operation was orchestrated by the U.S. State Department's Agency for International Development's "Public Safety Program" which in 1967 was operating assassination & dissent-suppressing programs in 32 countries other than El Salvador. Kill everyone in the country who wasn't on the C.I.A.'s side until the only one's left are the C.I.A.'s paid lackeys who rule the bungalow while the rest of the fine folk are out in the fields picking cotton or cutting cane or picking fruit for you white folks's pleasure.

In Guatemala the C.I.A. overthrew the freely elected government of Jacobo Arbenz and unleashed upon the Guatemalans a 30-some year period of military dictatorships and terror in which once again the United States trained 30,000 Guatemalan police in their expertise which cost the lives of tens of thousands of people over the years (50-75,000 from 1980-85 alone).

In Chile it was Richard Nixon, Henry Kissinger, Alexander Haig, the C.I.A., Richard Helms, Theodore Shackley, & I.T.T. which successfully plotted, funded, & watched over the overthrow of the government and the assassination of democratically elected Socialist leader Salvador Allende in 1973. This was Kissinger in one of his most Nazi-ish moves yet. Henry Kissinger- tyrannical diplomat, Secretary of State under Tricky Dick, dwarf womanizer. This is the cat who Nixon would not let the press record his real voice for month's because Kissinger's heavy German accent sounded just like a Nazi and Nixon knew that people would see right thru that one. Kissinger's a dead ringer for the role of Dr. Strangelove in which Peter Sellers played an ex-Nazi who was the demented mastermind behind America's nuclear forces. And ole Henry's not to be outdone in his own right; well, he's got more blood on his hands than the Manson clan, that's for sure. It was Henry who suggested to the Israelis that they should follow the example of the South Africans and restrict TV access to politically sensitive areas like the Occupied Territories, thus keeping the world from seeing what's really going on there and also allowing the level of violence unleashed upon the protestors to be increased.

They say that truth comes rolling down the tracks like a Hellbound Train and when it does, we're going to see the faces of Dick Nixon, Henry Kissinger, Allen Dulles, Richard Helms, William Colby, William Westmoreland, William Calley, Casper Weinberger, George Bush, Elliott Abrams,[3] David Rockefeller and friends all rolling straight to Hell.

Nazi tactics? Napalm in Nicaragua is kosher gas in Treblinka. And we learned from the best, the Nazis themselves. It seems that the very year that the C.I.A. was formed the U.S. State Department was busy assisting the Allies & the Vatican in helping some 7-10,000 Nazi war criminals escape Europe and join the ranks of the intelligence communities of France, England, Australia, Canada, West Germany, Italy, Austria, &, yes, the United States.

Who said history was nice?

And speaking of the Vatican, seems it's just another corrupt, power entity which has also been caught with its pants down as of late. An immense scandle involving some hanky panky with the Mafia and the Vatican Bank, lots of funny transactions and money being used to support South American right wing dictatorships, and the murder of a Pope all surfaced in 1982 with a resultant series of at least 10 murders &/or suicides strung along the way like sacrificial lambs. This includes the murder of Pope John Paul I just 30 days after taking office in 1978. John Paul was O.K., he even supported the Women's Rights Movement and promised to consider birth control for Catholics. But even more threatening was his expressed intent of checking out the Vatican moneytenders. On the nite before his death he gave his secretary of state Cardinal Villot (a vile & treacherous man) a list of names of people in positions of power at the Vatican who were to be dismissed or reassigned. All of these were supposed members of the secret Freemason group called P2. P2 is sort of the Illuminati's C.I.A., and after they killed the Pope they killed a judge, a journalist, the head of Rome security, & the head of the Palermo Intelligence division, all of whom had just got on their trail. Then with the murder of 2 witnesses and 4 principals in the case, all was hushed up as Pope John Paul II took the throne and the Vatican bank returned to its nefarious activities.[4]

      Cloak & Dagger, cape & coffin.
 Don't be surprised by any of this- absolute power corrupts absolutely. To kill a President, to kill a Pope; watch where thou doest tread, dear children, the demons fill the nite.

 And speaking of the Nazis, what makes the Nazis such an appalling spectacle before humankind? Or as Groucho Marx might say, "What have they ever done that we haven't done better?" Napalm just brings the ovens to the people. Maybe it was the Nazis' inhumane laboratory experiments upon human beings that made them such devils. Well, roll over Beethoven, tell Der Fuhrer der news. Good ole Uncle Sam's been doubling as the good Dr. Frankenstein and oh my, what hasn't gone on. The C.I.A.'s L.S.D. experiments on unwitting participants is pretty well known; as is the case of the C.I.A. doing germ warfare experiments on American civilians and releasing deadly bacteria in the NY subway, the tunnels of the Pennsylvania turnpike & the San Francisco harbor. People died as a result.

 But how about the real stuff, like the fact that the government conducted a 30 year (1940-71) series of radiation experiments on its own citizens, namely the homeless and people in prisons, old folks' homes, & hospitals. These tests included injecting people with uranium and plutonium, feeding normal adults and the elderly magnesium, uranium, radium, & thorium, and x-raying prisoners' testes repeatedly for eight years. Zeig Heil! <u>Never be too trusting of your government</u>, I found that out early on. I mean, x-rays below the belt anyone? "Here, Mrs. Henderson, another bowl of radium to get you off to a healthy start." And it wasn't too comforting when the Supreme Court ruled in 1988 that the U.S. government was not responsible for the thousands of people who, exposed to nuclear fallout in 3 states from 1951-62 due to atomic testing, developed cancer & leukemia because of it. And if your not righteously scared of that nuclear power plant down the street then pull up your chair a little closer to the TV & soak up them rays.*

 But let's get back to the Iran affair and on down the track.

---

 * And besides the radiation, the average American sees hundreds upon hundreds upon hundreds of commercials daily. Mindburn or what?

Chapter 42

So what's the big thing about Iran? The major thing about Irangate is that for one it exposed the whole international terrorist network run and financed by the C.I.A. and deeply involved in the smuggling of hard drugs, murder, & global mayhem for the past 25 years.

Selling guns to the god-crazed Ayatollah was nothing new. Since 1981 the United States had been selling arms to Iran via Israel via Zaire reportedly as a result of a pre-1980 election deal with the Iranians to prevent the release of the American hostages to help swing the election in Reagan's favor. The U.S. was also following its typical approach of selling guns to anyone for money (after all, armaments is and has been the #1 worldwide business of the U.S.) plus they were vaguely hoping for a coup of some kind if the guns got in the right hands. But things changed drastically in 1984.

In 1984 Beirut C.I.A. station chief William Buckley was kidnapped and taken to Iran, where he was extensively interrogated, tortured & killed. He told Iranians details of the C.I.A.'s entire Middle Eastern network and all of this was videotaped. The Iranians in turn blackmailed the U.S. into supplying top secret military intelligence (basically concerning Iraqi troop movements in the Iran-Iraq war) and into stepping up the secret arms shipments to Iran via Israel. Otherwise the Iranians were prepared to tip the Soviets off to the whole C.I.A. Mideast operation and screw everything up. But as cross turned to double cross we decided that if more arms were to be sold, then we'd inflate the price and make some bucks on the deal. But who was to handle all of this? Bingo.

Enter Lieutenant Colonel Oliver North, who with his gapped teeth & cowlicked hair & gee whizzes and all, kinda reminded one of Alfalfa from "Our Gang." Now Ollie North was from the old Al Haig "I am in command" school, and his tale's a strange one. It's reported that one time right before he was confined for his mental stress problems he ran around in the Virginia suburbs totally naked pointing a .45 to his head and screaming "I'm no good, I'm no good."[1] It was widely reported in the press at the time that North's "emotional stability was a concern." I mean this guy's got to be nuts to tell the Iranians during their dealings that Ronald Reagan was a "direct descendant of the God of Abraham" and expect them to believe that one. Who'd he think he was- Moses? Is this the kind of guy you'd put the entire Pentagon at his disposal?

What a Long Strange Trip It's Been

Well, this was just the kind of guy Ronnie & boys wanted, and it was all at his disposal: skimming money from the sales of arms to Iran then illegally funnelling the money to the murderous Contras, and then selling them shoddy guns at exorbitant prices to get the money back* were only some of his important functions.

Ollie North, all-American fascist. As we mentioned, one of his jobs was to draft a plan for martial law, suspending the Constitution, and allowing for the arrest & detention of dissenting Americans in the event of an unpopular military invasion abroad. Just like they did to Japanese-Americans in World War II. Reagan was to sign this and whip it out if necessary, while invading Nicaragua for example. It's not known if Reagan signed this in 1984 or not, but then Attorney General William French Smith flipped out when he saw it and sent a letter to Robert McFarlane, National Security Adviser and North's boss, telling him that this was way out of bounds. But in reality, this was only normal procedure.

From 1983 to 1986 North ran a series of illegal covert foreign policy actions around the world- he was his own little C.I.A. In fact he worked hand in hand with C.I.A. head William Casey on several things and as staff member of the National Security Council began running operations out of the White House the likes of which hadn't been seen since the days of Tricky Dick. This secret program of clandestine activities was called Project Democracy and even the televised Iran-Contra hearings failed to inform the American people of the depth of the nefarious activities which were involved in these projects, paid for by our tax dollars and arms sales rip offs. Every time something hot came up dealing with government drug running, etc.., the committee would go into "secret session."

So Ollie had his hands full. Planning the invasion of Grenada, and, more importantly, illegally breaking the ban on military aid to the Contras called the Boland Amendment, which Congress had passed in response to the American public's disgust of the Contras and their politics of death. What Ollie North was best at, it seems, was subverting the democratic process and the expressed will of both the Congress and the American people. Oliver North was a liar & a traitor. But one who was taking orders from other liars & traitors. Like Ronald Reagan.

When the Iran scandal erupted it was Reagan's ass that was really on the line. North had been acting under orders all along, and when a Lebanese newspaper blew the whistle on the secret arms shipments to Iran, the muddied footsteps led straight back to the White House, which had the same long shades drawn over the windows as in the Watergate

---

* With the same C.I.A. supply planes delivering arms to the Contras then running coke back to the U.S.

A Hippy's History of the Sixties

days. Shades of Watergate, indeed.

You betcha. Immediate scramble & cover-up. Contain the damage. At first the whole thing was laid at the feet of Ollie North- a rogue lieutenant colonel who they said took it upon himself to use the Army, Navy, Air Force, Marines, & C.I.A. to fight the Commies his own way. They said this was a result of Reagan's "hands off" management style, implying, of course, that the President didn't know what his subordinates were up to. Then they tried to make White House Chief of Staff Donald Regan the scapegoat, so he was tossed out the door. Then they used the excuse it was all an effort to free our American hostages in Lebanon which was pure bunk, cause the only hostage they were really worried about was William Buckley and he was dead.

Then it was a question of whether Ronnie had O.K.'d the arms sales or not. Laws had been broken and nothing could be admitted to without political fallout & considerable impact; perhaps even impeachment. The American people were pissed that we were sending guns to the Iranians when we were hounding the rest of the world to honor the arms embargo that we ourselves had called against these "terrorists." And it was Reagan who had always jumped up & down and howled about the Ayatollah, and selling guns to him seemed a traitorous move for sure.

So Ronnie's memory got cloudy and he couldn't remember if he had O.K.'d all this, or knew about this, or knew about that, or knew about anything, and after all he was an old man and after all he was only the President...

But that wasn't good enough. When the truth was demanded the only way Ronnie & the boys could think to stay in the clear was to say that Reagan did O.K. the delivery of arms to Iran but was on drugs at the time, recovering from one operation or another; thus, not only was he not responsible for remembering a thing about this, but he was also supposedly not responsible for the atrocious decision to be selling guns to Iran in the first place. On drugs? You expect us people really on drugs to believe that?

And when that ploy was not particularly well received, then Ronnie spent a couple of days ducking press questions by pretending to have laryngitis. Seeing the President on TV pointing to his throat and playing dead was one of the most disgusting pieces of bullshit I've ever seen coming from a politician. If this asshole can't stand up and answer for his actions and the illegal actions of the administrators of his policy, then get rid of the son of a bitch or tar & feather them all or something.[2] But don't expect me to be so stupid as to believe all the bullshit they're trying to pass off as truth.

What a Long Strange Trip It's Been

And alot of other people didn't believe it either. Congressional investigations were being formed and questions were being asked as to who knew what when, and how and why a strictly advisory group like the National Security Council was running covert operations which clearly violated a host of both U.S. & International laws. And things got especially serious when it was announced that money from the arms sales had been illegally diverted to the Contras. Even more so, is the fact that Felix Rodriguez accepted $10 million from the Medellin cartel on behalf of the Contras according to a Medellin accountant.

As with Watergate, there were numerous players whose silence was imperative if the truth of the involvement of the President was to be kept covered up. This time the boys didn't mess around with hush money. They moved fast. If you couldn't be trusted to perjure yourself, then it was best not to show up to answer questions at all. Like Bud McFarlane, for example.

Robert McFarlane was at one time the head of the National Security Council, jolly Ollie's boss, & privy to lots. According to Iranian sources it was McFarlane who cut the deal with the Iranians for the delivery of more arms to protect the C.I.A.'s Mideast operation. Although he resigned in December of '85, when the Iran story broke he figured squarely in all of this, and aided in the initial cover-up by helping to prepare a false chronology of the President's knowledge.

Bud had already lied to some persons investigating the matter, but when it came time for McFarlane to give further testimony in front of Congress it was as we said before- perjure or don't show up, so Bud didn't show. Seems that morning (whether on his own volition or not, we don't know) Bud had taken an overdose of valium in a pretty inept attempt to kill himself and thus spare the Presidency. But Bud failed and later told investigators he had taken part in an effort by White House aides to hide President Reagan's role in the initiation & private endorsement of the Iran arms sale. That left V.P. Bush, Ollie North, John Poindexter, who had replaced McFarlane as NSC head in '85, and William Casey, C.I.A. head who had to be worried about.

Of these Casey was by far the most dangerous. He was a codgey old man, a real life Professor Ludwig von Drake, if the Walt-Disney-in-the-Sky ever meant one. Casey'd already lied to Congress on several occassions & several issues, this included, and this time he was really going to be grilled. Now William Casey knew one hell of a lot of illegal things which the Reagan crew were up to cause he was in the middle of most of them. It was Casey, remember, who had the Carter debate papers stolen back in 1980, and he just loved stuff like this. It was Casey along with Attorney

General Ed Meese who endorsed a secret plan to pay the Israeli government yearly kickbacks out of the Pentagon budget so they wouldn't knock off a billion dollar oil pipeline which Meese's friend Robert Wallach was to build along the Iraqi-Israeli border. And you can bet Meese would have probably gotten millions once this little deal went thru. This involvement and illegal use of his office to arrange big-time business deals would be the political downfall of Attorney General Edwin Meese III.

But Casey's downfall was his knowledge and the fact that he was in with a bunch of cutthroats who were just a bit more heathen than he. So Casey, too, wouldn't make it to his Congressional grilling over the Iran affair. You see, the day before he was supposed to testify, ole Wild Bill Casey kinda had a brain seizure at work and when they got him to the hospital he had a brain tumor...and lo & behold they cut out part of his brain to get that nasty tumor and all the time Ole Bill ain't saying nothing to nobody, and damned don't you know it if old Bill didn't finally up and die due to all those goings on inside his brain & all. Murder would be more like it. A little C.I.A. poison in his morning tea, instant seizure, call the ambulance, slice, slice, a started but failed recovery, perhaps a nod in the nite to Bob Woodward, & a fine obituary for one of America's late grates. After living thru the Kennedy assassinations & subsequent cover-ups, Vietnam, Watergate, and a whole bunch more, there's no way you can tell me that William Casey wasn't killed to keep him silent. Don't waste your breath. And it worked. This alone more than anything else saved the Reagan Presidency from impeachment.

From then on everyone played dumb. Bush disappeared from public view to duck questions on his role in the Iran affair, and Reagan commissioned the Tower Commission to investigate the matter. Naturally the Tower Commission placed most of the criminal blame on Ollie North and at the dead feet of William Casey, and the President of course "did not seem aware" of how the weapons deal went down or the diversion of profits to the Contras.

Bush, of course, has yet to prove he wasn't neck deep in the drugs smuggling and the running of funds to the Contras after the Boland Amendment was in place. He met with Contra leader Max Gomez (also known as Felix Rodriguez one of the original members of Operation 40, the C.I.A. assassination team) in his office during this time and it would seem by all appearances that Bush himself was involved in co-ordinating things at the highest levels in the Reagan administration's end run around the ban on Contra aid. And more. Newsweek magazine reported in May of '88 that George Bush's national security adviser was the Washington co-ordinator for a secret guns & drug smuggling operation sending guns illegally to the Contras and bringing back cocaine to the United States. Oregon gun merchant Richard Brenneke testified to Congress that Bush's aide Donald Gregg helped run the venture out of Bush's office with help from the C.I.A., the Honduran military, the Israeli Secret Service, and financed by the Medellin cocaine cartel in Columbia which supplied the planes & cocaine.[3]

Well, they finally had both private & televised Congressional inquiries into the whole affair, and a whole bunch of people proceeded to perjure themselves and to implicate others in wrongdoing. What came to light, however, was this: an administration bent upon terrorizing the Nicaraguan people with all the resources it could secretly raise; and the individuals involved so greedy they even subverted their own far-right cause and ripped off their own supporters to line their pockets. It was the coup/coup Fawn & Ollie show, with Ollie North giving anti-Commie slide shows to right wingers, milking then for their bucks, and Richard Secord buying Porsches and sticking the money in Swiss bank accounts with the other money.* And as far as overcharging on arms deals, that was certainly defrauding the American people on the sale of items it owned let alone trading sophisticated weaponry with our supposed enemies, and in the real breach of national security, leaving our own stockpiles short. And all that money in Swiss bank accounts.

So Ollie marched into the televised hearings and gave his best John Wayne rendition of "let's support the freedom fighters, laws & truth be damned" speech and once again he won the hearts & minds of those political sheep who spend most of their lives glued to the tube and whose reality is based upon Republican-type TV scriptwriters whose job it is to pass off the elite's social prejudices as reality to be emulated & enforced at any cost.

But fact is fact and history is history, and history records the fact that the Contras were perpetually guilty of murderous acts of terrorism almost strictly against the civilian population. That was their job. The C.I.A. even provided them with manuals encouraging the assassination of civilian leaders and other such acts as standard operating procedure. And it was Ronald Reagan, George Bush, Ollie North & Co. who were directing these heinous atrocities against a civilian population whose crime once again was that their country ceased being a whore for America. And you know how Uncle Sam always hates to let a good fuck go. Especially Nicaragua. No, we'd been fighting too hard to keep El Salvador under control to let

---

* There's still 8 million dollars of U.S. money in Swiss banks controlled by them.

Nicaragua go under.

Our hands are so bloody from the hundreds of thousands of Central American citizens which U.S. tax dollars & C.I.A.-trained death squads have so brutally & unabashedly exterminated and continue to murder, that even Pontius Pilate couldn't get them clean. And shit, most people aren't even reaching for the soap.

So you can see why lots of people bought that Ollie North hero bullshit, cause hell, killing Commies is the American way. Always been. Least since World War II when the Commies & us sorta divided up the winnings and started the race to see who could cop the rest. An economic battle fought mostly on military & subversive terms in Third World countries and propaganda terms at home. That's why our government's so necessarily fostered hate & suspicion toward Communist nations; cause if we hate somebody then it's certainly alright to kill them. Or so goes the Republican's TV script spewed forth from the mighty vortex of international Whitey greed, feeding the minds too dulled to seek truth elsewhere and keeping them in fear of the Boogeyman.

Well, it would be one thing if we were really promoting democracy and all that, but it's the same old rape, pillage, & steal program that's been running since Genghis Khan. Only this time not only do we get all the natural resources from whichever country we're currently making safe for democracy, but the armament manufacturers are making a literal killing off of our fears, hatred, & inability to fathom political reality.

Running guns, hard drugs, & Contra operational death squads are not very heroic things for a flea-bitten lieutenant colonel & crew to be thumping their chests in public about; but if they're so proud of their betrayal to the people & principles of this country, then we should be no less proud to publically castrate these bastards and stick their genitals down their throats; which is one of the lesser atrocities which are routine events in Central America due to the likes of "heroes" such as these. Mea culpa, mea culpa, mea maxima culpa... anymore I'm a gun-toting pacifist.

So when the Reagan administration got caught violating the Boland Amendment, Reagan went ahead and said that this particular law didn't apply to him. (Just as he would later say of the War Powers Act when he sent the U.S. fleet sailing into the Persian Gulf using U.S. tax dollars to protect "our" oil, which in fact was going to Japan.) Which is exactly the point that Richard Nixon was trying to make when he was King- laws are to be followed by leaders of democracies, but not by dictators. And to hear Ollie tell it, we all knew that Congress, the People, & that law was wrong anyway, so what's the big deal? I'll tell you what's the big deal.

Look again, gang... Lady Justice ain't so blind, that's not C.I.A. coke on

What a Long Strange Trip It's Been

those scales, and that sword is hanging right above your necks...

Well Ronnie's neck slipped out from underneath the Irangate blade, but barely by inches and Bill Casey's last dying breath. After 15 months of investigation, criminal charges were then brought by Special Prosecutor Walsh against Oliver North, John Poindexter, Richard Secord, & Iranian arms dealer Albert Hakim among others in March of '88. Lawrence Walsh could have been the greatest hero in American history by also indicting Ronald Reagan or at least naming him an unindicted co-conspirator, but he didn't, and this supported the cover-up's assertion that Reagan didn't know of the diversion of funds to the Contras which is totally absurd.

In 1988 North petitioned to have charges dropped against him because he was not formally warned that lying to the government and destroying official documents could be illegal acts. The judge, Gerhard A Gesell, denied the request, noting that North had a "skewed attitude" toward Constitutional government. During North's trial in the spring of '89, documents revealed that both Ronald Reagan and George Bush knew of and approved illegal funding of the Contras and thus in their lies and silence were also guilty of cover up and impeachable offenses. A 42-page government document introduced as evidence in the trial, which the F.B.I. "failed" to turn over to the committee investigating the Iran-Contra affair, implied that Bush met secretly with the president of Honduras to increase American aid to Honduras in return for Honduran aid to the Contras. On May 4, 1989, North was found guilty of three felony charges and whether the others will be brought to task only time will tell.

They were, however, successful in having the trial postponed until after the presidential elections that year (a ploy used in earlier years by Richard Nixon to get re-elected when the Watergate scandal broke) and which certainly helped George Bush win in '88 by not having to address his role in the Iran scandal in court or in depth.

But in the end we all figured it'd be Ollie Ollie in free when the sentence came down with a swift flick of the Presidential pen. However, it was the Supreme Court in 1991 who let him off the hook by overturning his conviction (due to lack of their own) because Ollie had been promised immunity for his testimony and some of that was used against him.

Nevertheless criminal acts are nothing less, and this whole affair was a chorale of deception the least of which was a cover-up by all the parties involved, including Ronald Reagan. Reagan flat out lied and misled the American people more than once about his role in the Iran-Contra affair. No more so than when he read a false chronology of his knowledge of the Iran affair at a special press conference on the matter. He should have been impeached for that alone.

This was somehow part of his manner, though, to obscure the field of debate with pure bullshit for fact, and thru the ridiculousness of it somehow still survive. Misspeak. Doublespeak. Reaganspeak. A combination of half-truths, ignorance of the facts, folksy tales, & calculated lies. Lots of historical revisionism. This one, for example. That "all the waste (from a nuclear power plant) in a year could be stored under a desk." (Burlington Free Press, February 15, 1980)[4] Right!

But worst of all were the outright lies told the American people by the Reagan administration as a matter of intended policy to mislead and deceive them. This policy, called disinformation or "White Propaganda" by the administration itself, was soley intended to mislead the American people about the reality of foreign policy events in Nicaragua & elsewhere. In 1983 the Office for Public Diplomacy for Latin America was created in the State Department at the request of the C.I.A. and National Security Council. For the next four years this office was engaged in illegal, prohibited, & covert propaganda activities designed to influence the media and the public to support the administration's Latin America policies. Their stories were planted in the Wall Street Journal, Washington Post, New York Times, and on NBC News, all touting the Contra cause and oftentimes credited with being written by the Contra leaders themselves. But it was just more propaganda from the Ministry of Information, more lies to let the killing go on. I mean, what's it take to get impeached these days?

So lies & inaccuracies were common traits of the Reagan administration with Reagan himself remembered as the biggest perpetraitor of them all. Press conference after press conference Reagan would tell these tales, only to later have the White House release corrections or the press uncover the untruths. By 1983 it was so obvious to all that at a press conference Reagan quipped "Make sure I was telling the truth,"[5] in an effort to laugh it off. But the Iran affair brought these lies out, exposed the State Department's illegal shipping of arms to the Contras, and the total lawlessness on our government's part with regard to human rights.

And those Americans who saw thru these lies were themselves once again turned upon by the enforcement agencies of the state; the F.B.I. once again went back to its surreptitious means of wiretapping, break-ins, and unwarranted search & surveillance upon those individuals and organizations in active opposition against Reagan's policy of Latin American genocide & terror. This included over 100 groups such as the Maryknoll Sisters, the National Education Association, the American Indian Movement, the Quakers, the United Steelworkers, the United Auto Workers, &,

of course, legitimate American political organizations such as C.I.S.P.E.S. (the Committee In Solidarity with the People of El Salvador) were monitored and infiltrated with undercover agents, informants, and a network of conservative political spies which operated outside of Constitutional restraints but was illegally in league with the F.B.I. and gathering information illegally on its own.

But nevertheless six years of investigation of C.I.S.P.E.S. (from 1981-87) failed to show any terrorist inclinations or connections, or were any found in the other church, labor, or civil rights organizations that were targeted. Political censorship was the real goal. The clear lawbreakers in the truest sense of American law was once again the government and government only. If we were a Latin American country these same groups which had been monitored, identified, followed, and infiltrated, would then have been systematically exterminated by agents of the state. It's just that up to this time, the political climate in this country has not allowed for that, & even Kent State- had killing students become standard policy from then on, it would have caused such an uproar in this country that the government could in no way have banked upon winning. And that's exactly why you should never elect a person President of the United States who was once the head of the C.I.A. Just to insure that we don't all disappear in the nite sometime.

I mean, it was the same William Webster who as head of the F.B.I. ordered the opponents of Reagan's Central American policy be spied upon, that was appointed to head the C.I.A. when Bill Casey, ah...died. Musical chairs or what? I bet Webster fixed his own java in the morning...

And how about the L.E.I.U. as a perfect example of today's fascism? The Law Enforcement Intelligence Unit is made up of police officers from state & local governments who have been trained extensively in domestic intelligence gathering, namely surveillance and infiltratrion; watching the New Left, anti-nuclear activists, and similar groups in favor of democratic change. It operates as a private spy organization whose findings are shared among law enforcement agencies thru a computerized information network which although supported mainly by public tax money, is unaccountable to individuals, the public, or any level of government, including the Freedom of Information Act. It's activities began in 1970 when Richard Nixon began using funds from the Federal Law Enforcement Assistance Administration to arm local police to the teeth and teach them all about breaking & entering, phone tapping, and other unconstitutional surveillance techniques so that the rising tide of political activism could be curbed at the local levels. This would later come in handy in use against the opponents to Reagan's Latin American policies.

At any rate this bullshit's gotta stop. This whole damned bunch of law enforcement witchunters, genocidal politicians, & C.I.A. sleaze has just got to go so that Peace and Justice and Liberty can prevail in a humane climate in Central America & elsewhere. U.S.A. elsewhere. So whichever way it goes it's up to you. Vote, and if that doesn't work, run for office yourself. But don't just run. There's change that needs to be made, and we've gotta stop killing people with U.S. tax dollars, and repressing people abroad and at home.

Cause that's one of the things which the Reagan-Bush era will be remembered for- the Afghanistanization of Central America. The murder of countless tens of thousands of men, women, & children by forces armed, trained, paid, and directed by the U.S. government.

But there are other equally vile things for which Ronald Reagan will be remembered. The federal deficit, for sure. Voodoo economics. Never in the history of our country had one President racked up such a huge debt to the world. Under Reagan's reign the rich got richer and the poor stayed poor. Huge tax breaks to the rich corporations and the gutting of social programs. Like the Federal Reserve System bleeding the country dry.

Fifty of America's top profit-making corporations paid no income taxes at all in at least four of the Reagan-Bush years, including 40 companies which paid no taxes on more than 10 billion dollars in one year alone. All blueblood members of the Military-Industrial Complex. In 1988 both General Motors and I.B.M. were among at least a dozen big U.S. corporations which paid no taxes at all; yet G.M. and I.B.M. both got refund checks from the I.R.S.

And what about everyone else?

For the first time since I was born there's become masses of people across this country who are homeless- hundreds of thousands of people nationwide who have no job or home or income and began living in the streets & alleyways, in subways & bus terminals, & cardboard boxes, and eating out of dumpsters in America as a result of U.S. companies deserting its workers & moving overseas to exploit cheap labor and Reagan's heartless economic & social policies. During these years ten million factory workers lost their jobs due to these policies. He had no time to worry about old Joe from "South Succotash."[6] I mean, under Reagan ketchup was considered an acceptable substitute for vegetables in the school lunch program's nutritional guidelines. This shows you how much the guy really cared.

So aside from the Contras, his sleaze-drenched administration, the

What a Long Strange Trip It's Been

deficit, the homeless, & his habit of lying, Reagan will also be remembered for his firing of the country's air traffic controllers and undermining the safety of American air travelers for years to come. Once again it was a triumph of the tactics of brute force over those of diplomacy and reason. The air traffic controllers were on strike and Ronnie issued a Presidential directive which ordered them back to work pronto or they would be fired without chance of rehire. And what's more he dissolved their union in a move of pure fascism. Especially since at the very time Reagan was getting down on the Polish government for busting up the trade union Solidarity. No difference at all. So the controllers got fired, new, inexperienced people took the controls, and errors & fatalities increased. In 1987 the major airlines had 31 crashes in what proved to be the highest number of accidents in thirteen years. Another one for the Reagan record book.

Then there's South Africa. The blatant inborn racism of the Reagan administration could be clearly seen in their continual support of the white supremacist dictatorship there which has kept an entire nation of Black Africans enslaved. The struggle and sacrifice of the Black liberation movement in South Africa, and the jailing & murder of its most articulate leaders, especially the almost 30-year imprisonment of Nelson Mandella & the murder of Stephen Biko should have brought American-led sanctions against the white rulers there which would have brought them to their knees. But instead Reagan only paid lip service to the forces calling for democracy and the end to apartheid, thus ensuring the continuation of repression & racism there. It's that old American penchant for aiding governments whose skin & money's the same colour as ours. But in fact our money will turn anyone's colour white, so what's the dif?

And how about Israel? Right off, this is going to piss a lot of folks off who somehow think of themselves as the chosen race or those who constantly holler about the holocaust, but I don't care. Because the Israeli government's been acting like a bunch of Nazis for so many years with our money that the sacred Souls of all those burnt at Treblinka would turn over in their graves & haunt your seders forever if they could do so to register their dissaproval of what's going on.

The oppressed have become the oppressors.* Israel's been governed so long with this seige mentality that it somehow justifies whatever act of lawlessness or violence it cares to use against its neighbors, its citizens, or the world, in the name of national security. Sound familiar?

Cases abound, but the fact that Israeli secret agents stole its first bomb-grade plutonium from a Pennsylvania power plant in the late 60's* to

---

* An American history dejà vu.

develop its first atomic weapon & now has over 100 nuclear bombs secretly stockpiled to start World War III with if they get too paranoid is enough for me.

And their actions in the occupied areas of the West Bank & the Gaza Strip would make old Adolf himself proud. After 20 years of occupation by Israeli forces, the Palestinian citizens began rebelling in 1987 demanding the very thing which Israel itself was denied for so long and now were denying to others- a homeland.

So how did Israel respond? With force, of course. Killing over 140 West Bank & Gaza Palestinian demonstrators in the first three months of unrest, in a casually callous & brutal display of fascism. Some people died of beatings but most were a result of Israeli troops shooting live bullets against stone throwing youths...fair odds, indeed. But to be sure the Israelis adopted a policy of conducting midnite raids on Palestinian homes and breaking the hands, wrists, & fingers of all males of stone throwing age (15-35). The hospitals were overflowing with people beaten and with broken limbs, but when this didn't stop the protests, they just rounded up thousands of Palestinian youths and threw then in jail to thin out the ranks a bit. From there they started to deport unruly Palestinians from their birthplace, & then they started to get really inventive like burying four Palestinians alive with a bulldozer and leaving them to die as an example to others. A rule based upon a system of Palestinian collaborators much as the Nazi occupation of its neighbors was carried out. The basic policy in the field, however, was to kill 2-3 protestors a day in an effort to deter the inevitable. Just like South Africa.

So let's get a grip on these people. It's been our tax money that's kept them in existence for God knows how long (at least 10 billion dollars a year these days, all tolled some 45 billion dollars by 1989), so what gives? I mean, we're giving them $9,000 a year per Israeli citizen, so who's subsidizing the terror? It's these politicians of ours who are afraid of losing the "Jewish vote" (i.e., campaign contributions) who refuse to use their proper political influence to curtail either these gestapo actions by Israel or the flow of American bucks to the same. It's time for a change, which it hopefully may after the signing of the first Israeli-PLO peace accord on September 13, 1993, leading the way for the return of occupied Arab lands by Israel for calm relations. An excellent turnaround in Israeli policy.

So after his support of repressive regimes around the world, that probably leaves Ronnie's war on drugs for which he'll be least remem

---

* They've stolen at least 175 kilograms of enriched uranium from the U.S. to date.

bered. What a joke. Getting down on dopers, especially pot smokers, is hypocritical to the max when the government's running coke & smack galore into this country (coke to finance its covert Third World military ventures, and heroin and crack to keep the Blacks in the ghetto down). Like the downers & qualudes they used to flood campuses with in the springtime to keep activism down.[7] And then there's all the Afghani hash brokered in the U.S. during the 80's to pay for American weapons for the Afghani rebels. Let's be real. It was *great* hash, too.

The most addicting abused & destructive drugs in our society today are alcohol, TV violence, sugar, nicotine, caffeine, cocaine, prescription downers, & speed in that order. Over 1,000 people die a day due to cigarettes...over 30,000 a year slaughtered on the highways due to alcohol.

Ever see Nancy Reagan downed out on TV muttering how evil drugs are? Or Nancy on downers falling off her chair & off the stage onto the floor at a White House speech by Ronnie. Nancy. Miss Anorexic 1932. Seems she just couldn't say no to her addiction to 11 thousand dollar dresses she "borrowed" from top designers by the closetful & wouldn't return.

Instead of saying "Just say no," Nancy's slogan should have been "Just say blow." At least according to Patricia Lawford, widow of Peter Lawford and authoress of The Peter Lawford Story (Jove Books, 1988). It seems that when Reagan was crowned king in 1980, Peter Lawford revealed to his wife that "When she was single, Nancy Davis [Reagan] was known for giving the best head in Holywood." He himself was one of the many satisfied recipients of the first lady's early talents. And we can only assume that with the help of Poli-grip, she's still at it today. According to biographer Kitty Kelly, Nancy was having intimate lunches with Frank Sinatra, all the while Ronnie was playing emperor. Kelly also revealed that Nancy and Ronnie had themslves smoked marijuana. So what's all this hypocrisy about sex and drugs?   Just that.

Let's get real. Marijuana mellows you out & psychedelics properly used will reveal God.

The great drug hysteria is being perpetrated on us all by the media & the politicians leading to kids turning in their parents, just like pre-war Germany. The media to sell news & politicians to get elected. They're the real vultures of society. While recreational drug users become the scapegoats & prey: by uptight politicos into control & by those who for two decades have used drug charges as an easy way to jail & politically neutralize New Left activists.

The legal use of marijuana, psychedelics, & MDA at least is guaranteed in the Constitution under the right of the pursuit of happiness, and also by the separation of Church & State; that the government can make no law curbing religious freedom. For marijuana & psychedelics are Sacred in nature and sacraments of our culture. They've been valid and accepted medicinal & spiritual aids in human culture for at least 4,000 years, and ignorance of this fact is a gross misunderstanding of their nature due to fear and personal inexperience. This has led to a witch hunt.[8]

Surely urine testing for drugs is unconstitutional, a clear violation of the laws against unreasonable search & seizure and the 5th Amendment which protects against coerced self-incrimination. And as if school-workplace urine tests aren't enough of a government-corporate invasion of one's liberties & privacy, how about Channel One, the "educational" television programming offered to schools in exchange for free T.V.s & lots of in school time commercials. Or the replacement of cafeterias in our high schools with McDonalds fast food, plus the great opportunity for kids to earn their math credits not taking math, but while working for free for McDonalds in the school during lunch periods.

And what could be more misleading & insidious than the public school system's participation in the anti-drug D.A.R.E. propaganda program? Bringing cops into classrooms with loaded guns at their sides preaching their false indoctrination how marijuana'll make you go blind. Pure brainwashing to facilitate social control. And what of the 2,000 Deadheads in prison in 1993 on l.s.d. charges compared to the mere 100 four years before, many on mandatory no-parole prison terms of 10-20 years? Social control, alright. It's time to let these people be as free as they are. And how about the paraquat that the DEA's been spraying massively in other countries and here at home once again starting in the summer of 1988. Paraquat's just another Agent Orange which not only destroys the environment but will destroy your lungs if you inhale it. The government knows this but doesn't care... anything to win the "war on drugs." Incarceration, decimation, taking all our freedoms away. Again it's the people into control vs. the people into freedom.

The people into freedom want to explore, evolve, & transcend for educational and spiritual reasons. But the people in control cannot tolerate that, because not only are they afraid of such spaces themselves, but once people do grass & acid they begin to think for themselves and are no longer good subjects of control or good sheep to sell things to. All those years of control thru TV programming, debilitating the will thru nutritionally inert foods, & chaining the Spirit thru chemical dependencies on sugar, nicotine, caffeine, booze, etc. begin to disappear with the dawning of Consciousness; and the validity of the world of the people into control likewise disappears, so they try to control the rest of society so they don't stray too far from the norm and expose the untruths which are the very base of their lives. 1930 to be preserved at all costs! They are totally intolerant of anyone who is not just like them. How's that for the American tradition? At least some light was shed in this area by Surgeon General Joycelyn Elders, who on December 7, 1993, called for study of the legalization of drugs in America, stating that it would reduce crime and violence. Such a move would cut in on the money made daily by the government's cocaine and heroin trade. Coincidentally enough, two weeks later her son Kevin was arrested on drug charges stemming from an alleged sale of one-eighth gram of coke to a narc in a park nearly six months before.

The real danger to society comes not from recreational drug users but from those in power hooked on alcohol, violence, greed, & power.

So "don't lay no boogie woogie on the King of Rock-n-Roll;" just say no to genocide. Just say yes to life.

As for the glorious moment which Nancy had so hoped would get Ronnie the Nobel Peace Prize- the signing of the I.N.F. Treaty banning intermediate range nuclear weapons with Russian leader Mikhail Gorbachev in 1987 and work on a later treaty in '88 reducing the superpowers long range arsenals in half; well it was done, but primarily for vain reasons alone. Nancy wanted Ronnie to look good in the history books. (They even tried to get Ronnie the Nobel Prize the year before by sending Trilateral Industrialist Armmand Hammer to New York to talk to the Peace Prize Committee about giving the award to Ronnie for his great efforts at achieving peace in Central America. What a joke. Costa Rican President Arias, whose Peace plan for the region was adopted and which Ronnie did his best to subvert, justly won that year. The award that Ronnie finally got & deserved was in April 1992 in Las Vegas when as the recipient of a National Association of Broadcasters award, he was given a crystal-line statue that was summarily smashed to pieces on the podium by Rick Springer, an anti-nuclear protestor, who then tried to give a few words of his own but was pounced on by the Secret Service who as usual was a little late on the job. The 41-year-old activist got 4 months in jail.

The climate in America was for Peace at the time, in fact the Peace Movement had grown to be stronger in the Reagan Era than anytime since the 60's. The million person rally in N.Y.C. in 1982 for disarmament, the Great Peace March across America in 1986, and such events as the World Instant of Cooperation in 1986-87 and the Harmonic Convergence in '87, all in their way contributed to creating the climate which made dialogue & agreement on disarmament a politically desirable move as opposed to the old Reagan policy of badger, balk, & escalate. Next came Bush.

A Hippy's History of the Sixties

The election race of 1988 between Michael Dukakis and George Bush was called the most negative campaign in American history, and it was George Bush who led the mudslinging way as a matter of "practical" politics. As he slashed his way into the TV livingrooms of America with his razor-edged lies, the truth lay in shreds and once again proved how easily manipulated the American voting public can be thru the same formula of untruths, scare tactics, & coercion used by Reagan, Nixon, and like political scum before him. As Bush was facetiously calling for a kinder & gentler nation (kinder & gentler Death squads perhaps...), the first strike mentality of the viscious little wimp he really was lashed out at his opponent and with complete ease he justified his negative attacks as a necessary part of the game to get elected. And this kinder & gentler nature was displayed just weeks after the election when jogging in his hometown on Thanksgiving morning, George Bush was asked about his ties to Panamanian leader & indicted drug lord Manuel Noriega. The Reagan administration for the time being quit trying to oust Noriega* once he publicly stated that he had the goods on Bush and would make all known about Bush's knowledge of drug running, etc. if the Reagan-Bush administration moved against him. Upon hearing the inquiry as he jogged by, Bush immediately brought his hand behind his back and gave the finger to the person who dared ask the truth of his involvement as he kept right on running. Kinder and gentler indeed. I saw this myself on the Thanksgiving nitely news. Read my finger.

Another ploy Bush used to get elected was "liberal bashing", turning the rest of the county against those who professed liberal political beliefs. Since J. Edgar Hoover started rounding liberals up in 1919 we have seen an almost nonstop succession of right wing Republicans who have tried to round up and jail liberals because of their opposite political persuasions. From Hoover to Joe McCarthy, to Richard Nixon, to Gerald Ford (who led the attempt to impeach Supreme Court Justice William O. Douglas), to Ronald Reagan, to George Bush we have heard these intolerant totalitarian types saying that being liberal is unAmerican and unpatriotic and trying to turn the nation against liberal thinking and the liberal tradition. This in itself is unAmerican & unpatriotic, and overlooks the fact that many of the greatest Presidents in American history have been liberals. The definition of a liberal, by the way, is someone who is favorable to progress, open minded or tolerant, and free from prejudice or bigotry. And George Bush is certainly none of these. It seems hatred is his middle name (or one of them anyway).

---

* Bush would later invade Panama, kidnap Noriega, deftly grabbing both the canal and eliminating the middle man on the coke route.

What a Long Strange Trip It's Been

Bush's campaign was littered with people directly connected to WW II Nazi and anti-semetic groups, and even had Watergate felon & dirty trickster Dwight Chapin (an old hand at political sabotage) working as a senior advisor to the campaign's scheduling & events unit.

And with these tactics of lies and the manipulation of public opinion thru the manipulation of public opinion polls after the Republican convention, plus the early returns projected by TV broadcasters on the day of the election, Bush was able to win the election despite a track record which included a federal defecit greater than all other administrations in American history combined, the Iran-Contra scandal, a dangerously unsafe nuclear weapons & waste management program, his call for more "safe" nuclear power plants for the future, and his lame attempts to pass himself off as an environmentalist and an "education President."

And J. Danforth Quayle, Bush's Vice-Presidential choice, was clearly the most inept person to come before the political spotlite in two centuries of American politics. He couldn't spell his way out of a wet bag, let alone a potato, but as Vice-President, Quayle's Council on Competetiveness would seek to gut all environmental laws that stood in the way of economic "progress." (Hence, all environmental laws.)

The choice of Quayle was so bad that the Swedish Consul General in New York, Arne Thoren, called Quayle "an insult to the American voters and to the rest of the world." He later was reprimanded by Sweden and had to issue an apology... it seems someone always wants an apology when you tell the truth. And the truth is that Dan Quayle was lost. Here is a guy who said he could not understand why there were so many homeless people on the street when there were so many houses on the market! Out of touch to say the least. Perhaps just a bit too affluent to understand.

So Quayle came off as the spoiled little rich kid that he really was, and his money & position of privilege which got him to the White House was the same which enabled him to dodge the draft during the Vietnam War by special intercession allowing him to hide out in the Indiana National Guard, and also to get him into law school the same way. It's surmised that Bush picked Quayle as impeachment insurance against the revelations which were surfacing concerning his real role in the Iran-Contra affair, Contra drug running, and the charges that he had been the one to cut the deal in 1980 with the Iranians to not release the 52 American hostages during the election to the Carter administration. And something as treasonous as that would certainly deserve impeachment.

But the American public was once again royally fleeced, but not by the politicians spouting these same old lies, but by themselves, for being too politically ignorant to see the truth and to realize that by electing a ruthless former C.I.A. head and a preppie draft dodger to office that the rich would continue to get richer, the environment continue to worsen, and freedoms continue to erode. This election shouldn't have even been close! I guess it takes alot to cut thru the brainwashed state the American public's come to exist in. You wonder if people are ever going to wake up in time. You wonder if time is ever going to go to sleep...

Just shows you the wonders of TV, and perhaps this election reflects the choice of a viewing audience who did not want to be without something in front of them to scare them at nite or to laugh at for the next four years. Nihilist TV. Bad programming. Like the Moonies. Or Geraldo "Chairface" Rivera, trash TV to the max. Funny! George Bush puking all over the Japanese prime minister at a state dinner in Japan in 1992 on worldwide TV. Best TV since Nixon and the war that didn't have to be. More bad programming.

George Bush's mental state is best reflected in a bizarre series of statements he made in 1991-92 while apparently under the influence of the drug Halcion, a sleeping pill banned in 11 countries because of its adverse side effects (amnesia, confusion, hallucinations, hostility & violence). Totally ignored by the major media, his peculiar behavior and strange utterances were first revealed to the American people in the comic strip Doonesbury. Statements such as "So don't feel sorry for, don't cry for me Argentina. We've got problems...and I'm blessed by good health." But his health was questionable. Falling over jogging, for example. Conveniently, however, when questions were resurfacing about his role in Iran-Contra, shifting the press's attention on his health and with a miraculous recovery, no more tough questions asked, as if they were afraid he'd kick his ticker if put on the spot. And how about this: "I said to them, there's another one that the Nitty Ditty Nitty Gritty Great Bird and it says if you want to see a rainbow you've got to stand a little rain." So who's on drugs, George? The White House, of course, reported that the drug was not a factor in his performance, but if that's true I'd say that's even more cause to worry.

The war that didn't have to be. The U.S.-Iraq War of 1991 was essentially contrived by George Bush as a medium-risk gamble (his skin vs. WWIII). The war was a vehicle to, if maximally effective, get re-elected or, minimally, gain enough popularity to stay out of jail if all truths came to lite. Kind of acquire that political teflon that Reagan had worn so well and had also used to get re-elected.

In Bush's mind & for Bush's motives, this war was imperative. The economy was finally falling due to 10 years of Reaganomics; massive homelessness could no longer be ignored; hundreds of banks failing and hundreds of more on the way; the economic fallout of the H.U.D. scandal, the Savings & Loans bleeding the American taxpayers of hundreds of billions of dollars for years, all for a C.I.A.-drug-money laundering rip-off scheme, just as the BCCI banking scandal was; the F.D.I.C.. going dry; and the stockmarket giving its warning tremor in the fall of '89. Trouble was brewing!

There was the trickle down theory which in the end trickled nowhere but down America's leg...and with the shadow of the Iran-Contra case still stalking his political trail and with his sons, Neil and Jeb stuck middle in the web of the S&L scandal (Neil, in fact, up to his eyeballs in it), George Bush knew there was enough evidence to put both himself and his son in jail, & he knew that he had to do something to divert America's attention. And he did.

But it took a while. Bush at first had a hard time convincing America we needed to go to war. Nevertheless he sent 125,000 troops to "protect" Saudi Arabia even tho' they didn't want us there until we threatened to cut off their foreign aid. The day after Congressional elections, November 9, 1990, Bush authorized another 125,000 troops for the mideast. One day, one reason was found & if that didn't work the next day another reason was thrown out to the public like some smelly old fish bait. First it was to protect the Americans who were being detained by Iraq, but they were released. Then it was because of jobs. (Jobs?)

Then it was Saddam Hussein was on the verge of having nuclear weaponry- again untrue. He was a Hitler. A madman.

He had our oil. There we go. We all knew it was for oil, no matter what they said. Bush was an oil man & boy didn't Exxon and those other oil companies make a bundle off the Kuwaiti invasion and the paranoia they could induce in the American pocketbook.

And it was obvious that Bush had no intention of negotiating for peace with the Iraqis, especially when he sent Secretary of State Baker for a total of only one six-hour face-to-face talk with the Iraqis with implicit orders not to negotiate and just deliver Bush's ultimatum And Bush pushed on even in the face of the facts that international sanctions against Iraq were indeed working. Once Congress was on holiday recess, he got the U.N. Security Council to give its conditional nod and a Jan. 15 deadline for Hussein to get out of Kuwait, and he was all set.

But ask yourself this- If this was truly a U.N. operation, why was George Bush calling the shots? All the shots. An alliance was formed with foreign powers which was forged by forgiving debts owed the U.S. and promises of future arms shipments to countries in the region; remember, "money turns anyone's skin white," right?

A Hippy's History of the Sixties

When Congress reconvened January 8, they were faced with an international deadline for possible war, one week away and Bush directly asking them to give him that same power to wage war. After some limited debate on the subject, Bush's wish was railroaded thru Congress in shades of the Tonkin Gulf resolution. The same lame excuse as previously heard in votes on Contra aid, etc., that without the support of Congress, "the enemy" could perceive a divided camp and this would weaken the President's bargaining position for peace- He wanted peace about as much as he wanted brocolli.

The war. Despite the limited debate & approbation before the war, once it got going the government used the total illogical stand that since the war was on, the only moral and "American" stand was unconditionaly support of our troops and whatever they may have to do to end this unwanted war. Cries of "they don't want to be there, it's only their job," reminded one that in America, most people were still not ready to take a moral stand against War. They thought that the real lesson of Vietnam was don't let the troops come home to no support,when the actual lesson was don't let your government coerce you into accepting any war. The government played the theme that not supporting our troops would contribute to their defeat through the demoralization of their desire to kill & die for oil. Not much thought was seriously given towards peace nor the fact that the best way to support our troops was by bringing them home alive and with expediency. Unfortunately, most people, to our own future detriment, bought the government's line of thinking like sheep once again. The flags and yellow ribbons were brought out to be sold and patriotism was marched out from sea to blinding see.

So the shots began barely hours after the Jan. 15 deadline had passed. With Bush pulling the strings Operation Desert Shield mandated for protecting the Saudi border, became Operation Desert Storm, which was a purely offensive move against the Iraq.

So the war began the big time- at least for us. We began relentlessly bombing Iraq & Kuwait (causing, by the way, scads more damage & civilian deaths to the country than Saddam Hussein's "rape" of Kuwait ever did), as the Iraqis responded hardly at all. It was David & Goliath with Goliath jackhammering David's testicles right up his asshole & out his ears. Two thousand allied bombing sorties a day were flown for a month amid little or no resistance. Iraq would later launch its antiquated Scud missles against Saudi Arabia and Israel with little or no success due to advanced allied interceptory technology. It must be said that for all the brouha, Saddam Hussein never once resorted to chemical weapons when

What a Long Strange Trip It's Been

the entire world was throwing everything it could at him and his people. We opted out of this one easy, but if all the government programmed "patriots" don't wake up pretty soon, they'll be cheering on the real WWIII and still waving their American flags (made in Hong Kong) when the Nukes fall. The Peace Movement, however, was quick to mobilize with continual drumming (55-gal. oil drums) vigils outside the White House day and night, daily marches, a large march on the Pentagon, and once the war began, a huge national march in D.C. January 27, with over a million people present. The press reported the demonstrations at first, such as the blocking of the Golden Gate bridge in San Francisco, but rapidly dropped coverage and reported vastly lower protest numbers once again in an attempt to keep Americans uninformed of the level of dissent against the war & from joining that dissent. And with the programmed patriots, Etc., cranking out rally's of their own in support of the war, well, "News is news, folks."

To further distort and impede the progress the process of Democracy and the right of an informed constituency, the TV networks broadcast the war like it was the greatest football game or mini-series to come along in years. This should be no surprise since they're owned by major corporations and weapons contractors like General Electric owning NBC. (Tom Brokaw, the first night of the war, telling how nifty it was to sit in the cockpit of an F-15 & take off made me wanna vomit.) The true nature of the conflict and its deep and entwined roots were not disclosed to the American viewing public.

The Television Networks & the rest of the mainstream media totally left unchallenged the complete Pentagon censorship which the Bush government had imposed on them- "to protect our boys and girls over there." Likewise Congress hasn't the sense to protect the freedom of press here at home, especially during war time; especially knowing how many civilians we were senselessly slaughtering (collateral damage, our military termed them) & how many of our brothers, sisters, sons & daughters were among those in the military killed for Bush's political gain. No pictures of dead U.S. bodies like in the Vietnam war. No body bags either. That might encourage antiwar thinking or actions by our viewers at home.

Nothing of the sort would invade or violate the consciousness of America, plastered in front of the TV set like neon flies around electric shit. This time TV and the Generals were assuring that there was wide consensus for the war by nightly serving up opinion polls & reports of surgical strikes and precision bombing (80% on target- how many off?) so that no one woud feel bad about a few misfallen bombs. High-tech

A Hippy's History of the Sixties

automated warfare, so clean and easy with so few casualties on our side. Until we blew up a bunker full of 400 civilians and world attention was necessarily focused on how many innocent people we were killing. Whoops!

This was a war of carpet bombing, gas-air bombs, and a bunch of kowtowing to and by the American government. This was a war in which the rich Kuwaitis sat back and watched their Western lapdogs do their fighting for them while Israel, our ally(?), held the world hostage for 13.8 million dollars (and who knows what else) or it would enter the fracas & start World War III. So instead we paid & took out Israel's biggest military threat in the area- Iraq. We did this by "softening up" the Iraqis with the greatest military ferocity in history. Then the ground war began.

Another joke.

In the first two days of Operation Desert Storm, the U.S. buried over 6,000 Iraqi alive in over 70 miles of trenches with plows mounted on tanks and earthmovers. Earth First or what?

It's obvious by now the Iraqis were not the Viet Cong, their leader was not a brilliant war strategist, nor the desert the jungle. All plusses for our side. The ground war consisted mainly of 100 hours of rounding up Iraqi P.O.W.s who surrendered by the droves (when we weren't busy shooting them), blowing up mega-mile-long lines of retreating tanks with laser-guided missiles (I tell you this was a war of computer game heroes), and outflanking the main Iraq forces in Iraq till Hussein cried "Uncle!"

Actually, after the main forces had surrendered and it was obvious that the U.N. goal of freeing Kuwait was achieved (a country whose citizens were not exactly free under the old & soon to be reestablished monarchy), we continued pounding the shit out of the fleeing Iraqi troops. Finally, the British in a 3-hour conversation with General George demanded the Allied offensive cease as the U.N. objectives had been met, and nothing less than slaughter was going on.

Bush then told reporters the lie that General Schwarzkopf had told him that the job was done & a ceasefire was being called for humanitarian reasons. Only later, in an TV interview, did Schwarzkopf admit that he had actually advised Bush to keep pushing to Baghdad & all the way to Hussein's doorstep. After a few days media flap, he then of course had to apologize in public & say that's not what he really meant to say and another Bush lie stood on flimsy excuse. Remember No New Taxes? Kinder & gentler?

BUSH
LIAR

What a Long Strange Trip It's Been

In the days preceeding the ceasefire, however, the Soviets were negotiating intensely with the Iraqis and had gotten them to agree to a withdrawal from Kuwait and all terms and so the U.S. almost one way or another was forced into a ceasefire despite their desire to continue hostilities.

So what was left when it was all over was a Kuwait in rubble, oil fields afire, oil in the gulf, & Saddam Hussein still in power, as C.I.A.-encouraged rebellions were started in southern Iraq by Iranian-backed Shiite Muslims and in the north by Kurdish dissidents. But without the promised U.S. military assistance, the insurrection turned into "George Bush's Bay of Pigs." Saddam Hussein's forces were no longer engaged in fighting the Allied armies but were free to crush these rebellions, driving hundreds of thousands of desperate refugees fleeing Iraq along the Turkish & Iranian borders. In the ensuing weeks, with no food or shelter in primitive mountain conditions, thousands of people starved to death or died of exposure and as of April 26, '91, there were still 2,000 people a day dying along the borders. International aid finally responded with the U.S. Marines constructing tent cities for the refugees in Saudi Arabia and northern Iraq, but the refugees were reluctant to return for fear of renewed persecution by Hussein's thugs. These Kurdish people are from the same group that Hussein had killed with chemical weapons during Iranian-Iraqi war, but at the time Saddam was our ally, so we looked the other way. This time, they had no big oil like the Kuwaitis so a few tents sufficed. And the price of oil? It was kept "artificially" low during the war by the government releasing the National Oil Reserves so people wouldn't bum out, but a few months after the war, prices kept right on going up.

What everyone seemed to miss and still does is the fact that this & future wars would be totally unnecessary if the United States would completely convert to renewable energy sources to renewable energy sources like solar & hemp. (Hemp grows 4 times the amount of paper per acre than trees do and is renewable three times per year; plus, if only 6 percent of the continental U.S. was planted with hemp, it would provide all of America's energy needs and end forever dependence on fossil fuels- oil., coal, & other pollutants. It grows in virtually every state of the Union and could provide inexpensive clothing, oil, food, & medicine - all once commonly used but taken away by the DuPont Comapny in favor of their pollution-inducing, petrochemical alternatives. Rayon replaced marijuana as the main clothing fiber in the 1930's. Strangely enough, it was Robert DuPont along with former Reagan Drug Czar Carlton Turner and former head of the National Institue of Drug Abuse who cornered the market on urine-testing. (Turner was forced to resign after making outrageous statements that smoking pot leads to homosexuality and AIDS. Piss on them.) Rainforests could be saved, pollution exterminated and the quality of life return to the Earth and humans if only the oil companies were not in control of the U.S. government & so much of the world.

But no, like aliens from a mutant realm, they're polluting our once pure world to make it more like their own. It's only the first step in the alien takeover.

TV is the second step- leaving your psyche unnattended while the alien mind slips in.

So, yes, the U.S.-Iraqi war was a success in that we restored the oil-rich monarchy of Kuwait back to power & reduced the Iraqi military threat to Isreal, but it's improbable that the action did little to contribute to the long-term stability in the area. Did we get rid of Hussein's nuclear capability? Maybe, maybe not. But that still leaves Israel and a lot of other crazies around the world with the bomb (ourselves, the Soviets, N. Korea, etc.).

One plus is that it brought a needed spotlight on the oppressive policies in the Israeli "occupied territories" & the need for an immediate homeland for the Palestinian people.

As any use of force must ultimately be judged by whether it alleviated more suffering than it caused, this is no exception. In this case, it didn't. The suffering continues. A team from Harvard assessed the situation and announced that 170,000 Iraqi children would die in the year after the war from disease, inadequate health care and other consequences of the war that George built. And if this was the first step in George Bush's New World Order- then beware the future. And fuck the parades.

This country began, however, to march to the tune of a different drummer, a former draft resister in fact, due to a change in direction with the election of "Good Guy" Arkansas Governor Bill Clinton as President & Senator Al Gore of Tennessee as Vice-President of the United States in 1992. After a strange campaign against both Bush-Quayle & "my favorite Martian" Ross Perot, billionaire from another planet, the Democratic ticket of Clinton-Gore arose victorious. Meanwhile George Bush whimpered out of D.C. beneath the fireworks of celebration of freedom from 12 long & vicious years underneath the high-rolling wheels of the Reagan-Bush regime which ran America & so many Americans right into the ground.

Clinton got off to a good start with his wife's help, despite reports that as Governor he knew that Ollie North & crew were using the remote airport in Mena, Arkansas to run cocaine & guns as part of the illegal Contra resupply effort, but chose to look the other way, for whatever reason[9]. The reasons were that Bill Clinton too was an integral part of the guns and drug running of Ollie North & friends. It seems these days that cocaine & cocaine-derived campaign contributions are what fuels most politicians in D.C. & in this case, the big white line stretches all the way to Arkansas. Clinton knew and approved of the covert coke operation in his state, of the illegal arms shipments sent back down to the Contras & knew just how good that blow really was. He and his brother Roger had a nose for these things and didn't want to be left out of the action. Bill Clinton reportedly did a couple of detox stops on the way to the White House and Roger got busted for coke with Dan Lasater, one of Bill's best friends & whom Clinton later gave a full pardon.

The cocaine money was laundered through a firm set up under Clinton when he was governor called the Arkansas Development Finance Authority. This was set up to help with loans to schools and colleges in the state, but according to Larry Nichols, former director of marketing of ADFA, was actually set up to launder the millions of dollars of cocaine money coming into the state each month. (A hundred million per month coming in & out of the Mena, Arkansas airport.) From here the money went to banks connected to BCCI. The first loan ADFA was to Park-o-Meter, $2.85 million, of which nothing was paid back. In reality, the company didn't make parking meters, it was retrofitting airplane nose cones for smuggling coke into the U.S. through Mena. Another side of Iran-Contra. (See the video The Clinton Chronicles by Citizen's for Honest Government, 1-800-828-2290.)

The Iran-Contra affair itself would rest with nothing less than the truth coming out after all attempts. In November of '92, Bush pardoned former Secretary of Defense Casper Weinberger who was up on criminal charges stemming from Iran-Contra., along with three others involved. These Christmas eve pardons effectively blocked any trial testimony and notes which would have certainly implicated Bush in both the illegal arms sales to Iran and the resultant cover up. In February 1993 Iran-Contra Special Prosecutor Lawrence Walsh offered new evidence that confirmed that Vice-President Bush, SWeinberger, Attorney General Edwin Meese, National Security Adviser John Poindexter, Secretary of State George "Peanuts" Schultz, & of course Reagan himself had all participated in a shakey but till-then successful cover up. The Iran-Contra prosecutor's final report, January 18, 1994, implicated both Reagan & Bush as knowing of & condoning the illegal sales to Iran and that both had "engaged in a concerted effort to deceive Congress and the public." A cover up. Then Special Prosecutor Lawrence Walsh concluded that even so they didn't break any laws. This was totally untrue as the ban on selling arms to Iran was broken, the congressional ban on military support to the Contras was broken, perjury, obstruction of justice, & many other charges could and should have been brought against Bush and Reagan, the foremost being Treason. Instead the cover up was complete with the release of the report & the media convincing the American people that enough time (six years) and money (35 million) had been spent on this whole affair and it shouldn't be pursued further. Meanwhile, continued government drug running abounds.

The main element of Clinton's first six months in office was compromise and giving in to the powers that be. For example, his rejection of Zoë Baird as Attorney General nominee because she had ilegally employed an immigrant housekeeper, then rejecting Ms. Kimba Wood for the job because she too had a housekeeper but had paid her taxes but whose downfall had been an interview for a job with Playboy years before. Is this blatant sexism or what? Meanwhile Democratic Chaiman Ron Brown, who doubled as a lobbyist for Japan and who had not paid the slave-tax on his servants, sucked down the political plum of Secretary of Education which Big Bill let him keep because he didn't want to have to retrieve it. After all, a deal's a deal in a man's world.

His first hint of real controversy was when before his inauguration he reported that he would lift the ban on gays in the military. This freaked the right wingers right out! What could be next... The legally sanctioned right to alter one's consciousness by the ingestion of marijuana & psychedelics in the worship of God? The legalization of freedom?

Clinton fudged a bit on the gay issue. First he wanted gays to have full rights in the military, then he backed down to what amounted to putting a light bulb in their closet. He called for higher fees for cattle, timber, and mineral exploitation on government lands and backed off that one due to pressure from fat cat Western Democrats. When he tried to cut Political Action Committee funding to elected officials from $5,000 to $1,000 per person, the Democratic head of his own committee for campaign reform, who got bunches of his money from PACs, convinced him once again to back down.

Clinton also broke his very first promise to the American public in his first televised debate in Florida, which was to bring sanctions against China and refuse to renew its most-favored nation trade status unless it cleaned up its sordid human rights violations. China did not and he did not even though he delinked the topic of human rights to the stipulation.

The most prominent of Clinton scandals that wasn't sexually related was called Whitewater, after a failed Arkansas savings & loan company. Within the walls of this company went on deals which would not only profit the Clinton's personally and financially but also $12,000 of Cinton's campaign funds for governor were alleged by federal investigators to have come illegally from this institution. It, like so many other S&Ls that failed, was also involved in laundering drug money & providing huge loans to individuals to purchase weapons that went to the Contras in exchange for cocaine. According to Linda Thompson*, a $2.7 million loan was made by Webster Hubble (a creator of ADFA and later Clinton's Assistant Attorney General who resigned over Whitewater) to his son-in-law Skeeter Ward who them used the $$$ to buy bombs from a local munitions company for the Contras and shipped them out through Ollie North's network in Mena, Arkansas.

Gore, on the other hand, was known in Republican circles as "Woodsey the Al Gore" for his dangerous understanding of the environment and of the total ecological havoc humans are subjecting the Earth & themselves to. Gore, a former journalist, even wrote an excellent book about the subject.

The environment is probably the biggest area to see improvement under the Clinton/Gore administration. The EPA took significant steps to get a grip on the Department of Energy and its horrendous record with regard to its oversight of the nations nuclear installations and the public's health and safety. Clinton did, however, include a budget request of $60 million for existing and new nuclear reactors. The pattern here is obvious and the only thing we can do is once again organize and bitch when an issue comes up such as this or toxic waste incinerators.

Both Hillary and Bill had been on the board of directors of toxic waste incineration companies before assuming office as President. When it looked like a huge incinerator was going to be allowed to begin operation in Findlay, Ohio, by the federal government, after intense public sentiment against it, the White House put on hold any go ahead for 16 months & the EPA announced it was going to take a whole new look at even the benefit of the existence of toxic waste incinerators at all. Sure doesn't seem like burning that stuff's good for you.

Or burning kids in Waco, Texas, either. There's one that Big Bill wasn't ready for. Now here we have the perfect example of inept, improper, and lethal force used by the government pursuant to a crime that's not even a capital offense. The fact that this supposed wacked out religious cult had amassed weapons without paying the taxes on some I guess was a

---

* Radio interview 1-9-94 Station KGNU, Boulder.

justification for a hundred miscommanded agents of the Bureau of Alcohol, Tobacco and Firearms storming the ranch of the Branch Davidian Church in Waco, Texas, in early 1993 with the express intent of serving papers on its leader David Koresh. The ATF's goal from the start was to see that Koresh, whose followers believed him to be like Jesus Christ, got nailed to his own cross.

The raid turned ugly when the Branch Davidians turned out to have a .50-calibre semiautomatic machine gun mounted in their church tower & appeared to be not only smarter but better shots than the ATF forces. A standoff ensued but when the ATF & FBI agents got impatient after 51 days, they sent in the tanks and tear gas. After hours of pounding by tanks and armored vehicles, the structure caught fire and the church members were burned alive and perhaps shot themselves to spare themselves from the flames. Other evidence indicates that up to 30 people ran out of the burning building alive, were shot by an F.B.I. sniper team and drug back in the fire. The cause of the fire was immediately branded by the FBI as started by the "cult" members themselves in a mass suicide and had been started hours after the tanks had withdrawn. This is a lie.

The truth is, as stated by Tom Brokaw on NBC news, film footage showed spreading flames just 2 minutes 50 seconds after the tanks repeatedly rammed holes in the farm house walls & withdrew their barrels from the building. Thus, the contention by the few surviving cult members, given in independent reports, that the fire had been started by kerosene lamps used for lighting that had been knocked over by the intruding tanks is given far more credibility than any official report by the investigating fire or government agencies which followed. Other evidence surfacing since then is a videotape which many people saw live on CNN of tanks equipped with flame throwers torching the place. Linda Thompson of the American Justice Federation, is single-handedly responsible for bringing this tape to the public's attention and being shot at for it. A copy of this tape can be had for $20.00 from the American Justice Foundation, 3850 S. Emerson Ave., Indianapolis, IN 46203, and should be seen by everyone.

The cover up began immediately. Having with all probabilty caused the fire, the FBI immediately said that the "cult" had set the fire and it was David Koresh's fault for the death of 87 people, including 25 children.

This is bullshit! After attacking them with 100 cops killing church members in the initial assault then holding them in an armed standoff for a month and a half all the time buzzing the house with helicopters, spotlights, and Nancy Sinatra music at night to psyche them out and deprive them of sleep; then attacking them after vowing to "sit this one out until it's over." The FBI certainly should have seen the possibility of a mass suicide following such harassment, including cutting off their water, gas, and electricity and making them go to kerosene lamps for lighting. And if it was a mass suicide, which I highly doubt, the people inside certainly held to a higher code by taking their own lives & not coming out guns ablazing to take out a few cops with them. So who's the bad guys? Janet Reno, ill-picked bitch Attorney General with cold steel balls, will tell you the Branch Davidians were crazy, burnt themselves up, and it was herself who ok'd the flawed plan to attack and gas the place, and it was done to save the children. But wait, the next day Clinton took full responsibility for the inept and dubious scenario which so needlessly caused such carnage.*

The truth is there were no responsible decisions made by the ATF, or the FBI, or the Justice Department, or the White House at any time in this matter from day one, nor can anyone satisfactorily say why they had to move against the church on the 51st day, when the express policy had been one of negotiation not provocation following the initial assault on the Christians which had left 4 ATF agents dead at least one, if not all 4, shot by fellow agents (this was reported by Texas Rangers on the scene at the time). And why did they attack the church compound knowing that the church was heavily armed and had already been tipped off hours before the raid if they weren't out to cause a scene to kill David Koresh in the first place?

After seeing this inferno you can take the Constitution and all its guarantees say about due process, unlawful force and freedom of religion & wipe your ass with it. And that's what's wrong with this whole affair. It stinks. A bunch of macho, gun-toting, shit-for-brains at the ATF who didn't have a clue about the sensible way to handle a sensitive situation or at least arrest someone without roasting a bunch of kids to death. And that's as simple as it gets. If the issue was one of the stockpiling of illegal weapons by church members, if the issue was one of concern for reported sexual abuse of children within the church, and those were the only issues involved, then it sure was a funny way to approach the situation. But if they believed the situation was dealing with a group of people who truly believed their leader was sent by God, then, following the true Christian tradition of killing poor ignorant folk's leaders and saving them... they handled the situation perfectly. It also would serve as deterent for any other religious types that might stray from the norm.

In the wake of the debacle at Waco, Congressional investigations began, so in the words of my Representative, "we can learn a lesson from

---

* "Hey, Bungler Bill, who did you kill, who did you kill?"

all this and deal with the situation better next time." What short-term memory loss the people in power seem to have. (And obviously not from smoking pot!) This is the same lesson they so soul-searchingly pondered after Vietnam, Kent State, Jackson State, Attica State, and in every other state, so that it would never happen again. And that lesson is simply to negotiate not provovate in a touchy situation. The loss of life on either side was regrettable & unjustified in this case & in all the others and none of this would have happened if agents of the state knew in each case they couldn't get away with taking the lives of those whose political persuasions were not there own. But the agents of the state only were reaffirmed once more that if they do the intimidation and killing the politicians want done, then the politicians will cover up for them. And that's exactly what happened in Waco, Texas. Once again, the government got away with murder. In June of 1994, eight of the Branch Davidians were found guilty of manslaughter, two convicted of weapons charges, four acquitted altogether, and all acquitted of conspiracy to murder. Although these acquitals reaffirmed the legitimate use of self-defense against excessive government force the guilty were still given the maximum 40 years. The chairwoman of the jury was shocked and appalled afterwards saying that none on the jury wanted them to receive such harsh sentences. It was strange that the judge in the case would not show the jury any photos or evidence of the dead agents because he said that they were too grisly.

The Waco disaster was reminiscent of the Randy Weaver affair. In 1992 in Idaho, Weaver, an ex-Green Beret, refused to infiltrate a local white power church for the F.B.I. He was then set up by undercover agents he had met at the church years before to sell them two shotguns and sawed off the barrels for them. Weaver sawed them off illegally one-half inch too short, was issued a warrant for the offense & then, he didn't appear in court, the F.B.I. put his remote mountaintop cabin under 18 months of video surveillance them moved in force one day, ambushed the family, shot the Weaver's dog and killed Randy's son by shooting him in the back. Later an F.B.I. sniper shot Weaver, a family friend, & then blew Weaver's wife's head off as she held her baby in her arms. For the next 10 days, Weaver's two young daughters had to take care of the 18 month old baby & the two wounded men while the decaying body of their mother lay under the kitchen table. Within hours of the initial shooting the mountain was surrounded by hundreds of National Guardsmen and tanks. A stand off ensued & further bloodshed avoided when Weaver's ex-Green Beret commander intervened and Weaver surrendered. The government charged Weaver and his friend in the death of a federal agent in the original shoot out, but a jury acquitted both men of all charges except Weaver's failure to appear in court warrant. This sent a clear statement to both the government and U.S. people that self-defense in the face of excessive government force, even when serving a warrant, is an individual's right to protect themselves. Remember this.

Once he had gotten his first taste of blood Clinton became prey to what Timothy Leary once called The Curse of the Oval Room, fighting the temptation to take human life by the vast power one commands simply by being President. Clinton too had the curse. First by attacking a Somali warlord, then by bombing an Iraq intelligence building in June of 1993 for supposedly instigating a plot against ex-President Bush's life when he visited Kuwait months before. In an unbelievable defense Big Bill Clinton said he regretted the death of innocent civilians who had been killed by American ordinance but such a plot was an "attack against every American and could not go unanswered." I myself didn't feel attacked.

But I agree. He should have given the plotters all medals of valour and let it slide at that. At least an E for effort and F for failure. You'd think chopping their heads off would be good enough, but for the U.S. to bomb a purely symbolic target and again toss aside the pain and suffering of innocent people involved as a price they have to pay is faulty brain-thought. If Saddam Hussein is sending assassins out, and we must retaliate, then send some in in return.* But to kill a world-renowned sculptoress and children and like innocents, and to call that acceptable retribution destroys the last vestiges of moral self-justice that one who considers himself a liberal democrat is supposed to have. So that's the way it seems. Clinton's just another puppet on the strings of the military hoping to appease them by dropping a few bombs abroad & watching his approval ratings rise at home. It was Bush's best domestic policy. We can only hope that some of the kids that got burned up at Waco will invade Bill's dreams at night and squelch this evil curse preventing further acts of military voyeurism from occurring.

In 1993 Clinton also presided over the largest sellout of the American people to date- the North American Free Trade Agreement (NAFTA, giving the green light for American industries to race to Mexico & take advantage of the 30 cents/hr. child labor, the abolition of border tariffs & next to nonexistent pollution laws. The pollution when NAFTA was enacted was already so bad that over 50 babies had been born with no brains in the Brownsville, Texas, area which lies a death's throw from the border & the vast polluting toxically insidious U.S. industries already

---

* You'd think that if the CIA could kill John Kennedy they could get Saddam Hussein. But they couldn't even get Castro and he was only 90 miles away.

there. This was originally Bush's deal and key to the New World Order's plan on exploiting & trashing the entire planet. The NAFTA treaty was passed in a 240-189 House vote whch totally exemplified American politics as the Clinton administration openly bought votes with bribes and blackmail tactics reminiscent of the worst of political scum. And the Congress bought it. And the American people will pay for it. With lost jobs and fouler air to breath. Same with the GATT treaty.

Clinton's administration seemed plagued by indecisiveness. The Bosnian situation, for example. His reprehensible nonpolicy toward the Holocaustic genocide of the Muslims by the Serbs and Croats in former Yugoslavia also reflects this. Here the idea of Nazi death camps were revived for the purpose of ethnic cleansing while the United States and the world once again stood idly by.

Under Clinton other trappings of a police state were evident, including boot camps, more police & gun control & warrantless searches, all leading to a New World Order. Like the Orwellian Clipper chip, a surveillance device heading for all phones and computers able to monitor them at all times.

There's great danger on the horizon being orchestrated by the few to subdue the many. You should know and act against this threat. We are definitely in times of prophecy faced with the greatest threat to our lives, liberty, & pursuit of happiness. With no idea what to do with nuclear wastes (except Russia dumping 900 tons of liquid nuclear waste in one day off the coast of Japan in 1993 with plans for continual dumping for several years to come). Likewise the army now has plans to incinerate their voluminous & aging stockpile of chemical weapons over the next few years. Don't let them get away with that, especially you Vietnam and Persian Gulf vets who know the devastation of these deadly toxins. To show you how much they care, Clinton's head of the Department of Energy, Hazel O'Leary, revealled in 1994 that more than 800 secret radiation tests had been conducted on unsuspecting American citizens from the 1940's through the 80's. The parallel to Nazi Germany & their inhuman human experimentation is clear. People being injected with plutonium, even a person brought into a hospital unconscious from a car accident. Pregnant mothers were fed radium-filled cereal at government-sponsored prenatal care seminars, & some of the younger children who had accompanied their mothers there even had uranium pellets surgically implanted into their heads.

We haven't got much of a chance of survival if you look at the reality of the world around us. (You are our last chance.) How quickly the world is being devoured and devastated by these forces of evil. Yes, folks, the trumpet's at Gabriel's lips. Satan is on the loose, Revelations is on the marquee, the lights are down, the show's almost over & when the curtain falls, your fate is going to be determined by which side you're on.

What is apparent is that the world community needs to heed the grievances of their fellow planetary citizens & truly seek peaceful solutions to their problems. A switch to solar power & hemp & other renewables as well as a moratorium on chemical & nuclear weapons certainly couldn't hurt & it would be a step in the right direction for all of us.

> If only we could see thru the TV programming,
> it would be like peering through the Looking Glass
> instead of merely seeing reflections of what's been put before us.
> Try some Alice-tea.

And again that's why psychedelics & marijuana are so suppressed by the government, because they are the most effective deprogramming tools available to those seeking to free themselves from the web that's put forth as reality. Especially electoral politics. At the rate the human race has been going, I think that psychedelics, marijuana and the expanded understanding they contribute are the only real possibility we have to bring about the necessary alterations in comprehension & action which are needed on such a mass scale to save our planet and ourselves from self-annihilation. And I'm convinced that if it wasn't for the appearance of psychedelics on the scene some thirty years ago and the resultant change in consciousness this new beginning brought, that the world would have blown up by now.[10] This new awareness allowed new possibilities. One example, due mostly to Mikhail Gorbachev's radical and bold initiatives, along with Boris Yeltsin, is that the Cold War's melted, Eastern Europe is free, and the Berlin Wall has fallen. In the Soviet Union, power was turned upside down as the desire for freedom disnintegrated the U.S.S.R. in late 1991 into a complex & unstable situation with implication which only the future can tell. That's the biggest threat at the moment, all of the nuclear arms formerly held by the Soviet Union which have been sold to other countries. But still an undeniable shift has been made...

> A nice beginning.

But the beginning is not the end- just a start. The end is as near as the road leading there & the swiftness of the footsteps taken.

Which leads us to the future.

Chapter 43

And the future belongs to you. With all of its pollution, nuclear uncertainties, unswollen usurpities, & unclaimed destiny- it's yours to take by the hand and lead toward sanity.

Meditate, materialize Peace, nonviolently resist criminal authority, feed the hungry, OM intently, dose lightly.

The more people who work for Peace, the more peaceful the future will be.

You've the beauty, knowledge, strength, & goodness to do this; to not is to commit yourselves to more of the same or worse... a radioactive pall, the same never-ending emphysemic tree-eating greed, the same mind-bitten television drones never wondering if all that nitely TV violence doesn't return in the morning news.

There's a lot my friend that's left to be done.
If we survive.   If we are to survive.

And when we're done... as that long foretold final shore folds in over the immensity of it all;

When it is finished... when Destiny's door is reached, and the Emerald City is revealed as Peace, ...then we shall rest.

Then, arm in arm with those other
  Lost Angels & Dancers at the End of Time
we may all look back and see with tearstained eyes from afar-

WHAT A LONG STRANGE TRIP IT'S BEEN.

Epilogue

What the 60's revealed to me...

It's most important that history records the passing of this era with a canvas large enough to capture the aspirations, visions, accomplishments, & rainbows of those who forged together and facing impossible odds, endeavored to stick their finger in a gushing dike about as deep & wide as the Devil's Triangle.

The 60's will be recalled as the Great Awakening- an intellectual & spiritual maturation in which, largely due to the divine influence of psychedelics, the human experience was opened up to the possibility of a fuller and deeper existence. Thus a culture based upon the sane and serene principles of Peace, freedom, Love, non-violence, co-operation, compassion, happiness & being natural, came to be seen as a necessary alternative for the existing culture of war, control, hatred, violence, competition, greed, exploitation, intimidation, fear, commercialism, artificiality, contrived scarcities, & alcohol; which at best was making a grand effort at exterminating itself if not the rest of the world.

This mass change of consciousness was accompanied by further revelations on a physical & spiritual level. Enlightenment was sought.

It became understood that diet was of supreme importance to the attainment of a realized state of being and from freeing oneself from the Karmic trap of compulsive desire; that meat, white sugar, white flour, food additives, booze, coffee, cocaine, & nicotine were chemical agents of a toxic nature which were debilitating to the will, the nervous system, the health, & the Spirit. These are agents of a weakening effect upon the Self which when present in the blood stream of an individual makes it easier to be controlled by the government. They're not actually controlled substances but substances of control. That the quality of life and one's thoughts were directly linked to their chemical composition and level of toxicity at the time was a fact observable by oneself; and those truly serious about Spiritual Evolution worked first toward cleansing & gaining control of the body and then the Soul. In this way the first prerequisite for spiritual advancement was achieved which was discipline, thus leading the way for success on the further journey. And the second, weakening & Soul-binding temptations must not be given into at all costs if we are to get home. Knowledge, Discipline, and Love is the surest route.

Which is probably the greatest revelation of the 60's- the rediscovery of those overgrown yellow bricks which lead the Holy temple of the Soul back home. For with the 60's came the biggest wave of spiritual awakening that this world has ever seen, and the mysteries which had been held in the East and by the High Priests thru the ages became known to the seekers; and they too became High Priests & Priestesses in their own right. And what they learned was that yoga was the true path in this circled maze of illusion. That yoga, Kundalini Yoga, was the doorway to that orgasmic being whom we call God, and that discipline, patience, & practice were the keys to the door. A hardtrod shortcut for those who knew enough to reach for that brass ring deep inside to get off this reincarnary merry-go-round. That's what was really revealed in the 60's. God revealed Herself to those who were really looking. And will still in soft abide.

And for those who weren't looking then and aren't today, they may never know that their shoestrings were tied together thru their ears if they don't take their first step forward.

To Oz...

WHO'S WHO OF THE 60'S

Heroes

White Buffalo
Henry David Thoreau
Swami Satchidananda
Robert Kennedy
Uncle John's Band
Uncle John
Donovan
The Beatles
John Lennon
Jefferson Airplane
Jorma Kaukonen
Jack Casady-
Paul Kantner-   The Pepsi 3
Country Joe McDonald-
Robert Zimmerman
Jimi Hendrix
Joe Walsh
Les Paul
John Cipollini- unsung hero
Papa John Creach
Peter Max
Wavy Gravy- The greatest magician & rainbow maker of the 60's.
Ken Kesey
Stanley Augustus Owsley, III- Master Acid maker
William S. Burroughs
Neal Cassady & Jack Kerouac
Allen Ginsburg- The King of May
Harry Smith
Mr. Ken Nordine- The Psychedelic Dr. Seuss
Albert Hoffman- The father of L.S.D.
Gordon Wasson, Humphrey Osmond & Ralph Metzner
David Soloman, Alexander Shulgin & Stanislov Grof
The Harvard headmasters
Abbie Hoffman & The Yippies
Phillip & Daniel Berrigan & Daniel Ellsberg
Jane Fonda- Current killer of buffaloes.

The Quakers
The Diggers
Angela Davis
Ho Chi Minh
Vietnam Vets Against the War
Martin Luther King
A.J. Muste
Dick Gregory
Ron Dellums
George McGovern & Eugene McCarthy
George Wald- an excellent & compassionate man to lead this land.
David Dellinger- the same can be said of David.
Saul Alinski
William O. Douglas
Ralph Nader
Gore Vidal- should lead the world for civilization's advancement.
I.F. Stone
Buckminster Fuller
Harvey Wasserman & Howard Zinn
Phillip K. Dick- read his book *Ubik,* for sure.
Harlan Ellison
Edward Abbey
J.R.R. Tolkien
John Brunner- read *The Sheep Look Up*
Alan Harrington- read *The Revelations of Dr. Modesto*
Hunter S. Thompson & Larry Flint
Captain Kangaroo
Walt Kelly & Pogo
Odd Bodkins
Wonder Wart Hog
Cheech Wizard & Vaughn Bodé
Berke Breathed- a breath of fresh air.
Doonesbury
Patrick McGoohan- *The Prisoner*- he'll always be #1
Elvis (Elvis' pelvis did as much to loosen the youth up at the time as the Beat thing. Elvis set the stage for the floor-shaking 60's.)
Robert Anton Wilson
Rainbow Family
Daniel Sheehan & the Christic Institute
Phillip Agee & John Stockwell
Noam Chomsky & Alexander Cockburn & Helen Caldicott
Gary Null
Weird Norman

Martyrs

JFK
RFK
RFK's son David
MLK
MLK's mother
John Lennon
Abbie Hoffman
Norm Morrison
Sandy Schuer
Jeffrey Miller
Allison Krause
Bill Schroeder
Fred Hampton
George & Jonathon Jackson
Medgar Evers
Andrew Goodman
James Chaney
Michael Schwerner
Malcom X
Che Gueverra
Salvador Allende
Benjamin Linder
Bobby Sands
Steve Biko
Victor Jara
Norman Mayer
Karen Silkwood
Mae Brussell
Lenny Bruce
Phil Ochs
Jim Morrison
Tim Buckley
Nick Drake
Roy Buchanan
Tom Forcade
Richard Brautigan
Wilhelm Reich
Nikola Tesla

Villains

RMN
RWR-666
Agnew
Hoover
Mitchell
Kissinger
Westmoreland & Calley
Colby & Helms
Evil James Angleton
Bush-667
James Watt (If raping the Earth makes one a motherfucker, then history will record Watt, Reagan's former Secretary of the Interior, as one of the biggest motherfuckers in the world.)
Elliott Abrams- A 60's villain in the 80's
Donald Gregg-   Ditto
Rob Owen-   Ditto ditto
Ed the Sleaze Meese
G.G. Liddy
Wrongway North
Harry J. Anslinger (The man who made marijuana illegal.)
Bob Dole (Watch out for Bob; he can be a vicious dog.)

Sellouts

Jann Wenner
Jerry Rubin
Patty Hearst
Dave Mason (The first rock guitarist I saw on a beer commercial.)
Gregg Allman (He made "the junkie's choice"- see page 205.)
Michael "Whiter than thou" Jackson (He was never in to sell out but he did the best he could. Don't let him touch your Elephant, Man.)
Bill Graham ("The Grinch who stole Rock & Roll.")
Bill Cosby "Cosby can't make up his mind whether he's a black militant or a white millionaire." Phil Spector, *Rolling Stone, 1969.*

Nightmares

Michael Falzarano- Jorma's 3rd arm, polluter & ruin of Hot Tuna.

OM CIRCLE
FOR WORLD PEACE

The OM Circle is an ancient & sacred method of channeling peaceful healing energy to the inhabitants of Earth & to the planet itself. Like [pra]yer & meditation, OMing follows the Universal Principle that Energy [foll]ows Thought, & that willed thought & chanting can actually material[ize] Peace on the planet & physically heal the Earth.

OM is the God-sound of the Universe, the composite of the sounds of [all] substances in creation vibrating together. OMing acts in restoring the [vita]lity & balance of the natural electromagnetic field (the aura) around [li]ving object (be it the human body or the Earth) which has been [env]ironmentally distorted & shorted out from the effects of television, [ele]ctrical lines, radar, radioactive fallout from nuclear testing and acci[den]ts, metal-bearing air pollutants, stress, & violence. OMing cleanses the [bod]y by resonating the God-vibration thruout itself, thus temporarily [rais]ing its own vibratory rate to a higher level, clearing the mind & the [eth]eric channels. OM circles have been in use for thousands of years, are [qui]te effective, & have been holding the world together in ways unseen & [uns]ung save by those who know & participate. And today, more than [any]time on earth, the healing & Peace-bringing powers of the OM Circle [are] greatly needed.

In this time of need come OM for Peace.

FOOTNOTES

Chapter 3
1. Comedian Lenny Bruce was crucified for defending the First Amendment. Bruno was burned at the stake for declaring the truth of the world revolving around the sun. Galileo was put under house arrest for the last ten years of his life for espousing and failing to renounce the same theory. Wilhelm Reich was a brilliant cosmic energy scientist who was persecuted and died in jail for his beliefs in the United States.
2. William Morris along with other members of their organization called The Brotherhood, (the pre-Raphaelite painters Gabraeli Rossetti & Edward Burne Jones included), led the 19th century artists revolt against the Industrial Revolution at its early beginnings. Seeing that greed & industrialization had lead to a cheapening of spiritual values at the severe cost of the loss of quality of life, (stress, pollution, the reduction of the human being to a unit of work), they withdrew to the medieval city of Oxford and produced works of art & decor that harkened to an era more simple & pure and they politically & artistically tried to preserve the sanity of the world which they saw being raped by the nature of industrialization. Percy Bysshe Shelley was a utopian socialist who along with his wife had a commune at times, and being at political odds with the government was harrassed as such. Clark Ashton Smith (1893-1961) was a brilliant bohemian writer whose poem "The Hashish Eater" is an exquisite example of his skill & mastery of high fantasy.

Chapter 9
1. JFK did his fair amount of drugs in the White House. Not only did he partake in marijuana, L.S.D., cocaine, and hashish as related by Judith Campbell and Mary Pinchot Meyer, but he also was the nation's first president known to mainline speed. Check this out. In the latter part of 1960, before he had won the presidency, JFK began receiving treatments by Dr. Max Jacobson known to wealthy celebrities as "Dr. Feelgood." Now Dr. Feelgood made you feel just that- real good. Real good. His injections of amphetamines mixed with vitamins, steroids, live animal cells, and other goodies, made his clients feel so good that they wouldn't come down for three days. Full of vigor, euphoria, energy and enthusiasms just like the old JFK we all loved and remembered. But the crash was bad. JFK and Jackie had both developed a strong dependency on speed by the summer of 1961. And the shots continued sometimes three or four a week until the

end of his presidency. JFK took Jacobson with him when he traveled to Europe and also tried to get him to move into the White House. Of course. Speed's not the best thing for a person to be taking, especially that way. But burn and learn, an old drug-related adage, somewhat akin to stick to the weed. Information on Dr. Feelgood comes from *A Question of Character: A Life of John F. Kennedy*, Prima Publications., Rockland, CA, 1992, pp. 295-297.

2. For historical purposes it should be noted that the late Texas billionaire H.L. Hunt has been mentioned in many corners of the JFK assassination researchers & theorists ring as bankrolling the Kennedy hit. Hunt's money, the mob ties, & C.I.A. & Cuban exiles hit squad. Even a major movie on the lines of the JFK killing was made called Executive Action which suggested the same scenario with the President and immediate witnesses murdered.

Chapter 10

1. Marvin Miller, *The Breaking of a President: The Nixon Connection*, pp. 331, 364. All told the mob contributed $1,580,000 to Nixon's campaigns over the years according to Jim Keith in *The Gemstone File*.

2. *The Breaking of a President*, page 10, "Also there are some peculiar connections between participants in the original Watergate burgulary and the assassination of President Kennedy. Frank Sturgis, alias Frank Forini, for example was investigated during the assassination of J.F.K. and is also one of the Watergate burgulars."

According to testimony by Marita Lorentz before the House Assassinations Committee and to the press, it was elements of the same squad of mafia-backed C.I.A. and Cuban exile hit men who had been mutually recruited to kill Fidel, who had later knocked off JFK. She should know. She was Castro's mistress who had actually worked with Frank Sturgis on trying to bump him off. But that didn't work. So they decided to bump JFK off, make it look like Castro did it, and invade Cuba if they could. She named Frank Sturgis, Lee Harvey Oswald, E. Howard Hunt, Orlando Bosch, Ignacio & Guiellermo Novo, Pedro Diaz Lanz, & Gerry Patrick Hemming as the group who did John Kennedy in. Oswald, of course, was the patsy. Sturgis & Hunt would be later caught at Watergate, and Sturgis & Hemming would later be employed as representatives of a weapons company specializing in assassination equipment. They should know.

When the Kennedy assassination did not bring the imminent invasion of Cuba, Orlando Bosch & the Novo brothers kept up their terrorist activities. In 1967 they formed Cuba Power to further co-ordinate their efforts and in 1968 Bosch was given 10 years for shooting a bazooka at a

What a Long Strange Trip It's Been

Polish cargo ship in the Miami harbor. Released in 1972 he was arrested in Venezuela in 1974 for blowing up the Cuban Embassy there, but the C.I.A. & State Department saw to it that the charges were dropped. In March 1976 Bosch was arrested in Costa Rica after Frank Sturgis notified authorities of Bosch's plans to assassinate Secretary of State Henry Kissinger on a state visit. He was arrested then deported. He then masterminded the hit on former Chilean Foreign Minister Orlando Letelier who was blown up in his car just blocks from the White House in September of 1976. It was this hit which would send the Novo brothers to jail on murder indictments, but Bosch kept on until October 1976 when he was arrested for planning the bombing of a Cubana Airliner which had exploded in flight and killed 73 persons. Bosch was arrested in Venezuela, found guilty & jailed there. But none of them, although questioned about it, have ever been charged with the killing of JFK.

So it was Marita Lorentz, who had both known and worked with some of these same people, who placed Howard Hunt, Frank Sturgis, Bosch, the Novos, Pedro Diaz Lanz, & Gerry Hemming in two cars traveling from Miami to Dallas the weekend immediately before the assassination.

This information culminated from research and articles done by A.J. Weberman, Dana Beal, & others and originally printed in the *Yipster Times*. It was later compiled in a Yippie book *Blacklisted News: Secret Histories from Chicago '68 to 1984.* of which pages 123-135 were especially pertinent. Probably the book to read is A.J. Weberman & Michael Canfield's *Coup d'etat in America*. Activist Dick Gregory also was instrumental in 1975 in bringing to public attention photographs of two men whom he tentatively identified as Hunt & Sturgis who were dressed as bums and immediately after the shooting were led away from the grassy knoll area by police, supposedly to be booked on vagrancy charges but in fact safely escorted from the scene of the crime, with no record extant except for the photos. I bet Lee Harvey Oswald thought he was going to make a clean getaway too.

3. Frank J. Donner, *Age of Surveillance* (Alfred A. Knopf), p. 255.

Chapter 11

1. *Blacklisted News: Secret Histories from Chicago '68 to 1984* (Bleeker Press), p. 446.

2. LBJ may have been haunted by his war-related killings as the President insisted that the Holy Ghost visited him during the early morning hours when he received his daily briefings on Vietnam. He reportedly asked one ambassador if he thought God was making earthly visits. This further supports the contention made by an ex-aide that Johnson's "world started slipping from his control" and that he "had

become a very dangerous man." *The Denver Post*, August 19, 1988.

3. James Deakin, *Smiling Through the Apocaplypse: The Dark Side of LBJ*, p. 513.

Chapter 13

1. Marc Riboud & Philippe Devillers, *The Face of North Vietnam* (Holt Paperback, 1970).

Chapter 14

1. Members of the French intelligence blew up the environmental group Greenpeace's ship The Rainbow Warrior and killed a Greenpeace photographer in the process when the ship was protesting French nuclear bomb testing the Pacific Ocean in the 1980s.

2. *The Face of North Vietnam*.

3. William L. O'Neill, *Coming Apart: An Informal History of America in the 1960s* (New York: Quadrangle/New York Times Books), p. 132.

4. One thing revealed in the unravlings of Watergate was the fact that Howard Hunt had "doctored" some State Department cablegrams to make it look like JFK had ordered the death of South Vietnamese President Diem.

Chapter 18

1. *Acid Dreams*, p. 271.

Chapter 19

1. Dr. John Beresford, "Introduction," in *The Psychedelic Encyclopedia*, by Peter Stafford (San Francisco: And/Or Press 1977) and "Who Turned Who On," *High Times*, Oct. 1977, p. 41.

2. This came from an article entitled "The Killing of Robert Kennedy" by William McGaw & Thomas G. Whittle which appeared in the January 1986 issue of *Freedom* magazine, pp. 4-14.

This same information in expanded detail is found in the excellent book *The Assassination of Robert F. Kennedy* by William Turner & John G. Christian (New York: Random House 1978).

Also the book *Coroner* by Dr. Thomas Noguchi who did the autopsy on RFK also affirms that Kennedy was shot from the rear and not from the front where Sirhan Sirhan was.

3. *The Assassination of RFK* by Turner/Christian, p. 216. It should also be noted that Jerry Owens was close friends with Artie Bremer's sister, who worked for Owens's brother for eight years before her brother Artie shot presidential contendor George Wallace. Now you don't have to wonder where they get these "lone, crazed assassins."

Chapter 22

1. *Blacklisted News*, p. 337.

2. Frank J. Donner, *The Age of Surveillance: The Aims and Methods of*

America's Political Intelligence System (New York: Alfred J. Knopf), p. 215.

3. Jay Pound, "Who told the Truth about JFK?", *Critique*, Spring/Summer 1986, p. 81.

4. Martin Lee & Bruce Shlain, *Acid Dreams: The C.I.A., L.S.D. & the 60s Rebellion*, p. 85-86.

5. This information was read in an article entitled "Jonestown—C.I.A. Assassinations, Drugs & Mind Control", by John Judge wich appeared in the Spring/Summer 1986 issue of the journal *Critique*.

6. Donner, The Age of Surveillance, p. 237.

Chapter 23

1. Aryeh Neier, "Surveillance as Censorship", *UnAmerican Activities: The Campaign Against the Underground Press*, ed. Geoffrey Rips, p. 11.

2. Ibid, p. 160.

3. *UnAmerican Activities: The Campaign Against the Underground Press.*

4. *Blacklisted News*, p. 433.

5. Neier, "Surveillance as Censorship", *UnAmerican Activities: The Campaign Against the Underground Press*, p. 9.

6. Pound, "Who Told the Truth About JFK?", p. 87.

Chapter 26

1. *Prairie Fire: The Political Statement of the Weather Underground*, p. 65.

2. *Blacklisted News*, p. 149

Chapter 29

1. *The Sixties*, Rolling Stone Press., p.266.

2. Dougan & Lipsman, *The Vietnam Experience: A Nation Divided*, p. 136.

Chapter 31

1. Quotes appeared in the press and Peter Davies' *The Truth About Kent State*, pp. 21-22.

2. *The Movement Toward a New America* (Pilgrim Press, 1970), p. 594

Chapter 32

1. Miller, *The Breaking of a President*, p. 361.

2. *Blacklisted News*, p. 337.

3. Groden and Livingston, *High Treason*, Conservatory Press, 1989.

4. *Blacklisted News.*

5. Miller, *The Breaking of a President*, p. 10.

6. *Blacklisted News*, p. 350, & Miller, *The Breaking of the President*, p. 10-11.

Chapter 33

1. Miller, *The Breaking of a President*, pp 508-518.

2. Ibid., p. 11.

3. Ibid., p. 397.
Chapter 35
1. Miller, *The Breaking of a President*, p. 674.
Chapter 36
1. *Blacklisted News*, p. 465.
Chapter 37
1. Miller, *The Breaking of a President*, p. 677.
Chapter 38
1. Andreas, *The Incredible Rocky*, p. 16 & 17.
2. *Blacklisted News*, pp. 111 & 113.
3. Ibid. Also information by Robert A. Manning, "The Making of a President: How David Rockefeller Created Jimmy Carter," *Penthouse*, n.d..
4. William Randolph Hearst, grandfather of Patricia, is the perfect example of an American corporate scumbag who raped this nation and helped deprive all Americans of the truth & their full rights & got away with murder. Owning the Hearst newspaper chain, he was the pioneer of yellow journalism; reporting his sole intent was to create and perpetuate racism against Blacks, Hispanics, and Orientals to keep the white elite in power in America by causing dissension among and repression of these minorities. Hearst was instrumental in making marijuana illegal because he wanted to protect the monopoly he had built over the timber & paper industry and feared competition from hemp. So he peddled the story of the hopped up Black men who raped white women while high on pot. Hearst also shot in the head and killed Hollywood director Thomas Ince, mistaking him from the back for Charlie Chaplin who was fooling around with actress Marion Davies, Hearst's girlfriend. The press originally reported that Ince was shot then, of course, changed their story and said Ince had died of indigestion on Hearst's yacht. Indigestion of the head. This story can be found in the excellent book *Hollywood Babylon*, by Kenneth Anger.
Chapter 39
1. A pre-election drug bust of members of the Allman Brothers family almost caused Carter not to be elected. This was the infamous case of Gregg Allman narking on his road manager Scooter Herrring, with Herring receiving a 75-year sentence. The inside story (according to current Allman Bros. road manager Kirk West in a personal interview 6/18/94) is as follows:

Once Macon druggist Joe Fuchs got caught by an anonymous tip freely supplying Scooter Herring with pharmaceutical coke for Gregg in Feb. '76, Fuchs was sentenced to 10 years (6 of which he served). Fuchs told all

What a Long Strange Trip It's Been

he could to involve Scooter, Gregg, and Phil Walden, head of Capricorn Records. The Allman Bros. had raised a million dollars for the Carter campaign when it was desperately broke in a series of benefit concerts in which Capricorn Records matched dollar for dollar all proceeds brought in over a 4-month period of shows. This bust was naturally the green light for the Republicans to tie Jimmy Carter's presidential campaign to cocaine money, which the Justice Department quickly began to do. Knowing that all this was going down, and with only months to the election, there was a meeting between Scooter, Gregg, Phil Walden, and their lawyers. In order to save the Carter campaign from going under, Scooter willingly took the rap (which included two grams being sold out of Capricorn's offices) and got the maximum penalty of 75 years, which automatically set his case up for appeal in 6 months (which otherwise could have taken years). After serving 6 months, he spent another 6 months in rehab and was set free. Meanwhile, Capricorn Records bought Scooter a new home worth several hundred thousand dollars & once out Gregg set him up with several tour busses which he and other rock bands leased from Scooter for the next 5 years. Transcripts of the trial show that Gregg made, in West's words, "the junkie's choice," receiving immunity for his testimony against Scooter as did Phil Walden, head of Capricorn Records. Once out, Scooter became the road manager of the Allman split-off band Sea Level. Capricorn Records cut away Gregg and 18 months later the Allman Brothers Band was back together with Scooter back in the family and Gregg having himself & bad press to live with to this day.

I must say that this hardly lets Gregg totally off the hook, but it was Scooter who said that he would willingly "take the heat" and he was well taken care of. Gregg, an immense junkie at the time of the grand jury investigation and the subsequent trial, could have gone down too & probably should have (public outcry and the justice system not wanting to create a rock star martyr would probably have minimized his sentence). At any rate that was the deal and one thing's for sure - it did save Jimmy Carter's presidential bid and gave us at least for four years the only decent presidential leader we have seen since John F. Kennedy. And last heard, the Allman Brothers Band were back together as a kickass band. Gregg totally clean & Dickey Betts playing some of the best mushroom-inspired leads I've ever heard. An excellent comeback.

John Phillips of the Mamas & Papas, however, went a bit further when caught for his pharmaceutical misadventures by not only narking but immediately turning anti-drug zealot & showed up on every TV talk show this side of needle park with his daughter Mackenzie preaching the evils of drugs. For his sellout efforts he got 30 days, 5 years probation, and a chance to do 250 more hours of public drug repentence in the year to come. How's your joints taste today, Papa John?

2. The Other Americas Radio, "The October Surprise," cassette documentary tape.

Chapter 40

1. Miller, *The Breaking of a President,* p. 403.

2. Empowerment Project, "Cover Up: Behind the Iran-Contra Affair," documentary film.

Chapter 41

1. It was under the evil genius of Allen Dulles (Director 1952-1961) that the C.I.A. moved from its outlined realm of quiet intelligence gathering into the murky realms of assassination, espionage, and most importantly counter-insurgency programs designed to assure the U.S. complete control over a growing string of third world countries whose mineral wealth and natural resources was desired by the ravenous corporate appetite. This was done by circumventing the legal limitations in place and attaining the power & authority necessary to carry out special operations. Thru Special Operations it was possible to subvert governments in secret and continue the Military Industrial Complex's plan of world domination. By 1954 there were almost no restrictions on the C.I.A.'s operations, Dulles having been able to limit the operational control the National Security Council had over the C.I.A. He was also instrumental in placing C.I.A. agents & their allies inconspicuously throughout the many levels of government, the military, the media, and the business & academic community both at home and abroad, in a calculated and long range bid which would make it possible for the C.I.A. to have the power & resources to carry out any operation it wished. The C.I.A.'s power grew so large that with the assassination of John F. Kennedy it successfully took over the reins of power of the U.S. government, and thru General Maxwell Taylor's philosophical & informational manipulation of L.B.J. was able to ensure that the U.S. moved deeper and deeper into Vietnam; thus ensuring a high economic income to those corporations supplying the military, plus an unending cash flow to the military itself with which to continue the colonialistic & expansionist policies it carried out in the name of fighting Communism.

It was Allen Dulles who with his brother among others, had fostered and preached the post WWII doctrine of containment which led to the creation of the C.I.A. in 1947 and its early targeting of the Soviet Union.

This is where one of our best chances for world peace was blown. After WWII President Truman abolished the O.S.S. (forerunner to the C.I.A.) and deactivated the military as swiftly as possible. The Secretary of State was calling for peace with the world and with the Russian people who had fought beside us in crushing Hitler's war machine and whose country had suffered far greater destruction than ours in the war. And in 1946 the United Nations was formed in order to provide a forum with which to hopefully prevent future wars.

But Peace was only beginning to awaken when those militaristic paranoids convinced Truman that the possibility of the Soviet Union attaining the atomic bomb made them & Communism the supreme enemy of the Universe and that the proper stance towards them should not be one of peaceful co-existence, but one of a Cold War. No wonder the world today's held in the grip's of nuclear terror when for the last 45 years our aim has not been on Peace, but on continually escalating military budgets & actions and ensuring that Peace doesn't happen. For Peace is bad for business. Thus for America's wartime footing to continue in "peacetime", a cold war had to be invented and a constant threat (whether real or imaginary) identified & pursued. In this case Communism. It was Allen Dulles who helped raise the spectre of the Cold War and thru its self-created presence was able to multiply the power & authority of the C.I.A. in the years he was its director from 1952-1961, when he was fired by President Kennedy for lying to him.

2. Alan Nairn, *Colorado Daily* (May 4, 1984), p. 10.

3. Elliott Abrams, former Assistant Secretary of State for Latin American Affairs, who reportedly lied to Congress and the American media about the illegalities and atrocities being committed by the American government. in Latin America. Elliott's all for the "Kill A Commie A Day For Christ Crusade" and was pivotal in executing American Terror Politics in the region. The National Reporter dubbed him "Beasty Boy" and quoted him as saying "the purpose of our aid is to permit people on our side to use more violence." As the Reporter said, "Once in a while even Elliott Abrams strays into telling the truth." They also noted the Abrams career is involved in the promotion of murderous violence. *The National Reporter*, Vol 10, number 4 & volume 11, number 1, p. 64. In the fall of 1991 Abrams pleaded guilty to 2 criminal charges of withholding information from Congress about the contras.

4. John Hogue, *Nostrodamus and the Millenium*, pp. 114-117.

Chapter 42

1. Norman Aikens, "Oliver's Twists," *Rolling Stone*, July 16 - July 30, 1987, p. 104. Also, *Brought to Light*, p. 13, Eclipse Books, Forestville, CA.

2. Perhaps corrupt politicians should follow the lead of R. Bud Dwyer.

3. It was the downing in Nicaragua of a C.I.A. supply plane & the capture of American Eugene Hasenfus which initially revealed the exist-

ence of illegal aid to the Contras. Hasenfus was carrying George Bush's office card and phone number on him at the time.

4. Mark Green & Gail McCoy, *Ronald Reagan's Reign of Error*, p. 104.

5. Ibid., cover.

6. Ibid., p. 71. "Is it news that some fellow out in South Succotach someplace has just been laid off?" President Ronald Reagan, March 16, 1982.

7. From *Blacklisted News, The Secret Histories*: "The pharmaceutical executives & government agents who flooded Miami, Columbus and other freek scenes with sopors [downers] as a riot control technique knew what they were doing. I understand that 10,000 ludes hit Columbus days before the Yippies' first anti-McDonalds action where 500 showed but no more than 10 of us could stand up." p. 354.

Fact. The government used to flood the campuses with downers in the spring to cut student activism. I saw this firsthand at Kent State.

8. A perfect example is Operation Greensweep of August 1990 in Northern California. This government operation violated civil rights and represents the first time the army was used against its own citizens within the borders of the United States. Headed by the Bureau of Land management, this operation netted the paltry fruits of only 28 hemp gardens, cost $700,000 and resulted in a class-action law suit against the government for illegal search and detention.

9. *High Times*, May 1992.

10. L.S.D. was first synthesized in 1936. Its hallucinogenic properties weren't discovered until 1943, the same time as the development of the first atomic bomb. This wasn't a cosmic coincidence; it was meant to be. Only awareness can prevent nuclear devastation.

Author's All-Time Favorite Political Quote:
"That Bitch set me up!" -Marion Berry, mayor of Washington, D.C., as D.E.A. and F.B.I. agents ran in from the adjoining motel room, wrestled the crack pipe from his hands and, twisting his arms behind his back, put on the cuffs.

Bibliography

American Friends Service Committee. *The Police Threat to Political Liberty.* Philadelphia: American Friends Service Committee, 1979.

Andreas, Joel. *The Incredible $Rocky$ vs. The Power of the People!* New York: NACL, 1973. 151 West 19th Street, New York 10011.

Beckett, and Murray. *Government Lawlessness in America.* New York: Oxford Press, 1971.

Braden, William. *The Private Sea: LSD and the Search for God.* New York: Bantam, 1968.

Brunner, John. *The Sheep Look Up.* New York: Ballentine Books 1972.

Cook, Bruce. *The Beat Generation.* New York: Charles Scribner's Sons, 1971.

Cooney, Robert. *The Power of the People.* Philadelphia: New Society, 1987.

Copeland, Alan, ed. *People's Park.* New York: Farrar, Strauss, Giroux, 1973.

Davis, Angela. *If They Come in the Morning.* New York: Bantam, 1971.

Del Tredici, Robert. *The People of Three Mile Island.* San Francisco: Sierra Club Books, 1980.

Dobrovir, William; Gephardt, Joseph; Buffone, Samuel; and Oakes, Andra. *The Offenses of Richard M. Nixon: A Guide to His Impeachable Crimes.* New York: Quadrangle/ New York Times Book Co., 1974.

Donner, Frank J. *The Age of Surveillance: The Aims and Methods of America's Political Intelligence System.* New York: Alfred A. Knopf, 1980.

Dougan, Clark, and Lipsman, Samuel. *The Vietnam Experience: A Nation Divided.* Boston: Boston Publishing Co., 1984.

Esler, Anthony. *Bombs, Beards and Barricades: 150 Years of Youth in Revolt.* New York: Stein and Day, 1971.

Fairfield, Dick, ed. *The Modern Utopia Community.* New York: Penguin Books, 1971.

Foner, Phillip, ed. *The Black Panthers Speak.* New York: J.B. Lippincott Co., 1970.

Forcade, Tom. *Underground Press Anthology.* Ace, 1972.

Freedom. North Star Publishing, January 1986.

Furst, Peter. *Hallucinogens and Culture.* Chandler, 1988.

Ginsberg, Allen. *Howl.* San Francisco: City Lights Books, 1956.

Glessing, Robert. *The Underground Press in America.* Indiana University Press, 1970.

Gold, Robert. *The Rebel Culture.* New York: Dell, 1970.

Goodman, Mitchell, ed. *The Movement Toward a New America: The Begin-*

nings of a Long Revolution. New York: Alfred Knopf, Inc., 1970.
Green, Mark, and McCall, Gail. *Ronald Reagan's Reign of Error*. New York: Pantheon Books, 1983.
Groden, Robert, and Livingstone, Harrison. *High Treason: The Assassination of President Kennedy and the New Evidence of Conspiracy*. Baltimore, MD: Conservatory Press, 1989.
Hayes, Harold. *Smiling Through the Apocalypse: Esquire's History of the Sixties*. New York: McCall Publishing Co., 1969.
Heinlein, Robert. *Stranger in a Strange Land*. New York: Berkeley Medallion Books, 1961.
High Times 50th anniversary of LSD issue. June 1993.
Hilgartner, Bell, and O'Connor. *Nukespeak*. San Francisco: Sierra Club Books, 1982.
Hoffman, Albert. *LSD: My Problem Child*. New York: St. Martin's Press, 1983.
Hoffman, Abbie. *Woodstock Nation*. New York: Vintage Books, 1971.
Hoffman, Abbie. *Square Dancing in the Ice Age*. New York: G.P. Putnam and Sons, 1982.
Hoffman, Abbie. *Soon to be a Major Motion Picture*. New York: G.P. Putnam and Sons, 1980.
Hoffman, Abbie, and Silvers, John. *Steal This Urine Test: Fighting Drug Hysteria in America*. New York: Penguin Books, 1987.
Hogue, John. *Nostradamus & the Millennium*. New York: Dolphin/ Doubleday, 1987.
Hollingshead, Michael. *The Man Who Turned on the World*. New York: Abelard Schuman, 1974.
Hopkins, Jerry. *The Hippie Papers*. New York: Signet, 1968.
Huxley, Aldous. *The Doors of Perception*. New York: Harper and Row, 1954.
Huxley, Aldous. *Island*. New York: Harper & Row, 1962.
Huxley, Aldous. *Moksha: Writings on Psychedelics and the Visionary Experience*. Los Angeles: J.P. Tarcher, Inc., 1977.
Kelly, Walt. *We Have Met the Enemy and He Is Us*. New York: Simon and Schuster, 1972.
Kerouac, Jack. *On the Road*. New York: Signet Press/Viking Press, 1955.
Kerouac, Jack. *Dharma Bums*. New York: Signet Books/Viking Press., 1958.
Kerouac, Jack. *The Subterraneans*. New York: Grove Press, 1958.
Kleps, Art. *Millbrook: The True Story of the Early Years of the Psychedelic Revolution*. Oakland, CA: Bench Press, 1975.
Kornbluth, Jesse. *Notes from the New Underground*. 1968.
Leary, Timothy. *The Politics of Ecstacy*. New York: Putnam and Sons, 1968.

Leary, Timothy. *Confessions of a Hope Fiend.* New York: Bantam Books, 1973.
Leary, Timothy. *The Curse of the Oval Room.* High Times Press, 1974.
Leary, Timothy. *Jail Notes.* New York: Grove Press, 1970.
Leary, Timothy. *Flashbacks: An Autobiography.* Los Angeles: J.P. Tarcher Press, 1984.
Lee, Martin, and Shlain, Bruce. *Acid Dreams: The C.I.A., L.S.D., and the Sixties Rebellion.* New York: Grover Press, 1985.
Lesberg, Sandy. *Assassination in Our Time.* London: Peebles Press International, 1976.
Lipton, Lawrence. *The Holy Barbarians.* New York: Julian Messner, 1959.
Mailer, Norman. *Miami and the Seige of Chicago.* New York: Signet Books, 1968.
Miller, Marvin. *The Breaking of a President: The Nixon Connection.* Corvina, CA: Classic Productions, 1975.
Moore, Alan. *V for Vendetta.* Forestville, CA: Eclipse Books, 1988. READ.
Newfild, Jack. *A Prophetic Minority.* New York: Signet, 1968.
Noguchi, Thomas. *Coroner.* New York: Simon and Schuster, 1983.
O'Neill, William L. *Coming Apart: An Informal History of America in the 1960's.* New York: Quadrangle/New York Times Book Co., 1976.
Obst, Linda, ed. *The Sixties.* New York: Rolling Stone Press/Random House, 1977.
Perry, Charles. *The Haight-Ashbury: A History.* New York: Rolling Stone Press, 1984.
Pichaske, David. *A Generation In Motion: Popular Music and Culture in the Sixties.* New York: MacMillan Publishing Co., 1979.
Pound, Jay. "Who Told the Truth About JFK?" *Critique: A Journal of Conspiracies and Metaphysics.* Spring/Summer 1986. Critique Publishing, P.O. Box 11451, Santa Rosa, CA 95406.
Prouty, L. Fletcher. *The Secret Team: The C.I.A. and It's Allies in Control of the United States and the World.* Englewood, NJ: Prentice-Hall, 1973.
Riboud, Marc and Devillers, Philippe. *The Face of North Vietnam.* New York: Holt, Rhinehart, and Winston, 1970.
Rips, Geoffrey. *UnAmerican Activities: The Campaign Against the Underground Press.* San Francisco: City Lights Books, 1981.
Rolling Stone, ed. *The Age of Paranoia.* New York: Pocket Books, 1972.
Rubin, Jerry. *Do It!: Scenarios of the Revolution.* New York: Simon and Schuster, 1970.
Rubin, Jerry. *We Are Everywhere.* New York: Harper Colophon Books, 1971.
Sale, Kirkpatrick. *SDS.* New York: Random House, 1973.

Satchidananda, Swami. *Beyond Words*. Drawings by Peter Max. New York: Holt, Rhinehart, and Winston, 1977.

Satchidananda, Swami. *Integral Hatha Yoga*. New York: Holt, Rhinehart, and Winston, 1970.

Satchidananda, Swami. *To Know Your Self*. New York: Anchor Books/Doubleday, 1988.

Schultes and Hoffman. *Plants of the Gods: Their Sacred Healing and Hallucinogenic Powers*. Atrium Publications, 1992.

Scott, Peter Dale; Hoch, Paul; and Stettler, Russell. *The Assassinations, Dallas & Beyond*. Vintage Books, 1976.

Shapiro, Harry. *Waiting for the Man: The Story of Drugs & Popular Music*. New York: William Morrow, 1988.

Shulgin, Alexander. *Phikal*. Transform Press, 1991.

Sinclair, John. *Guitar Army*. New York Douglas Book Corporation, 1972.

Snyder, Don. *Aquarian Odyssey*. New York: Liveright, 1979.

Stafford, Peter. *Psychedelics Encyclopedia*. Berkeley: Ronin Press, 1992.

Stausbaugh, J. *Drug User*. Blast Books, 1990.

Stevens, Jay. *Storming Heaven: LSD and the American Dream*. Perrenial, 1988.

Thompson, Hunter S. *Fear and Loathing on the Campaign Trail 1972*. Warner Publications, 1972.

Trumbo, Dalton. *Johnny Got His Gun*. New York: Bantam, 1970.

Turner, William; Christian, John. *The Assassination of Robert F. Kennedy*. New York: Random House 1978.

Unger, Irwin. *The Movement: A History of the American New Left, 1959-1972*. New York: Harper and Row Publishers, 1974.

Vankin, Jonathon. *Conspiracies, Cover Ups and Crimes*. Pargon House, 1991.

Watts, Alan. *The Joyous Cosmology: Adventures in the Chemistry of Consciousness*. New York: Vintage, 1962.

Weather Underground. *Prairie Fire: The Political Statement of the Weather Underground*. San Francisco: Communications Co., 1974.

White, John. *Kundalini Evolution and Enlightenment*. Anchor, 1979.

Wolfe, Tom. *The Electric Kool-Aid Acid Test*. New York: Bantam Books, 1968.

Wyden, Peter. *Bay of Pigs: The Untold Story*. New York: Simon and Schuster, 1979.

Yablonsky, Lewis. *The Hippie Trip*. Western Publishing Co., 1968.

Youth International Party. *Blacklisted News: Secret Histories from Chicago '68 to 1984*. New York: Bleeker Publishing, P.O. Box 392 Canal Street Station, New York 10012.

Miller, Henry. *The Air-Conditioned Nightmare.* New York: New Directions, 1975. I especially urge you to read this book. It is America at its truest by perhaps the greatest American writer of times.

Webster's Dictionary: <u>Television</u>-*Idiot box*

Hendrix, Jimi. *Electric Ladyland.* Polydor Records.
Jefferson Airplane. *After Bathing at Baxter's.* RCA Records.
Jefferson Airplane. *Volunteers.* RCA Records, 1969.
Jefferson Starship. *It's a Fresh Wind that Blows Against the Empire.* RCA Records, 1971.
Kantner, Paul. *Sunfighter.* Grunt Records, 1972.
Steppenwolf. *Monster.* 1968. This tells the tune.

And last but not least, if you really want to understand what's happening in this epic era (1960-2010), then you would do well to check out the song "Badge" by Eric Clapton & Cream:

> *Yes, I told you 'bout the love comes tumbling down.*
> *Don't you notice how the wheel goes 'round?*
> *And you better pick yourself up from the ground,*
> *Before they bring the curtain down.*

Appendix

According to a person I trust & believe, her relative at one time was part of the military force which guards the National Archives in which is stored evidence of the Kennedy Assassination which was not to be released to the American public for 75 years, until presumably all involved in the assassination were dead. He said the person who masterminded the assassination thru the government & outside agencies was none other that LBJ himself who, it must be remembered, had more to gain thru the death of John Kennedy than any person on Earth.

It should be noted that the remains of John Kennedy's brain were stolen from the National Archives, presumably to destroy the last remaining shreds of evidence of there being more than one gunman in on the shooting. The Yippies had a song called "Who Stole John F. Kennedy's Brain?" which never topped the charts but lasted longer than Nixon did.

So if the Kennedy assassination was initiated, as opposed to perhaps merely facilitated, by LBJ, then we must expand our list of conspirators accordingly.

In this area we can look to research done by one time New Orleans District Attorney & now deceased Jim Garrison, & like information in other books reviewed by Jay Pound, "Who Told the Truth About JFK?" in *Critique: A Journal of Conspiracies and Metaphysics*, Volume VI, numbers 1 & 2.

These researchers implicate:

1) The Free Cuba Committee, a Cuban exiles group whose leader worked with both Jack Ruby & Frank Sturgis.

2) Texas billionaire H.L Hunt & Reverend Carl McIntire acting thru a division of the American Council of Christian Churches.

3) Division 5 (Internal Security) of the F.B.I. headed by William Sullivan & working with & thru the intelligence agency of the Military-Industrial Complex (the Defense Industrial Security Command) also headed by Sullivan. DISC agents directly involved with the assassination were said to include Clay Shaw (C.I.A. agent) Guy Bannister (C.I.A. & F.B.I.), David Ferrie (C.I.A.), Lee Harvey Oswald (F.B.I., C.I.A.), & Gordon Novel (C.I.A.).

4) Elements of the mafia already working with American intelligence agencies, especially the Army and Navy intelligence.

5) The Swiss corporation Permindex (one of the directors was Clay

What a Long Strange Trip It's Been

Shaw), which allegedly tried to assassinate French President Charles de Gualle in 1961 & '62. When this failed and Permindex & NATO were tossed out of France by de Gualle, they may have brought their work home with them.

Whatever the total truth of LBJ's involvement, it's perfectly clear that the assassination of John Kennedy was planned & executed by members of the American intelligence community (F.B.I., C.I.A.), Cuban exile movement, American oil, & the Mob, in an attempt to regain Cuba, take direct control of American policy, & to continue the Vietnam conflict and the Cold War in order to keep the cash rolling to the arms makers of the Military-Industrial Complex and the heroin flowing to the C.I.A.

Hollywood producer Oliver Stone really stirred things up in late 1991 when his movie JFK came out, which blew the Warren Report's credibility right out of the water- despite intense efforts by the established media to discredit both Stone and his movie. This lead to a move to open up the investigation files of the assassination (sealed until 2029) and rekindled America's interest in past history & future justice. If the files are opened up, let us hope that the material has remained untouched.

An interesting note, here, is that Lee Harvey Oswald's assassin Jack Ruby, who started out as an errand boy for Al Capone, worked for then-senator Richard Nixon in Chicago in 1947 performing "informational functions" for the staff. This and more fun stuff can be found in the *Coup D'etat in America* trading cards by Eclipse Publishing, Forestville, California. Lee Harvey Oswald also trained as a teenager in the Civil Air Patrol in New Orleans with David Ferrie, Jim Garrison's prime witness who was murdered before he could be made to testify.

Another interesting note is that Lee Harvey Oswald had Jack Ruby's unlisted phone number on him when he got arrested for shooting JFK.

Imagine this- Secret Service agents physically overpowered the Dallas County Medical Examiner & illegally moved the corpse from Texas to Maryland where the cover up could be performed. All medical personnel from Dallas were sworn to secrecy & Lt. Cmdr. Wm. Pitzner, who filmed the autopsy was later killed at Bethesda Medical Hospital to set an example for everyone there who had already been threatened with court-martial to keep their mouths shut. This correlates with the fact that over 100 witnesses died unusual deaths after the assassination of JFK, of whom 27 key witnesses died of cancer within six weeks of the assassination. The odds of this many people dying connected so close to the murder who had all been interviewed by the government was computed by the *London Times* to be 100,000 trillion to 1. More strange deaths would follow like the plague when the House Assassinations Committee of 1976 was set up to reinvestigate the killing. These new murders would include Carlos Prio, the former president of Cuba, top-ranking members of the F.B.I. (six top men died in six months in 1977), in what Groden and Livingstone in *High Treason* called, "appeared to be a liquidation of the entire high-command of the F.B.I." Also shot at the time they were being interviewed by the committee where Sam Giancana and John Roselli, top mafiosos who with Richard Nixon and Robert Maheu formed the orignal hit squad for Castro which was later turned against JFK. The House Select Committee on Assassinations did conlcude that due to acoustical and other evidence under scrutiny that there was more than one gunman shooting at JFK, thus blowing to shreds the findings of the Warren Commission. On July 18, 1979, the committee announced they had found evidence indicating a conspiracy in the murders of both John F. Kennedy and Martin Luther King. They named no names and then sealed their files. A cover-up covered up.

Imagine this- The President's autopsy redone at Bethesda naval Hospital falsifying such crucial elements as to cover up the evidence of a second gunman in front of the motorcade. As part of this, X-rays and photos were deliberatly forged to suppor the cover up story of the lone gunman from the rear. When the original X-rays and photos had been destroyed by the Secret Service on the spot and clearly showed the massive headwound caused by a shot from the front.

Imagine this- Immediately after the shooting stopped, the entire telphone network in Washington, D.C., went out of service for an hour. So did the telephone in the press car traveling with the motorcade and the police radio which was the only other communication from the motorcade, also went dead.

Imagine this- both Richard Nixon and J. Edgar Hoover met with Texas oil millionaire & right-wing zealot Clint Murchison in Dallas before the assassination.

Or this coincidence- Both Jack Ruby and one Jim Braden met at the office of big time right-wing Nixon backer and perhaps the richest man in America at the time H. L. Hunt the day before the killing.

H. L. Hunt himself was hustled by the F.B.I. out of the country an hour after the shooting to hideout in Mexico for a month until things cooled off.

Jim Braden was arrested on the scene under an alias for the assassination but was later released then indicted by a New Orleans grand jury for conspiracy in the killing. Braden (aka Edgar Eugene Bradley) was the Hollywood-based West Coast representative of Dr. Carl McIntyre, the anti-Catholic, anti-Kennedy three million dollar a year fundamentalist preacher whose name comes up in connection with not only the assassination of JFK but John Lennon as well. Braden, who was also had connections to the RFK killing, was in Dallas the day of the shooting wearing a big leather hat band

What a Long Strange Trip It's Been

marked with conspicuous X's. Police, according to the Gemstone File, had been instructed to let anyone with an X-marked hatband through the police lines. Some may have been told they were Secret Service. What is known was that Dallas police officer claims that it Bradley who flashed his Secret Service badge on the grassy knoll and kept spectators and police away. One last mention Bradley was also a founding member of La Costa Club, the big Mafioso retreat twenty miles from San Clemente, where Richard Nixon first poked his nose out months after he was thrown out of office. The evidence & web of involvement in this matter is so overwhelming as to still require the pursuit and accountability of those persons involved. Suggested reading & further evidence of those responsible for killing JFK can be found in:

Coup d'Etat in America by Alan Canfield and A. J. Weberman, Quick Trading, 1992.

High Treason: The Assassination of President Kennedy and New Evidence of Conspiracy by Robert Groden and Harriston Livingston, Conservatory Press, 1989.

Conspiracies, Cover Ups, and Crimes by Johnathon Vankin, Pargon House, 1991.

For any of you trying to get to the root of the Long Strange Trip of American history, you cannot leave out one of the most shadowy & important figures of all- the reclusive billionaire Howard Hughes. My understanding of his role is sketchy at best but Howard Hughes was the epitome of the military industrial complex. Hughes's empire thrived off C.I.A. money and provided cover for countless C.I.A. operations. Charles Colson said that "it was impossible to tell where the Hughes Corporation left off and the C.I.A. began." A perfect example of this is the C.I.A.'s use of Hughes's deep-sea Glomar Explorer to retrieve two nuclear warheads from a sunken Russian submarine.

It was ex-F.B.I.-C.I.A. agent Robert Maheu who formerly was employed by Aristotle Onassis who Hughes hired in 1955 and later chose to run his Las Vegas holdings & it was Maheu who recruited Chicago mobster John Roselli for the C.I.A. to assassinate Castro. Maheu was fired by the Hughes Corporation in 1970 but was an important player in Watergate and the downfall of Richard M. Nixon.

General Caball, former deputy director of the C.I.A. by JFK following the Bay of Pigs, was then also hired by Howard Hughes and worked closely with Maheu.

Guy Bannister, whose office address was the same as Lee Harvey Oswald's (and E. Howard Hunt!) in New Orleans, 544 Camp Street, was a major suspect in Jim Garrison's JFK investigation and who died suspiciously before anything became known. He worked closely with Maheu. In fact, Maheu worked during World War II in Chicago in the FBI under none other than Guy Bannister. Others with whom Bannister was connected with were Howard Hunt, Frank Sturgis, Lee Harvey Oswald, Jack Ruby, and David Ferrie, a C.I.A. pilot who also died mysteriously during the Garrison investigation.

Maheu's first job for Hughes, by the way, was to neutralize the rumor, which was true, that Howard Hughes had given a $205,000 "nonrepayable" loan to Nixon's brother Donald.

Hughes pursued an ambitious game plan by buying judges, Senators, Governors, even a Vice-President (young Dick Nixon), And would later contribute heavily to all presidential candidates just to ensure he had the job in his pocket. It's interesting to note that it was Larry O'Brien's office (the Chairman of the Democratic Party), which was broken into at the Watergate hotel, obstensibly to see if O'Brien, who had worked for years as publicity manager for Hughes, had any knowledge of the Hughes-Nixon loan or of the $100,000 that Hughes had given Maurice Stans that year for Nixon's election and if O'Brien would use it against him in 1972.

So Howard Hughes had considerable access and influence on American politics with extensive connections to the C.I.A. on one hand & the ability to interface with the mafia to whatever degree was necessary on the other. And just as we said, the C.I.A. and the Hughes Corporation were one and the same, Sentaor Henry Gonzales, one of the truer of all American patriots, stated these days, "the mafia and the government were one and the same." Thus, we have a government run by the C.I.A., mob, and rich industrialists.

The best articles available on Hughes's extent of control would be "Strange Bedfellows: The Hughes-Nixon-Lansky Connection; The Secret Alliances of the CIA from World War II to Watergate," by Howard Kohn in *Rolling Stone*, 5/20/76. Avialble from Prevailing Winds Research, P.O. Box 23511, Santa Barbara, CA 93121. Send for a catalog.

"The Puppet, Uncovering the Secret World of Nixon, Hughes and the CIA" by Larry Dubois & Laurence Gonzales, *Playboy*, Oct/Nov n.d.

The Gemstone File, Inspiracy CAD, P.O. Box 523, Columbia Station, OH 44028. $2.

The Gemstone File, edited by Jim Keith, IllumiNet Press, 1993. ISBN 0-902626534-5-4. Recommended reading.

Also highly recommended is the mind-blowing book entitled *Behold a Pale Horse* by ex-Navy intelligence agent William Cooper, which deals with everything from the JFK assassination to alien penetration of our government.

What a Long Strange Trip It's Been

The Gemstone Files

A real mind expander is the Gemstone Files which gives a strange twist to the Hughes affair. These files were supposedly written by a disgruntled phycsicist, Bruce Roberts, whose synthetic rubies the Hughes Corporation ripped off and used for laser research. Roberts wrote 1,000 hand-written pages of information outlining the Hughes power structure and more. And what more!

According to this scenario, Hughes was kidnapped in a power play by Aristotle Onassis in 1957 but was shot in the head and severely hurt in the capture. Onassis was the source of Joe Kennedy Sr.'s illegal booze and subsequent fortune in 1932. Once Onassis had absorbed the Hughes Corporation & had the American crime syndicate under his wing, he fulfilled an old deal with Joe Kennedy- the presidency of the United States would go to one of the the Kennedy sons. In return, the mafia would get their casinos back from castro. JFK won, but two months later, his totally domineering father had a stroke which left John and Bobby on their own. They changed direction & sought to regain the reigns of power from the mob. The Bay of Pigs invasion of Cuba failed & JFK didn't see fit to launch a full-scale invasion against Castro & that pissed Onassis off. The Kennedy brothers arrested mafia teamster Jimmy Hoffa and put him in jail. They shut down paramilitary anti-Castro training camps in the southern U.S. They arrested Wally Berg, the owner of Air Thailand, which had been transporting heroin out of southeast Asia to Aristotle Onassis for the CIA and that really pissed Onassis off! So he used the mafioso-CIA Castro hit squad, including Howard Hunt, to bump off JFK. In that way, the power of the presidency was returned to the military, corporate gangster element which so desperately seeks the seat of power knowing the more power you have the bigger profit potential you'll have. The Gemstone Files are in depth & with the amount of material in them which has since been proven by history, at least a significant part are to be deemed highly accurate. And seeing how Aristotle ended up marrying Jacqueline Kennedy after JFK was blown away, I wouldn't doubt any of it with perhaps the exception of the contention that Daniel Ellsberg blew the lid off the Pentagon Papers to help distract the American public from the truth of Hughes, Onassis, and the true reason we were in Indochina which was for heroin and oil. It is interesting to note that the Watergate operation was codenamed Operation Gemstone by G. Gordon Liddy.

Another unseen and evil influence on American politics is the Nazis- yes, some of Hitler's original crew who were repatriated into the U.S. intelligence agencies after the war under the code name of Operation Paperclip. In fact it was ex-Nazi General Reinhard Genheln who helped form the C.I.A with

Allen Dulles after World War II.

The religious right is another frightening partner in the march toward American fascism. Take them seriously, folks.

Media censorship- It's a known fact that corporations for years have owned large segments of the media so they could control the information which gets to the American public. Examples of this are NBC TV being owned by General Electric and ABC News being bought by Cap Cities whose executives included the late C.I.A. director William Casey. I saw two blatant examples of T.V. censorship right before my very eyes. First off on NBC News when reporter Tom Brokaw was sighting a new report proving household radiation-producing objects were a far greater danger to human health than first thought. He listed those objects of greatest danger such as computers, microwaves, etc., but when he started to utter the words "color television sets" he was instantly cut off & a commercial appeared on the screen. When Tom reappeared, he was under control & no more lip slips were made.

The most glaring example of T.V. censorship showing who's really in power was when then-President Jimmy Carter strayed away from his prepared text during a live speech and began to tell the American people about the JFK assassination. This time only the power to the microphone was cut of so all you could see was Carter up there jabbering away, then when he realized he was cut off, he just sat there looking foolish as the cameras rolled for almost half an hour. "In fact each President upon entering office was destabilized by this Secret Team- shots were taken of them & things done to them. Presidents were mistranslated, intimidated, controlled & actually terrorized in some cases so that they got the message that the power lay beyond the White House gates." (*High Treason*, p. 417). The "suicide" death of no. 2 White House lawyer and childhood friend of Bill Clinton and former law partner with Hillary Clinton before the election is in the same vein. Vincent Foster, Jr., was found shot dead in a D.C.-area park on July 21, 1993. It seems suspicious that someone so close to the President and at the peak of his career just six months into the presidency would have such grave reasons to die. Clinton seemed to know this too, for at the funeral he said that Foster was "a great protector." "One of the things that has made us feel badly in the last few days is that we could never remember a time when he asked any of us to protect him." (7-23-93). But then again, Vince, and a whole lot of others, may well have been killed to save Clinton from impeachment and his wife and others in the White House from jail.

DEPARTMENT OF DEFENSE APPROPRIATIONS FOR 1970
NINETY-FIRST CONGRESS FIRST SESSION
House Bill 15090

In 1969 the US Department of defense asked for (and received) $10 million to create a virus in the laboratory for which there was no natural immunity to be used against those deemed politically and socially incorrect. The virus was to be made ready between 1974-1979. In 1977 the World Health Organization began injecting AIDS-tainted smallpox vaccine into over 100 million Africans and also people in Haiti. In 1978 some 2,000 white male homosexuals were given AIDS-tainted hepatitis B vaccine through the Centers for Disease Control under the project named Trojan Horse. It is now said the AIDS virus is in the drugs on the streets.

House Hearing Transcript 7/1/1969:

"There are two things about the biological agent field I would like to mention. One is the possibility of technological surprise. Molecular biology is a field that is advancing very rapidly and eminent biologists believe that within a period of 5 to 10 years it would be possible to produce a synthetic biological agent, an agent that does not naturally exist and for which no natural immunity could have been acquired.

Mr. Sikes: Are we doing any work in that field?

Dr. MacArthur: We are not.

Mr. Sikes: Why not? Lack of money or lack of interest?

Dr. MacArthur: Certainly not lack of interest.

Mr. Sikes. Would you provide for our records information on what would be required, what the advantages of such a program would be, the time and cost involved?

Dr. MacArthur: We will be very happy to."

(This information follows:)

"The dramatic progress being made in the field of molecular biology led us to investigate the relevance of this field of science to biological warfare. A small group of experts considered this matter and provided the following observations:

1. All biological agents up to the present time are representatives of naturally occurring disease, and are thus known by scientists throughout the world. They are easily available to qualified scientists for research, either for offensive or defensive purposes.

2. Within the next 5 to 10 years, it would probably be possible to make a new infective microorganism which could differ in certain important aspects from any known disease-causing organisms. Most important of these is that it might be refractory to the immunological and therapeutic processes upon which we depend to maintain our relative freedom from infectious disease.

3. A research program to explore the feasibility of this could be completed in approximately 5 years at a total cost of $10 mllion."

--Reprinted from <u>Documentation of the Theft of our Nation</u>. 1994, World News Insight.

INFO ON THE PREVENTION AND CURE FOR AIDS:
(reprinted from Life Times, Issue No. 4, pp. 27-32)

It's purportedly simple- oxygenation of the blood. <u>Food grade</u> hydrogen peroxide in small daily doses has been reported to be EXTREMELY EFFECTIVE.

CONTACTS:

Walter Grotz	Father Richard Wilhelm	Dr. Kurt Donsbach
Box 126	Box 18 Union Road	Bio-Genesis Institute
Deleano, MN 55438	California, KY 41007	Rosarita Beach, Baja, MEXICO
(612) 972-2144	(606) 635-9297	(714) 964-1535

Reprinted from Now What Magazine, Issue No. 1:
Waves Forest, P.O. Box 786, Montery, CA 93942

INDEX

A

Abbey Road, 39, 194
Abrams, Elliot, 150, 209
Abzug, Bella, 75
acid, 2, 8, 13, 41, 43-44, 46-48, 50, 76, 94, 166, 193, 204-205, 213
activist(s), 23, 26, 71, 77, 83, 90, 93, 102, 109, 111, 113, 144, 161, 165, 167, 203, 210
agent provacateurs, 31, 46, 57, 63, 70, 72-73, 77, 98, 100, 102-103, 107-109, 112-113, 116, 131-136, 139, 161, 163, 166, 180-182, 190, 208, 210, 216-217, 219-220, 223
AIDS, 82, 166, 176, 223
Alaskan oil spill, 92
Ali, Muhammed, 23
alien(s), 176, 220, 230
Allende, Salvador, 148-149, 195
Amerika, 58, 74
Angleton, 196
anti-war, 23-25, 57, 63, 65, 73, 75, 85, 87, 89, 96-97, 99, 102-103, 107-109, 144, 173
apocalypse, 37, 40, 204, 212
assassination(s), 1, 11, 19-22, 35, 51-52, 63, 65-67, 76, 88, 96, 116-118, 132, 132-134, 146-149, 156-157, 183, 202-205, 208, 211, 216-220, 222
Attica, 130, 182

B

Babylon, 31, 130, 206
Baez, Joan, 38
Banisadr, 140
Bay of Pigs, 19-22, 111, 117-118, 145, 147, 175, 211, 219, 221
beat, 5, 7, 46, 49, 109, 123, 194, 213
Beatles, 39, 49, 67, 94, 193
Beatnik, 42
Berkeley, 46, 80, 85, 119, 134, 213-214
Bhopal, 92
Black Panthers, the, 13, 38, 46, 67, 70, 78-81, 83-84, 108, 132, 134, 212
blacklisting, 203, 205-206, 210-211
Boggs, Hale, 63
Boland Amendment, 153, 156, 158
brainwashing, 26, 44, 52, 135, 146, 166, 170
Branch Davidian(s), 72, 180-182
Bremer, Arthur, 52, 204
bribes, 124, 184, 230
Brookings Institute, 112-113
Brotherhood of Eternal Love, 46-47, 201
Brown, H. Rap, 90, 207
Bruce, Lenny, 5, 94, 195, 201, 205, 213, 221
Buddhist, 84
Bush, George, 67, 140-141, 147, 150, 155-157, 159, 167-178, 183-184, 210

C

Calley, Lt. William, 150, 196
Cambodia, 31, 97, 129
capitalism, 27, 74, 84, 132-134
Carmichael, Stokley, 80, 135
Carter, Jimmy, 52, 76-77, 106-107, 130, 136, 139-141, 155, 169, 206-207, 221-222
Castro, Fidel, 17, 19-20, 22, 183, 202, 218-219, 221
censorship, 50, 85, 127, 161, 173, 205, 222, 230
Checkers the Dog, 106
Chernobyl, 92-93
Chicago Conspiracy Trial, 91
Chicago Democratic Convention, 48, 56, 88-90
Cleaver, Eldridge, 46-47, 79-80
clipper chip, 184
cocaine, 20, 48, 77, 94, 139, 146-148, 153, 157-158, 165, 167-168, 176-177, 179, 190, 201, 207
COINTELPRO, 65, 70
Colby, William, 76, 150, 196
collateral, 173
comics, underground, 43, 77
commercialism, 49, 93, 95, 151, 166, 190, 196, 222
commune(s), 43, 92, 201
conditioning, 26, 42, 82, 95, 132, 171, 175
confines, 25
confrontation(s), 60, 85, 96, 103
consciousness, 3, 8, 24, 39, 44, 93, 166, 173, 178, 185, 190, 213, 230
conspiracy, 21-22, 60, 64, 90-91, 113, 122, 127, 133, 182, 211-212, 216, 218-219
Constitution, 71, 77, 79, 97, 128, 134, 141, 143-144, 153, 159, 161, 165, 181, 230
Contras, 32, 127-128, 145-146, 153, 155-160, 162, 169, 172-173, 176-179, 209-210
corruption, 14, 17, 88, 141, 150-151, 210
Council, see Foreign Relations
counterculture, 43, 53
coverup, 17, 104-105, 115, 117, 122, 128, 154-156, 159, 218
CREEP, 115

D

Davis, Angela, 194, 213
Deadheads, 166
Dealey Plaza, 20, 110
Declaration of Independence, 11, 20, 34-35, 134, 180, 235
decriminalization, 139
Dellinger, David, 77, 90, 194
Dellums, Ron, 119, 194
Democratic Convention, see Convention
demonstration(s), 56, 67, 86-87, 96-100, 103, 105, 112, 164, 173
deprogramming, 8, 185
Desert Storm, 140, 172, 174
dictator(s), 19, 70, 139, 158
dictatorship(s), 148-150, 163
dissension, 46, 54-56, 63, 65, 70, 84, 87, 95-97, 100-101, 103, 111, 144, 149, 153, 173, 206, 230, 232
dissident(s), 72, 84, 109, 175
Doctor Feel Good, 201
Dohrn, Bernadine, 60
Donovan, 39, 193
doublespeak, 160
draft, 8, 23, 25, 56-57, 65, 96-97, 120, 129, 132, 144, 153, 169-170, 176, 231
drivel, 11, 106
drones, 187
Dulles, Allen, 21, 150, 208-209, 222
Dylan, Bob, 38-39, 56, 66, 139

E

Ehrlichman, John, 108, 110-111, 115, 117, 122-123, 126

Eldridge, Cleaver, 46-47, 79-80
Ellsberg, Daniel, 111, 117, 123, 193, 221
enlightenment, 13, 43, 190, 215
entrails, 82
eradication, 24, 99, 230
Execute, 131
Executed, 24, 66, 128, 148, 217
Execution, 20
Executive, 25, 116, 122, 202
Executives, 106, 210, 222
exploitation, 27, 133-134, 162, 178, 184, 190
Exxon, *see also* oil spills, 92, 171

F

F.B.I., 21, 47, 51, 58, 60, 63-73, 79, 83, 101-102, 104, 108-111, 113, 115-118, 123, 128, 132-135, 142, 159-161, 180-182, 210, 216-218, 220
fascism, 96, 109, 134, 141, 146, 153, 161, 163-164, 222
Federal Bureau of Investigations, *see* F.B.I.
Federal Reserve System, 74, 86, 111, 131, 162, 166, 179
Feel Good, Doctor, *see* Doctor
FEMA, 41, 49, 85, 94, 100, 113, 144, 175, 179, 184, 200-201
Fillipinos, 82
Forcade, Tom, 76, 195, 213
Ford, Gerald, 21, 75, 125-126, 128-132, 134, 136, 139, 168, 202-203
fraggings, 23-24

G

Gandhi, 54
genocide, 8, 81-83, 88, 146, 160, 162, 167, 184, 230
Ginsberg, Allen, 7, 91, 213
Grateful Dead, The, 8, 13, 40
Greenpeace, 92, 204
Greenwich Village, 24, 38, 47
Gregg, Donald, 157, 196, 206-207
groove, 31
Gueverra, Che, 19, 195
Gulf War, *see* Desert Storm

H

Haight-Ashbury, 46, 94, 213
Hakim, Albert, 140, 159
Haldeman, H.R., 108, 110, 115-118, 123-124, 126, 128, 148
hallucinogen(s), 112, 170, 210, 214
Hampton, Fred, 79, 195
Hasenfus, Eugene, 210
Helms, Richard, 66, 71, 117, 147-150, 196
Hendrix, Jimi, 38, 74, 94, 193, 215
Hesse, Herman, 45
Hinckley, John, 67, 124
Ho Chi Minh, 34-35, 65, 194
Hoffman, Abbie, 46, 66, 74, 76-77, 90, 193, 195, 214
Hollingshead, Michael, 44, 213
Hoover, J. Edgar, *see also* F.B.I., 51, 63-65, 69-70, 79, 88, 108-110, 115, 168, 196, 218
Hughes, Howard, 114, 219-221
Huston Plan, 65, 109-110
Huxley, Aldous, 44, 214

I

I.R.S., 19, 31-32, 69, 83, 109, 114, 119, 124, 128, 131, 148-149, 153, 158, 161-162, 164, 171, 174, 178-179, 230
incineration, 179, 184
India, 44, 92
Indian(s), 11, 24, 32, 46, 81-83, 160, 169, 180, 213
Indochina, 11, 23, 34, 36, 55, 57, 84, 145-147, 221
Industrial-Military Complex, 19, 42, 56, 69, 105, 162, 185, 208, 216-217, 219, 230
industrialist(s), 167, 220
industrialization, 65, 92, 94, 201, 208, 216, 219, 230
industry(ies), 63, 92, 130, 133, 183, 206
Iran-Contra, *see also* Irangate, 143, 145, 153, 159, 169-171, 177, 208
Irangate, 139-140, 143, 145-147, 151-156, 158-160, 169-172, 176-178, 208
Iranian(s), 140, 147, 152, 154-155, 159, 169, 175

J

jazz, 7-8
Jefferson Airplane, 8, 14, 38, 50, 193, 215
Johnson, Lyndon B., 23-25, 35-37, 51, 88, 90, 139, 204, 208

K

Kennedy, Jacqueline, 201
Kennedy, John F., 14, 17-18, 20-23, 35, 44, 51-52, 63, 65-66, 106-107, 116, 118-119, 148, 183, 193, 195, 201-205, 207-208, 211, 216-222
Kennedy, Robert, 51-53, 64, 66, 88, 96, 193, 204, 211
Kennedys, the, 1, 17, 20-22, 25, 35, 51-53, 63-66, 78, 88, 96, 106, 117-119, 147, 156, 183, 193, 202, 204, 207-209, 211, 216-219, 221
Kent State, 14, 17, 46, 58, 70, 72, 78, 95-99, 103-106, 131, 161, 182, 205, 210, 231
Kerouac, Jack, 7, 193, 212-213
Kesey, Ken, 13, 43, 193
King, Martin Luther, 7, 12, 25, 47-48, 51, 54, 64-65, 70, 74, 78, 82, 88, 96, 122, 124, 165, 167, 193-194, 218
Kissinger, Henry, 32, 120, 129, 147, 149-150, 196, 203
Kleindienst, William, 104, 123, 127
Krause, Allison, 101, 195
Krogh, Egil, 110, 117
Kundalini Yoga, 191, 215, 231

L

Leary, Timothy, 1, 43-48, 59, 65, 110, 183-184, 214
Lennon, John, 38-39, 49, 66-67, 94, 193-195, 218
LSD, 1, 8, 13, 17, 39-41, 43-45, 47, 51, 65, 76-77, 112, 151, 166, 193, 201, 205, 210, 213-214

M

Magical Mystery Tour, 39
Mandella, Nelson, 163
marijuana, 39, 46, 139, 165-166, 175, 178, 185, 196, 201, 206
massacre, 24, 32, 83, 99
Max, Peter, 39, 43, 156, 165, 170, 193, 201, 215
Maxfield, Parrish, 39
McCarthy, Eugene, 25, 88-90, 108, 120, 168, 194
McGovern, George, 34, 52, 89-90, 105, 119-120, 124, 126, 132-134, 140-141, 147, 150, 156-157, 159, 168, 170-171, 174-177, 194-195, 204, 210
Meese, Edwin, 156, 177
Merry Pranksters, The, 13, 43, 74, 128
Millbrook, 45-46, 110, 213
Miller, Jeffrey, 72, 101-102, 195, 202, 205-206, 208, 212, 215
Mitchell, John, 86, 104, 108, 111-112, 115-116, 123, 144, 196, 211
MKULTRA, 66
Mobil Oil, 18, 21, 27, 45-46, 52, 92, 117, 126, 130, 135, 147, 156, 158, 171-173, 175-176, 217-218, 221, 230
Morrison, Jim, 38, 84, 94, 195
Muhammed Ali, 23

N

Nader, Ralph, 194

napalm, 31, 150-151
Nazi(s), 34, 97, 149-151, 163-164, 169, 184, 221
Newton, Huey, 79-80
Nicaragua, 11, 32, 84, 144-147, 150, 153, 157-158, 160, 210
Nixon, Richard Milhous, 17, 19-22, 31-32, 44, 51-52, 63-66, 71, 75-76, 90, 92, 95, 97-99, 103-129, 139-142, 144, 147-150, 157-159, 161, 168, 170, 195, 202, 212, 216-220
North, Ollie, 31-32, 35-36, 58, 81, 97, 103, 120, 123, 130, 140-141, 143-144, 152-159, 175-177, 179, 183, 196, 204, 211
Nostradamus, 209, 212
nukespeak, 212

O

Ochs, Phil, 38, 91, 195-196, 207
October Surprise, 140, 208
oil spills, 92, 130, 171
Olympic(s), 23
Oswald, Lee Harvey, 20-21, 73, 202-203, 216-217, 219-220
Owens, Rob, 52, 204
Owsley, Stanley Augustus III, 13, 43, 46, 76, 193

P

pacifist(s)Pacifist, 108, 158
PACS, 178
Parks, Rosa, 54
Pentagon, 8, 58, 75, 87, 95, 110-112, 152, 156, 173, 221
pesticides, 81, 92, see also toxins
petrochemical, 18, 21, 27, 45-46, 52, 92, 126, 130, 147, 156, 158, 171-173, 175-176, 217-218, 221, 230
Phillipines, 59, 82, 140, 147
pilgrim(s), 45, 82, 205
plumbers, 110-111, 114-115
plumbing, 115
Plutonium, 151, 163, 184
police, 12, 14, 57-58, 60, 63, 67, 69-73, 75-76, 79-80, 85-90, 98, 102-104, 108-111, 113, 124, 128, 130, 132-136, 142-144, 147-149, 161, 184, 203, 212, 218-219, 228, 230
pollution, 34, 81-82, 92, 94, 175-176, 183, 187, 196, 200-201, 230
Port Huron Statement, 56
pranks, 13, 43, 74, 128. See also Merry Pranksters
Pratt, Geronimo, 80
programming, 11, 32, 52, 66, 120, 166, 170, 173, 185
provocateurs, see agent provocateurs
psychedelic(s), 178

Q

Quayle, Dan, 169

R

radiation, 81, 92-94, 120, 151, 184, 222, 230
radical(s), 12, 47-48, 54, 57, 69, 71, 94, 107, 113, 132-133, 185
radio, 48, 50, 76, 112, 179, 208, 218
radioactive, 92-93, 187, 200
Radium, 151, 184
Reagan, Ronald, 32, 67, 72, 103, 107, 111, 124-125, 139-145, 152-165, 167-168, 170, 175-178, 196, 210, 212
Reagan-speak, 160
revolution, 8, 19-20, 37, 40, 47-49, 58-59, 66, 89, 92, 134, 201, 211, 213-214
revolutionary(ies), 34, 59, 68, 73, 80, 99, 132, 134-135
Rockefeller, Nelson, 130
Rockefellers, the, 27, 130-131, 139, 150, 206
Rodriguez, Felix, 95, 155-156

S

S.L.A. communique, 38, 134
San Francisco, 5, 7, 13, 38, 41, 43, 71, 83, 132, 135, 151, 173, 204, 212-213
Sandoz Chemical Company, 44
Satchidananda, Swami, 193, 215
Savio, Mario, 85
Schroeder, Bill, 101, 195
Schuer, Sandy, 195
Seale, Bobby, 79-80, 90-91
Seberg, Jean, 68
Secord, William, 140, 147, 157, 159
self-defense, 182-183, 230
Shackley, Ted, 147, 149
Shulgin, Alexander, 193, 214
Silkwood, Karen, 63, 195
Singlaub, Gen., 147
Sirhan, Sirhan, 51-52, 204
Slick, Grace, 48-49, 76, 108
Smothers Brothers, The, 23
smuggling, 46, 76, 140, 146, 148, 152, 156-157, 177
Soledad, 132
Spock, Dr. Benjamin, 23, 195
St. Marie, Buffy, 38
Sturgis, Frank, 20, 115, 122-123, 202-203, 216, 220

T

Tackwood, Louis, 113, 133, 135-136
Tienanmen Square, 54
Tonkin Bay Resolution, 32, 172
toxins, 81, 179, 183-184, 190
trial, see Chicago Conspiracy Trial
Trilateral Commission, 130-131, 139, 167, 230
Trudell, John, 83
Trumbo, Dalton, 213
TV-programming, 11, 17, 23, 32, 37, 49, 52, 66, 70, 74, 77, 89-90, 95, 106-107, 112, 120, 124, 127-128, 150-151, 154, 157-158, 165-166, 168-170, 173-174, 176, 185, 187, 200, 208, 215, 222

U

Underground, The Weather, see also Weathermen, 46, 57-60, 205, 212
urine-testing, 175

V

Viet Cong, 24, 35, 174
Vietnam, 17, 23-26, 31-36, 54-58, 72, 76, 84-85, 88, 95, 97, 100, 103, 111, 116, 120, 129, 145-147, 156, 169, 172-173, 182, 184, 194, 203-205, 208, 211, 217

W

Waco, Texas, 179-180, 182
Watergate, 19-20, 63, 104-106, 110-128, 153-156, 159, 169, 202, 204, 219-221
Wavy Gravy, 193
Weathermen, the, 46, 56-60, 74, 205, 212
Weaver, Randy, 182-183
Weinberger, Casper, 150, 177
Westmoreland, Gen., 150, 196
Whitewater, 179
wiretapping, 58, 160
witchhunts, 162
Woodstock, 38, 48, 91, 214
Wounded Knee, 83

X Y Z

Yippies, 74-78, 84, 88, 90, 128, 193, 203, 210, 216
Yoga, see also Kundalini, 191, 215, 231

A Truly Free Society Has

NO SECRET POLICE

What the Future Means to You - the New World Order

The Game- MONOPOLY, Power, World Domination.
THE PLAYERS CHANGE BUT THE GAME REMAINS THE SAME

The Players- An elite mixture of the forces of Greed & Evil. International bankers, oil slicks, the Militatry Industrial Complex. The Council on Foreign Relations, The Trilateral Commission, The C.I.A., the U.N.

The Pawns- You & I.

The Plan- Total control of world's wealth, natural resources, governments, police & military forces, people. Instrumental in the plan is population control- A.I.D.S., famine, disguised genocide, ethnic cleansing (Bosnia & Rowanda), supply guns, ignite situations. Massively reduce the resistance to their totalitarian state thru death squads, supplying communications, weapons, training military forces worldwide in political repression, torture, & counter-insurgency techniques.

Formula for Total Control- Media- Corporate owned & censored. Propaganda, half-truths, & lies. Political system- Control thru Assasination, bribes, and blackmail. Source of funds- American tax dollars, guns & drug running. Control over laws & judges. Control of economy- The World Bank, Intn'l. Monetary Fund. Eradicate dissent- Surveillance, make populace criminals (drug war). Create atmosphere in country for frightening people into giving up their Constitutional rights- gangs.

RESULT- Worldwide simultaneous "Development" resulting in ecological rape of world & the destruction of the eco-system necessary for minimum human survival. Extreme poisoning of air, water, soil...radiation bombardment.

THOSE PERHAPS FURTHEST BEHIND IT ALL- Either perverse greed-soaken humans or an alien plot to pollute the world until it's more like their home planet and we die out.
A Total Alien-Nation.
You choose.

SOLUTION- Expanded consciousness, knowledge, dissent, after all non-violent means expended, self-defense.

About the Author

The author grew up in the 60's, attended Kent State, was drafted & resisted, maintains a diet free of meat, sugar, salt, white flour, additives, preservatives, nicotine, & caffeine, has long hair, lives in the country, smokes pot, drinks Irish Cream on occasion, and continues to be active in the areas of environmental protection, the Peace Movement, Yoga & Inner Exploration.

See you there.

RESIST CRIMINAL AUTHORITY

The author expressing his dissent at a nuclear weapons plant protest.

Published by
Still Steaming Press

"So hot, our shit's still steaming..."

For additional copies, send $13.95 plus $2 shipping & handling.
Make check or money orders payable to:
Still Steaming Press
637 South Broadway, Suite B-317
Boulder, Colorado 80303
(303) 271-7633

For additional trips, you know where to start...

Declaration of Independence

"Governments are instituted among men, deriving their j
powers from the consent of the governed; that whenever any fo
of government becomes destructive of these ends, it is the righ
the people to alter or abolish it, and to institute new governme
laying its foundation on such principles, and organizing its pow
in such form, as to them shall seem most likely to affect their saf
and happiness...

...But when a long train of abuses and usur
tions, pursuing invariably the same Object evinces a design
reduce them under absolute Despotism, it is the right, it is th
duty, to throw off such Government, and to provide new Gua
for their future security."

—— July 4, 1776

Remember Kids, Protest Works.